Janet Walker is one of Britain's leading authorities on vegetarianism and cooking without meats. She has made many appearances on BBC Television and has demonstrated her style and techniques of successful modern vegetarianism at the big food fairs at Olympia, at the Electrical Development Association, and before a large conference of senior trained cookery demonstrators from all over Great Britain. She is considered a pioneer in a field of culinary health that is becoming more and more popular to aware folk who wish to blend concern for their general health with appetising and satisfying eating.

JANET WALKER

Vegetarian Cookery

GRANADA

London Toronto Sydney New York

Published by Granada Publishing Limited in 1973
Reprinted 1975, 1977, 1978, 1979, 1981, 1982

ISBN 0 583 12192 6

First published in Great Britain by
Neville Spearman Limited 1959
New Impressions 1962, 1968
Copyright © Janet Walker 1959

Granada Publishing Limited
Frogmore, St Albans, Herts AL2 2NF
and
36 Golden Square, London W1R 4AH
866 United Nations Plaza, New York, NY 10017, USA
117 York Street, Sydney, NSW 2000, Australia
100 Skyway Avenue, Rexdale, Ontario, M9W 3A6, Canada
61 Beach Road, Auckland, New Zealand

Printed and bound in Great Britain by
Cox & Wyman Ltd, Reading
Set in Monotype Times

Granada ®
Granada Publishing ®

fruits, the dried fruits, and winter salads. Spring brings the cleansing foods that refresh us and clear away the stuffiness after a winter of indoors. Each season calls for rejoicing, even winter once we have noticed that it was the new bud that pushed off the old leaf!

This book is dedicated to vegetarians everywhere;
to all who prepare and serve vegetarian meals,
to all who seek harmless living.

And last but not least to my family, but for
whom I should certainly never have done all this
cooking, and in spite of whom, if I may say so
kindly, I have at last achieved such a book.

J.W.

Contents

INTRODUCTION

When I decided to serve only vegetarian meals to my family I had no guidance, no vegetarian cookery book, and I had never heard of a vegetarian restaurant. I enjoyed the adventure of devising new dishes and the family much approved the change. I should have welcomed a comprehensive book of vegetarian recipes, and that is one reason why I have plodded along for several years to produce this one. The other reason is that Mrs. Jenny Fliess of the Vega Restaurant in London recommended me for the job, when she was approached, since she had not the time to do the work herself. I made a good start on the book, then was overtaken by illness and had to commence all over again when I took it up later for my present publisher.

That I am a self-trained cook will, I expect, be all too obvious to the trained eye. That there was nowhere to train will not at first be realized. In recent years I have served on a panel of advisers to the educational side of the Vegetarian Catering Association, and although the members of the panel were setting and marking examination papers, and indeed giving pupils an excellent training in vegetarian cookery, none had the diploma they were hoping to award, and for the reason that they were founding a new line of cookery. There had to be a beginning and this was it.

For some years I have been demonstrating vegetarian meals as a freelance, to small or large groups in electricity showrooms, gas showrooms, large exhibitions and tiny halls with neither gas nor electricity. I have also taught students in my own home, in schools and colleges.

It has long been an established fact that a good vegetarian diet with dairy produce, cheese, eggs, and plenty of fresh fruit and vegetables is really adequate for the promotion of health and fitness. Mostly vegetarians will be careful to plan for adequate nourishment, and will look to vitamins also. I do wish to point out the necessity of allowing for fresh ripe raw fruit and fresh raw vegetables as well as the conservatively cooked ones. A healthy body is an alkaline body, and a sick body will be found to be very acid. The perfect balance would be 80 per cent alkaline food and the remaining 20 per cent acid making.

Those embracing a vegetarian diet will do well to partake of a reputable yeast extract daily such as Yex, Yeastrel, Barmine or Marmite. This is a necessity.

I have used 100 per cent wholewheat flour throughout the preparation of my recipes. This is not only stone ground but has been grown by compost means. This is easily obtainable and will provide the basis of sound nutrition. The flavour will be a new experience to many who have never known the meaning of bread as our forefathers knew it. The soil, a grain of wheat and the human body are composed of the same elements. By the time the good grain has been turned into white flour it has not only lost many of these elements completely, but has lost the germ or life of the wheat berry, and mainly starch remains.

My own wholewheat loaf, devised so that it will take little time or energy to prepare, cannot take more than 10 to 12 minutes to prepare, is proved once only, when in the tins, and requires but 30 seconds kneading. As one student remarked at the end of her first batch of bread, "It's such a soothing thing to do."

Very little salt has been used in preparing these recipes. I hope more will try to allow the natural flavours a chance to delight the palate. If salt seems necessary to you at first, then do allow for the salt in cheese and yeast extracts.

Throughout this book I have advised using demerara, barbados and pieces sugar. Since the recipes were prepared I have discovered that in the course of refining, an animal "char" is used as a filter in the production of demerara and of course, white sugars. I have been rather shattered by this. I have not altered the recipes, those who follow them will please themselves; we have at least, the barbados and pieces sugar.

It will be noted that recipes for pastas have found no place here. Whilst I am assured that these are prepared from a very nutritious part of the wheat berry, I have never been a great user of them, and so have not prepared more than an occasional spaghetti meal. Those who wish to use pastas will find excellent recipes on the packages, and, substituting nuts, nutmeats and vegetables for meat, will produce the kind of dish they require.

The frontispiece of this book is intended to show how adequately and artistically nature provides for us. May we show our appreciation by serving the lovely foods with as little damage to them as is possible.

In summer we have light, refreshing and cooling salads and fruits. In winter the more warming roots pulses, and the stored

"A SQUARE MEAL"

1 FOODS SUPPLYING VITAMINS

	A	and D
Cod & Fish Liver Oils	★★★	★★★★
Liver, Fish	★★★	★★★
Liver, Animal	★★★	★
Kidney, Heart	★★	?
Flesh, Animal	★	?
Flesh, Fatty Fish	★★	★★
Fish, Roes	★★	★★
Egg Yolk	★ to ★★	★★
Milk	★	0 to ★
Butter	★ to ★★	★★
Vitaminized Margarine	★★★	★★★
Cheese	★	0 to ★

	A	D
Green Vegs	★★	0
Carrots, Tomatoes	★★	0
Dried Apricots	★ to ★★	?
Fresh Fruits	★	?
Whole Cereals	★	?

Axerophthol ⇌ A comes from carotene
Activated Ergosterol ⇌ D or Calciferol

VITAMIN K
Liver	★★★
Green leaves	★★★
Animal fats	★

2 FOODS SUPPLYING VITAMIN B or B_1 (Aneurin)

Yeast, Dried	
Germ of Cereals, "Bemax"	★★★★
Yeast Extract, "Marmite"	

Middlings, Bran	
Buckwheat, Peanuts	★★★

Dried Peas, Beans, Lentils
Nuts (not coconut)
Wholemeal Wheat & Barley
Rye, Oatmeal, Maize
Whole Rice (brown)
Lean of Pork, Ham, Bacon, Liver, Heart, Kidney (esp. Pig)
Egg Yolk, Hard Roe (Fish) } ★★

VITAMIN E
Wheat germ oil	★★★★
Cereal germ	★★
Whole wheat	★
Green leaves	★★
Some vegetable oils	

Fruits
Vegetables
Lean Meat
Soft Roes } 0 to ★

3 FOODS SUPPLYING VITAMIN C (Ascorbic Acid)

Apple, Banana, Plum, Dandelion, Onion, Beet, Carrot, Parsnip, Milk	★
Tomato, Raspberry, Bean, Lettuce, Swede	★★
Loganberry, Gooseberry, Grapefruit Juice, Rhubarb, Lemon Juice, Red Currant, Potato (new) Liver	★★★
Orange juice, Strawberry Watercress, Broccoli Cauliflower, Spinach, Cabbage, Asparagus tips, germinated Peas	★★★★
Black currant, Kale, Brussels sprouts, Parsley	★★★★★
Rose hips	★★★★★★

VITAMIN P
Oranges	
Lemons	★★★
Grapes	
Plums	★★
Prunes	
Grapefruit	★
Rose Hips	

OTHER B GROUP VITAMINS
Yeast	★★★★
Liver	★★★
Meat	★
Cereals	★

4 FOODS SUPPLYING VITAMIN B_2 COMPLEX

	Nicotinic acid	Riboflavin	Adermin
Yeast, dried	★★★★	★★★	★★★
Yeast, extract	★★★	★★★	★★★
Liver	★★★	★★★	★★
Heart, Kidney	★★	★★	
Meat, lean	★★	★	★
Fish	★★	0	★★
Egg	★	★	
Pea meal	★	★	
Wheat germ	★	★	
Wheat meal	★★	0 to ★	★★★
Maize meal	0 to ★	0 to ★	★★★
Rice meal	0 to ★	0 to ★	★★★
Oat meal	0 to ★	0 to ★	
Potato, Spinach			
Other vegetables	0 to ★	0 to ★	0 to ★

The numbered squares indicate the four classes of food in a complete Diet:

FATS— 1
SEEDS— 2
VEGETABLES and FRUITS— 3
MEAT— 4

In the numbered squares are listed (irrespective of class) vitamin-giving foods graded in value, the more stars the more vitamin.

In the larger squares are the foods with the major vitamins that prevent deficiency diseases. Small inner squares show the foods with minor vitamins preventing certain special symptoms.

ACID-ALKALINE CHART

Column 1. Non-starch foods		Column 2. Proteins and fruits		Column 3. Starchy foods	
AL	Alfalfa	AC	Beef	AL	Bananas
AL	Artichokes	AC	Buttermilk	AC	Barley
AL	Asparagus	AC	Cottage cheese	AC	Beans (lina)
AL	Beans (string)	AC	Eggs	AC	Beans (white)
AL	Wax	AC	Honey (pure)	AC	Bread
AL	Beets (whole)	AC	Nuts	AC	Cereals
AL	Beet leaves	AC	Raw sugar	AL	Chestnuts
AL	Broccoli	AL	All berries	AC	Corn
AL	Cabbage (white)	AL	Apricots	AC	Corn meal
		AL	Apples	AC	Crackers
AL	Cabbage (red)	AL	Avocados	AC	Cornstarch
AL	Carrots	AL	Cantaloupes	AC	Grapenuts
AL	Cauliflower	AL	Cherries	AC	Gluten flour
AL	Celery knobs	AL	Cranberries	AC	Lentils
AL	Chicory	AL	Currants	AC	Macaroni
AL	Coconut	AL	Dates	AC	Maize
AL	Corn	AL	Figs	AC	Millet Rye
AL	Cucumbers	AL	Grapes	AC	Oatmeal
AL	Dandelions	AL	Grapefruit	AC	Peanuts
AL	Eggplant (aubergines)	AL	Lemons	AC	Peanut Butter
		AL	Limes	AC	Peas (dried)
AL	Endive	AL	Oranges	AL	Potatoes (sweet)
AL	Garlic	AL	Peaches		
AL	Horseradish	AL	Pears	AL	Potatoes (white)
AL	Kale	AL	Persimmons		
AL	Kohlrabi	AL	Pineapple	AL	Pumpkin
AL	Leek	AL	Plums	AC	Rice (brown)
AL	Lettuce	AL	Prunes	AC	Rice (polished)
AL	Mushrooms	AL	Raisins	AC	Roman meal
AL	Okra	AL	Rhubarb	AC	Rye flour
AL	Olives	AL	Tomatoes	AC	Sauerkraut
AL	Onions			AL	Squash
AL	Oysterplant			AC	Tapioca
AL	Parsley				

AL Parsnips
AL Peas (fresh)
AL Peppers
AL Radishes
AL Ruta-bagas
AL Savory
AL Sea Lettuce
AL Sorrel
AL Soybean
AL Spinach
AL Sprouts
AL Summer squash
AL Swiss chard
AL Turnips
AL Watercress

These tables are taken from the work of Ragnar Berg of Germany.

Foods preceded by the letters AL are alkaline forming and those preceded by the letters AC are acid forming.

For the arrangement of combinations of foods that will be easily digested we are advised that whilst columns one and two will combine very nicely, as will columns two and three, columns one and three will not. Ragnar Berg does not advise the combination of acid with sweet dried fruits, and says that berries and melons are best eaten alone.

I have included this part of Ragnar Berg's chart partly to help those wishing to maintain correct balance and partly for the benefit of food reformers and those following nature cure diets.

OVEN TEMPERATURES

As this book neared completion I became a little anxious about my ability to guide the housewife in the matter of absolutely infallible temperature settings for her oven.

I have experienced a very large number of cookers on my travels, but have not stayed with them for long enough to do any research since I have known them for but one day each.

When I mentioned my anxiety to my good friend Miss Ena M. Eaves, of the British Electrical Development Association, she told me of the work done on oven temperatures by Miss Bee Nilson, lecturer in Nutrition at the Northern Polytechnic, and reproduced in her work, *The Penguin Cookery Book*.

I am very grateful to Miss Eaves for pointing out the work, to Miss Nilson for the really valuable help, and to Penguin Books Ltd., for allowing me to reproduce the part relevant to oven temperatures.

I have been very careful in compiling the recipes and instructions, but I would advise those using the book, and any cookery book for that matter, since many cookers have their little discrepancies, and pressures do seem to differ in districts, to use the given temperatures as a guide only, carefully noting at the foot of the recipe in the book, the result, and later if the first result is not perfection, any adjustment that has been found necessary.

The following is taken from Miss Bee Nilson's Penguin Cookery Book: *Oven Temperatures*. Ovens vary a great deal, and it is always advisable to follow the advice of the makers. If the oven has no thermometer or heat control, it is well worth buying an oven thermometer, which may be stood on the oven shelf in the centre of the oven or where the food is to be placed. The heat should be adjusted until the thermometer remains steady at the required temperature. You will find temperatures are given with the individual recipes. The "Mark" numbers are those for gas cookers with standard markings.

The following table gives the corresponding markings for other cookers.

Corresponding temperatures in °F	Mark in recipes	Regulo, Cannon and Flavel	Autimo
250-325	2 or under	2 or under	4 or under
325-375	2-5	2-5	4-7
375-475	5-9	5-9	7-10
475-550	9 or over	9 or over	10 or over

Corresponding temperatures in °F	Mainstat	Adjusto	Parkinson Renown
250-325	C or under	4 or under	3 or under
325-375	C-E	4-6	3-5
375-475	E-G	6-8	8 or over

Most thermometers and thermostats on electric ovens are marked as follows:

Mark	Corresponding temperatures in °F
Slow	200-300
Moderate	300-400
Hot	400-475
Very Hot	500 or over

ACKNOWLEDGMENTS

Vitamin chart from "Food, Health and Vitamins" by Dr. and Mrs. Plimmer.

When I commenced feeding my young family upon a strictly vegetarian diet I had no ideas as to how the meals should be balanced in order to ensure correct vitamin intake. Many years later I came upon Dr. and Mrs. Plimmer's very excellent book and having prepared these recipes for publication it occurred to me that their chart, "A Square Meal," would make a very useful guide for others. I am most grateful to Dr. and Mrs. Plimmer for their work and to Messrs. Longmans Green & Co. for their kind permission to reproduce the chart.

Oven Temperatures chart taken from Miss Bee Nilson's "Penguin Cookery Book".

I am very grateful to Miss Ena M. Eaves of the British Electrical Development Association for having told me of the chart in Miss Nilson's book when I expressed my anxiety about giving really accurate guidance on oven temperature settings. I am exceedingly grateful to Miss Nilson for her research and also to Penguin Books Ltd. for their kind permission to reproduce the chart relevant to oven temperatures.

Ragnar Berg's Acid Alkaline chart.

I have had this chart for some ten years. I copied it in full from a book by Bernard Jensen of California, I think the title was *Live Foods and Total Health*. The book disappeared from my care and appreciation some time ago and this has made it rather difficult for me to obtain the source of the chart, and also to obtain permission to use it here. I am still, at the time of going to press, trying to do both. May I here express my real gratitude to Ragnar Berg for her work, to Bernard Jensen for having made it known to me through his book, and to assure both that if I succeed in tracing them, or should this meet them first, I shall be only too pleased to make the usual payment should it be required. Perhaps I shall have the opportunity of meeting Mr. Jensen and so discover more when I fulfil a promise to go to the U.S.A. to train some vegetarian cooks there.

The Jackson Stove Co. Ltd.

I would like to record here my gratitude to Jacksons. particularly as a housewife who has had wonderful and absolutely trouble free service from two of their cookers over a period of twenty-two years. I literally have never had to have a single repair or replacement. In fact that is my trouble. Since my last new cooker three years ago they have now lovely automatic cookers... and I have not a single excuse for scrapping mine. . .

As a demonstrator I have enjoyed using all electric cookers, but confess to a special soft spot for the Jackson. To the cynical may I say that as a freelance this acknowledgment was in no way expected of me.

To the makers of all the lovely electrical equipment it has been my pleasure to use in the course of my work, my warmest thanks.

Again as a freelance and under no obligation I would like to thank all the growers of wheat by compost means, all the millers who use the good method of stone grinding, and make the continued effort to better the nation's bread. I would particularly like to mention Messrs. Prewetts, as without their knowledge I used their products throughout my demonstrating years. I have in all cases found the flour perfect, and can honestly say that I have never failed to turn out the perfect loaf, cake or pastry in any demonstration.

It gave me real pleasure to find that Messrs. Allinsons were selling a compost grown flour at the Food Fair before last. It was the first time that I had seen any flour worthy of demonstration in any exhibition and I was glad to show the members of the public how it cooked.

I would like to acknowledge here all the work done for our good by the very many health stores all over the country. A visit to one cannot but leave one with better means of nourishment, and it gives me pleasure to use this means of expressing gratitude.

Lastly I would like to acknowledge the work done in this country by the members of the Vegetarian Catering Association, each in their own special field as well as in their corporate efforts. As a freelance demonstrator of a comparatively new line I have had to have something I could pin myself to, and it has been most useful to mention my membership of that association. I hope that members will feel that my time spent on this book has been of use to us in our aims.

JANET WALKER
Vegetarian Catering Association

ALMOND AND ONION – No. 1

2 pts white stock No. 35: 2 Tbs Almond cream or blend as advised in No. 557: 1 bay leaf: 1 medium potato: 1 clove of garlic or ½ tsp garlic powder: 1 large onion: 1 Tbs honey: 1 Tbs fresh chopped mint or 1 tsp mint and gooseberry jelly No. 615

Shred onion and scrubbed potato and add to stock in pan with bay leaf and shredded garlic. Simmer 20 minutes then remove bay leaf, sieve soup and return to pan keeping back one cup of liquor for blending with nut cream and honey as in Recipe No. 2.

Bring soup to boil, then remove from heat – add cream and honey blend and do not boil again. Season, if required, but do not spoil delicate flavour. Garnish with chopped parsley and serve with croutons No. 695.

ALMOND AND TOMATO – No. 2

6 large ripe tomatoes: 1 onion, medium sized: 2 Tbs Almond cream or (1 Tbs almond kernels with 2 Tbs water blended to a cream in an electric liquidizer): 1 Tbs honey: 1 bay leaf: 2 pts white stock No. 35: fresh chopped parsley to dress

Into a pan put quartered tomatoes, sliced onion and stock with bay leaf and bring to boil and then simmer for 20 minutes. Remove bay leaf and sieve and return to pan and bring to boil, but keeping back a cup of liquor for blending with nut cream. If you have a liquidizer, add cup of liquor and blend, otherwise blend with fork or rotary whisk, including honey, and add to pan. Reheat but do not boil after adding almond cream. Serve garnished with chopped parsley and with fingers of wholewheat toast.

APPLE – No. 3

4 good sized cooking apples: 3 pts hot water: ½ oz butter: 1 Tbs sago: 1 Tbs lemon juice: ½ tsp cinnamon: 1 Tbs honey

Well wash, halve and shred apples without peeling. Simmer for 10 minutes in pan with water and lemon juice then sieve. Return to pan with lemon, honey, sago, butter and cinnamon, bring to boil then simmer for 15 minutes, stirring well at first. Serve either hot or very cold.

CREAM OF ARTICHOKE – No. 4

2 lb Jerusalem artichokes: a few sticks of celery: paprika: 2 pts milk: 1 oz butter (or 2 pts white stock No. 35): ¼ pt top milk or cream: seasoning

Scrub artichokes and before peeling have a pan of cold water in which is a lemon skin or a slice of lemon. As each is peeled, dip into water and slice under it, leaving slices till all are done. Chop celery into small pieces.

Melt fat in pan, drop in artichoke slices and celery and turning about, let simmer in fat for a few minutes without browning. Pour on stock, or milk, bring to boil then simmer for 30 minutes. Sieve and return to pan, season to taste and boil. Remove from heat, add top milk or cream, and pour into tureen. Garnish with paprika, and serve with croutons No. 695.

WHOLE BARLEY – No. 5

1 cup brown barley: 1 cup new milk: 2 pts white stock No. 35: 1 onion: 1 carrot: 1 turnip: fresh parsley or chervil: 1 oz butter or margarine

Cook barley, simmering gently for 1½ hours in stock with lid on pan. Add vegetables diced and cook for further 20 minutes. Sieve and return to pan to re-heat with milk and butter. Stir well and serve in hot tureen garnished with finely chopped parsley or chervil. Season if liked.

FLAKED BARLEY – No. 6

1 cup barley flakes: 1 oz butter or margarine: 1 onion: 1 carrot: 1 turnip: 2 pts white stock No. 35: ½ cup top milk: 1 tsp fresh or ¼ tsp dried herbs: seasoning

Melt butter in pan, add finely shredded onion and diced vegetables, and shaking frequently over gentle heat simmer for 5 minutes. Add barley flakes and hot stock and herbs, and simmer further 20 minutes, after stirring. Season as desired, add top milk and serve in tureen garnished with parsley or chervil.

BROAD BEAN PURÉE – No. 7

2 large cups shelled broad beans: 2 large cups hot white stock No. 35: ½ large cup top milk: 1 medium onion: 1 oz butter or margarine: 1 Tbs semolina: nutmeg: salt as required: paprika: parsley to garnish

Boil beans in water or stock until skins can be removed. Cool and remove skins. Chop onion. Cook onion in fat in pan, till golden, over gentle heat, add semolina and stir. Add stock and hot milk, beans and nutmeg. Bring to boil and simmer for 15-20 minutes, sieve, return to pan to boil, seasoning to taste. Add top milk, serve in tureen with parsley and paprika to garnish, and with croutons No. 695.

HARICOT BEAN PURÉE – No. 8

2 cups haricot beans soaked overnight: 2 pts white stock No. 35: 1 medium onion: 1 carrot: 1 oz butter or margarine: 1 cup top milk or cream: salt and nutmeg: ¼ tsp dried or 1 tsp fresh chopped herbs: fresh chopped chives to garnish

Melt butter in pan and cook onion and diced carrot together for 2 minutes without allowing to darken. Add stock and a pinch of nutmeg and after boiling simmer for 2 hours. Sieve and return to pan to boil. Season, remove from heat and add top milk or cream. Serve in tureen garnished with finely chopped parsley and fingers of fried bread No. 696.

BEETROOT – No. 9

1 large raw beet: 2 pts stock or hot water: 1 shallot: 2 sticks celery: 1 small or ¼ lettuce: 1 oz butter: 1 Tbs wholewheat flour: ½ tsp marjoram: 1 clove or pinch of powdered clove: fresh chopped parsley to garnish: ¼ pt cream or top milk

Melt butter in pan, cook finely chopped shallot and celery for 2 minutes, stirring. Add flour and stir, add beet finely shredded and hot water, clove and marjoram. Bring to boil, then simmer 20 minutes. Sieve, return to pan, season to taste and bring to boil. Remove from heat, add cream or top milk. Into tureen place very finely shredded lettuce and pour soup over. Serve with croutons of bread No. 695.

CARROT AND RICE – No. 10

½ lb carrots diced small: 1 medium onion, sliced thinly: 2 pts white stock No. 35: 1 Tbs wholewheat flour: ½ cup cooked rice No. 68: ½ oz butter: seasoning, and a pinch of nutmeg: ½ tsp sugar: chopped chives to garnish

Cook onion in butter in large pan till golden, add flour and stir, then add carrots then gradually, stock. Bring to boil and then simmer, covered, for 20 minutes. Season, add sugar and nutmeg, and rice, bring to boil again, and serve with chopped chives, and fingers of wholewheat toast.

CREAM OF CARROT – No. 11

½ lb diced or sliced carrots: 1 small onion or leek sliced: 1 pt white stock No. 35: 1 pt hot milk: ¼ pt top milk: ½ tsp sugar: 1 Tbs semolina: 1 oz butter: seasoning, nutmeg: fresh chopped chives to garnish

Gently cook onions in butter in large pan till golden, add semolina and stir, add carrots and stir, then gradually, stock and hot milk and boil for 20 minutes. Pass through sieve or mouli, season, add sugar and nutmeg, return to pan and bring to boil. Remove from heat, add top milk and serve in hot tureen garnished with chives and with croutons No. 695.

CREAM OF CAULIFLOWER – No. 12

1 small cauliflower: 1 medium onion: 1 Tbs wholewheat flour: 1 oz butter or margarine: 1 tsp sugar: 1 pt water: 1 pt hot milk: ¼ pt top milk: fresh chopped parsley or chives to garnish

Cut cauliflower into really small pieces. Slice onion. Place fat and onion in large pan and stir about then gently cook for 2 minutes. Gradually add flour whilst stirring, then water, cauliflower and hot milk. Bring to boil and then simmer for 15 minutes. Sieve, season if liked, return to pan and boil, then remove from heat, add top milk and serve in hot tureen with parsley or chives to dress, and accompanied by toast or croutons of fried bread No. 695.

CREAM OF CELERY – No. 13

2 pts white stock No. 35: 1 medium head celery: 1 cup top milk: 1 Tbs semolina: 1 saltspoon garlic salt: chopped parsley to garnish

As above with addition of semolina and garlic salt until celery is cooked, then pass through sieve to purée, and re-heat without boiling, with top milk added. Garnish with finely chopped fresh parsley and serve in hot tureen with fingers of fried wholewheat bread No. 696.

CELERY BROTH – No. 14

2 pt white stock No. 35: 1 small head celery

Thoroughly clean and chop celery really fine, simmer together for 30 minutes, add extra seasoning, if necessary, before straining and serving.

CREAM OF CHESTNUT – No. 15

2 cups chestnuts: 1 oz butter or margarine: 2 sticks celery and chopped green to garnish: 1 carrot: 1 medium onion: 2 pts white stock No. 35: ¼ pt top milk: salt, nutmeg, paprika

Place chestnuts in grill pan under heat for a few minutes, shaking about occasionally to prevent burning. Soon it will be found possible to remove shells and skin easily. Pass through nut mill or fine mincer. Melt butter and cook sliced onion for 2 minutes, stirring, until golden, add milled nuts, diced carrot, nutmeg and stock, and bring to boil. Simmer 45 minutes, sieve and return to heat and bring to boil. Remove from heat, add top milk and season to taste. Pour into tureen, add chopped celery green and paprika to garnish and serve with toast fingers.

CREAM SOUP – No. 16

2 pts hot white stock No. 35: 2 oz wholewheat flour: ¼ pt yoghourt: 1 cup top milk: 2 Tbs cream cheese: 1 oz butter: 1 Tbs chopped fresh chives: pinch of nutmeg

Melt butter in pan over gentle heat. Gradually stir flour and cook for 1 minute whilst stirring. Add hot stock very gradually whilst continuing to stir. Simmer for 15 minutes. Beat cream cheese and yoghourt together with chives and nutmeg and stir in a cup of the hot liquor, then when really blended, add to main liquor and stir well. Serve with croutons No. 695.

CONSOMMÉ – No. 17

Brown stock No. 34 or white stock No. 35: with added yeast extract or Vecon

Or good vegetable liquor with added yeast extract or Vecon. Use hot or cold.

CREAM OF CUCUMBER SOUP – No. 18

2 good-sized cucumbers: 1½ pts white stock No. 35: 1 large cup hot milk: 1 small cup top milk: 1 oz butter or margarine:

> 1 *rounded Tbs wholewheat flour:* ½ *tsp sugar: a few spinach leaves or some green vegetable colouring: salt, nutmeg, pepper*

Peel both cucumbers, cut out, with a vegetable cutter, about a dozen small balls or other shapes, to garnish. Grate remainder of cucumbers finely and add to most of the butter melted in stew pan with shredded spinach leaves. Cook gently without browning for 5 minutes then add flour and cook further few minutes with sugar. Gradually add stock and bring to boil, then simmer for 15 minutes. Pass through sieve to purée and re-heat again, adding hot milk, seasoning and if necessary, colouring to delicate pale green tint. Finally, add top milk and serve in hot tureen adding cucumber balls to garnish, with croutons of wholewheat bread fried No. 696.

Gelozone or agar-agar may be used instead of flour for thickening according to instructions, when this soup could be served chilled in hot weather.

COLD FRUIT – No. 19

> To 1 *pt tin or bottle of fruit juice (not cordial) add:* 1 *pt water boiled for* 10 *mins with* 1 *heaped Tbs of either powdered barley or semolina, or* 2 *level tsp agar-agar: and adding either* 1 *Tbs sugar, or after cooling a little,* 1 *Tbs honey*

Add some finely diced fruit of the flavour–or to contrast, as available, garnish with mint leaves or flower petals (i.e. marigold, nasturtium, primrose, rose or violet). Any number of soups can be made, but they must be very fresh–really chilled–and attractively served. Tomato juice may be used, but with less dilution and preferably thickened with agar-agar.

JULIENNE SUMMER – No. 20

This is nicest in summer when peas, carrots, onions, French and broad beans etc. are in season, but I have made it very satisfactorily with Swell mixed vegetables soaked for 1 hour. It is quickly made by preparing and then very finely shredding all vegetables but peas and the smallest of onions. Vegetables should not be thicker than a match stick.

> 1 *large cup prepared vegetables:* 2 *pts brown stock No.* 34: ¼ *oz butter:* 1 *tsp honey: fresh chopped mint to garnish: (In winter* 1 *tsp of mint and gooseberry jelly No.* 614 *could be substituted)*

Gently boil vegetables in stock and when tender add butter-mint

and honey and season to taste. The flavour should be delicate.
Serve with fingers of fried wholewheat bread No. 696.

LEEK – No. 21

*1 lb leeks: 2 pts hot white stock No. 35: 1 oz butter: ¼ cup top
milk: 1 large potato: paprika: salt, if needed: chopped parsley
to garnish*

Scrub potato till like parchment, then thinly slice. Remove any
unworthy parts of leek–then cut through centre lengthwise, which
makes it easier to clean thoroughly. Keeping them in tidy halves,
clean well and rinse, then cut into ¼ inch slices. Melt fat in pan,
add leek and potato and simmer, shaking occasionally, keeping
covered. After two or three minutes add stock and stir well, bring
to boil and simmer for 30 minutes. Add top milk and season to
taste. Garnish with parsley and paprika and serve with wholewheat toast.

LENTIL AND TOMATO – No. 22

*8 oz lentils: 1 medium onion: stick of celery: ½ lb tomatoes:
1 clove of garlic: 2 oz margarine: 1 Tbs wholewheat flour: 2 pts
brown stock No. 34: a little lemon juice: seasoning: chopped
chives to garnish*

Slice onion and "sweat" in large pan with butter till golden. Add
flour and stir, add stock and lentils, sliced tomatoes and celery.
Bring to boil and simmer, covered, for an hour. Sieve and re-heat,
add lemon juice and season to taste, serve in hot tureen garnished
with chopped chives and with fingers of fried bread No. 696 or
toast. Finely grated cheese may be passed with the soup, especially if second course is a light one.

MUSHROOM – No. 23

*½ lb mushrooms: 1 medium onion: 1 oz butter or margarine:
2 pts white stock No. 35: 1 Tbs wholewheat flour: salt and
paprika: chopped parsley to garnish*

Melt butter in pan and simmer sliced onion for 2 minutes with lid
on pan, shaking occasionally. Add flour and stir, then herbs and
stock and very finely chopped mushrooms. Simmer for 30 minutes. Season as desired and serve with chopped parsley and
paprika and accompanied by fingers of fried bread No. 696.

CREAM OF MUSHROOM – No. 24

½ lb mushrooms: 1 large onion: 2 oz butter or margarine: 1 Tbs wholewheat flour: 1 pt white stock No. 35: 1 pt hot milk: 1 cup top milk: salt and paprika: chopped parsley to garnish

Finely chop mushrooms after washing but not peeling. Dice onion. Melt butter in stew pan and cook onion until tender, but brown – add mushrooms and continue to cook– stirring frequently. Add flour and stir well then stock and hot milk and simmer for 30 minutes. Sieve and return to pan and re-heat with seasoning. Finally add top milk and serve in hot tureen garnished with chopped parsley and accompanied by fried wholewheat bread croutons No. 695.

BROWN ONION – No. 25

2 large onions: 2 pts brown stock No. 34: 1 oz wholewheat flour: 1 oz butter or margarine: ¼ tsp nutmeg: ¼ tsp marjoram: chopped chives to garnish

Sweat sliced onions in margarine in pan for several minutes, shaking pan to prevent burning, and keeping heat very gentle. Add flour and stir, add stock and nutmeg and bring to boil. Simmer for 20 minutes then add herbs, and season to taste. Serve garnished with chives and pass croutons No. 695.

PEASANT ONION – No. 26

2 large onions: 1 clove of garlic: 1 carrot: 1 medium potato: 1 oz margarine: 1 bay leaf: 2 pts white stock No. 35: 1 oz finely grated cheese: 2 thick rounds toast, diced: chopped chives or chervil to garnish: seasoning, powdered sage

Sweat sliced onions and shredded garlic in margarine, shaking frequently, for 5 minutes over gentle heat. Add diced carrot, sage and bay leaf with stock. Bring to boil, then simmer for 25 minutes. Place toast in tureen and sprinkle with cheese. Pour soup over and give a minute under hot grill. Garnish with chopped chives or chervil and serve.

CHEESE AND ONION SOUP – No. 27

3 good-sized onions: 2 pts white stock No. 35: 2 Tbs wholewheat flour: 3 heaped Tbs grated cheese: seasoning: 4 rounds wholewheat toast cut into triangles: 2 Tbs margarine

Peel and slice onions, place in stew pan with margarine and cook to golden brown, turning about frequently. Add flour and stir well, add hot stock and bring to boil, then simmer for 30 minutes. Season with herbs, (marjoram goes well with cheese, but flavouring can be varied) and salt if needed. Add cheese to hot tureen and serve with toast. Remember that cheese is salty, so spare the salt.

GREEN PEA – No. 28

> 3 cups shelled or soaked dried green peas: a few spring onions or a small shallot: 1 oz. margarine: 1 oz semolina: ½ tsp sugar: 1 cup top milk: 1 bunch green mint some (chopped for garnish): 2 pts white stock No. 35 (or 2 pts of stock made by boiling pea pods)

If using fresh peas, boil pods in 2 pts water for 15 minutes and mash down well before straining to make stock. Make up to 2 pts if necessary.

Melt fat in pan and cook onions, chopped, or shallot, for 1 minute, add semolina then peas, stir, add stock and bring to boil. Simmer for 15 to 20 minutes according to whether fresh or soaked peas are used, with some of mint added. Sieve to purée, keeping a few peas back to garnish, if liked. Re-heat, add top milk and serve garnished with finely chopped mint and some peas and croutons No. 695.

SPLIT PEA SOUP – No. 29

> 1 cup split peas: 1 leek: 1 carrot: 2 pts brown stock No. 34: 1 cup tomato juice: 1 oz butter or margarine: 1 tsp chopped fresh or ¼ tsp dried herbs: seasoning: chopped fresh parsley to garnish

Soak peas overnight. Scrub and dice carrot. Split leek down centre and thoroughly clean without spoiling halves. Cut into thin slices. Heat butter in stew pan and cook leek turning about with spoon to prevent burning. Add carrot, herbs, stock and peas and simmer for 1½ hours. Sieve to purée and return to pan and re-heat with tomato juice and seasoning. Serve in hot tureen with parsley for garnish, and accompany with wholewheat toast fingers.

POTASSIUM BROTH – No. 30

A very valuable drink for the healthy or sick alike. Invaluable in fasts and simply prepared.

If cooking green or root vegetables without salt, the liquor may be used. If preparing specially, use any green vegetable leaves and stalks, cabbage, watercress, celery, lettuce, sorrel, dandelion, mint, etc., and a carrot, turnip, etc., minced after cleaning. Do not cook long, 10-15 minutes boiling then strain off liquor, add level teaspoon yeast extract, and drink hot. This makes a delicious drink for mid-morning or bedtime and is a vital food containing necessary mineral salts.

If you possess a liquidizer there is no need to cook, but add water to vegetables in machine and when reduced, strain, add yeast extract and serve.

POTATO SOUP – No. 31

4 medium – sized raw potatoes: 3 sticks celery or 1 celeriac: 1 medium onion: 1 rounded Tbs butter or margarine: 1 pt white stock No. 35: 1 pt hot milk: 1 level Tbs semolina: salt, paprika, nutmeg: chopped chives to garnish

Well scrub and dice potatoes, celery or celeriac and onion. Melt butter in stew pan and add celery or celeriac and onion and cook for a few minutes, turning about frequently. Add semolina and stir well, then stock and milk and potato and simmer for 30 minutes. Sieve and return to pan to re-heat, adding seasoning. Serve in hot tureen garnished with chopped chives and paprika, accompanied by croutons of fried wholewheat bread No. 695.

SORREL, LETTUCE AND CHERVIL – No. 32

A handful each of sorrel, lettuce and ⅓ cup chopped chervil: 2 egg yolks – or 1 would do if large: 2 pts white stock No. 35: a little cold water or stock: 1 tsp cider vinegar: 1 oz butter

With fingers tear washed lettuce and sorrel into smallish pieces and with chervil, simmer in butter, in pan for 10 minutes, over very gentle heat, frequently shaking. Add stock, bring to boil and simmer for 20 minutes, then add cider vinegar and egg yolks beaten in cold stock or water – ½ cupful – heat again but do not boil. Season if required, and serve with croutons No. 695.

SPINACH PURÉE – No. 33

2 lb spinach: 1 clove of garlic: 1 pt white stock No. 35: 1 pt hot milk: 1 rounded Tbs butter or margarine: 1 rounded Tbs wholewheat flour: salt and nutmeg

Have ready a large thick-bottomed stew pan. Pick over then wash spinach in 4 to 5 waters before lifting, wet, into stew pan. Cover with lid and stew gently until tender, stirring occasionally. A very little water may be necessary, but under $\frac{1}{2}$ cup should suffice. Press cooked spinach through sieve to purée and whilst it is in the basin, melt butter in stew pan and add finely minced garlic clove. Stir about well whilst cooking but do not brown. Shake in flour and mix well then add gradually a cup of hot milk to make a sauce and boil for a minute, very gently. Add rest of milk gradually, while stirring, and then hot stock and purée. Bring all to boil and season before serving in a hot tureen with croutons of fried whole-wheat bread No. 696.

BROWN STOCK – No. 34

As for White stock No. 35 but with the addition of pieces of car-rot, carrot tops, shredded lettuce and cabbage, watercress stalks, pea pods, green beans, tomatoes and swedes.

Note on Stock: If no stock available use hot water and a good yeast or vegetable extract, taking care not to use so much as to kill the flavour of soup. It will be understood that the bouquet garni No. 762 and other herb flavourings will be missing from soup–so these will have to be added in order to achieve a soup of any flavour. Read both stock recipes in order to get the idea of flavour for soups. These flavours are far superior to the slapdash salt and pepper only, and are the reason why I do not give quan-tities of salt and pepper throughout. Try the fine and delicate flavours and cultivate a palate for them. So many palates today only respond to shocks!

WHITE SOUP STOCK – No. 35

Can be made from trimmings from leeks, celery, celeriac, cauli-flower, turnips, onions, potatoes, mushroom stalks, or the water from cooking any of these vegetables. Any untidy-looking pieces that are not presentable for the table can be used. Well scrub, and cut into tiny pieces and place in a large pan with water only just visible from the top. Put on to simmer, adding a few peppercorns and a couple of cloves, with a bouquet garni No. 762 and a bay leaf.

Cover and simmer for not longer than 30 minutes. Press well and give a good stir–then strain and use liquor for white stock. For illness egg shells may be added, crushed. The liquor may be used as it is for broth, or with added yeast extract makes a good drink for a fasting person, to take every few hours. Do not keep longer than 2 days – it is easy to make fresh.

TOMATO SOUP – No. 36

1 lb tomatoes (or a small tin tomato purée): 2 medium onions: 1 medium potato: 1 medium carrot: 2 pts vegetable stock No. 34 or 35: 1 oz wholewheat flour: some cleaned celery trimmings: ¼ pt top milk: 1 oz butter or margarine: marjoram or basil: seasoning as required: 1 oz finely grated cheese: chopped parsley to garnish

Slice onions and scrubbed potato, celery trimmings, carrot and tomatoes and "sweat" together in large pan with butter. Add flour and stir about, then gradually add water and extract, or stock, and if purée used, add this now and not at the first stage. Bring to boil then reduce to simmering and add herbs, continuing to simmer for 20 minutes. Put through sieve or mouli and return to pan to re-heat. Season as required, add top milk and do not boil. Turn into heated tureen and add grated cheese, stir well, add chopped parsley and serve with croutons No. 695 or pulled bread No. 698.

CREAM OF TOMATO – No. 37

2 lb ripe tomatoes or a large can of tomato purée: a small leek or a medium onion: ½ clove of garlic or a pinch of garlic powder: 1 pt white stock: 1 pt hot milk: ¼ pt top milk: ½ oz butter: 1 Tbs semolina: 1 tsp marjoram: a small bunch of parsley: some chopped parsley to garnish: seasoning as required

Melt fat in a large pan, add sliced onion or leek and garlic, and "sweat" over a gentle heat for a minute, shaking pan occasionally. Add sliced tomato and stir, add semolina and stir, then stock and hot milk, and finally herbs. Boil then simmer with lid on for 10 minutes. Season, then sieve, and return to pan to re-heat, adding top milk and not quite boiling. Serve in hot tureen with croutons No. 695 or toast.

TOMATO AND VERMICELLI – No. 38

1 lb tomatoes: 1 oz vermicelli: 1 medium onion: ½ oz butter: 1 clove of garlic: ½ tsp sugar or honey: seasoning: 2 pts white stock No. 35: chopped parsley to garnish

Thinly slice onion and garlic, peel and quarter tomatoes. "Sweat" onion and garlic in butter for 2 or 3 minutes, shaking pan occasionally, then add stock, bring to boil and simmer for 15 minutes. Add vermicelli and simmer again for further 10 minutes before serving. Add sweetening and season to taste, serve in tureen dressed with parsley and hand fingers of wholewheat toast.

AUTUMN VEGETABLE WITHOUT THICKENING – No. 39

2 large carrots: 1 large onion: 1 small leek: 1 stick celery: 2 turnips – medium – or 1 large: 3 Tbs peas: 12 French beans: seasoning: 2 pts brown stock No. 34: 1 oz butter or margarine: Dice all vegetables – keep peas and diced beans separate. Melt fat in pan, adding a handful at a time and stirring all the while, gently start vegetables simmering in butter. Simmer and stir for 10 minutes, then add stock and stir again. Bring to boil and simmer for 5 minutes more, add peas and beans and again simmer for 10 minutes. Season to taste, and serve with croutons No. 695.

NUT SAVOURIES

ALMOND ROAST – No. 40

*4 oz milled almond kernels without skinning: 1 thick slice whole-
wheat bread weighing same as almonds: 1 oz butter or margarine:
half a cup of boiling milk or tomato juice: 1 grated shallot or
piece of onion: 1 medium carrot, grated: 2 tsp chopped fresh or
½ tsp dried herbs to flavour: 1 beaten egg to bind: seasoning if
required: baked crumbs, No. 699 to coat: 1 oz fat for roasting*

Place bread in bowl, pour over boiling milk or juice, add butter,
cover and leave whilst milling and grating nuts, carrot, etc. Mash
bread firmly with potato masher, add other ingredients and shape
into a roll. Roll in crumbs. Heat cooking fat in baking dish, when
melted roll roast in this and baste, then bake at 400°F or Mark 5
for 1 hour. Serve with mint jelly No. 614 or mint sauce No. 361 or
any hot sauce selected, and hot vegetables. Serve also hot or cold
with salad.

ALMOND RISSOLES – No. 41
Make as for roast No. 40 then shape into individual rissoles or
sausage shaped rolls, about 3 by 1½ inches.

Melt fat in grill pan and about 1½ oz., and when melted roll
each rissole in it to baste; for flat ones, lay in, then turn over at
once – then grill for a few minutes at maximum heat and about
10 minutes at low heat.

Serve hot with sauce or jelly and vegetables, or cold with salads.

BRAZIL ROAST – No. 42
Make as for almond roast No. 40, substituting brazil kernels and
omitting carrot and adding 1 level tablespoon wholewheat flour.

BRAZIL NUT RISSOLES – No. 43
As brazil nut roast No. 42 mixture, and method for rissoles as
almond rissoles No. 41.

CASHEW NUT ROAST – No. 44
As brazil nut roast No. 42 or almond roast No. 40, substituting

milled cashews and keep back a few kernels to press on top to
decorate.

CASHEW NUT RISSOLES – No. 45
As cashew roast No. 44 for mixture, and almond rissoles No. 41
for process of making and cooking rissoles.

HAZEL ROAST – No. 46
As for almond roast No. 40 but substituting hazel kernels for
almonds. Hot water and 1 teaspoon yeast extract may be used to
soak bread.

HAZEL RISSOLES – No. 47
As for hazel roast No. 46, making as almond rissoles No. 41.

STUFFED PINE KERNEL ROAST – No. 48
A special roast for Christmas Day meal or any celebration.

½ lb milled pine kernels (saving 1 Tbs whole for decorating roast):
½ lb wholewheat bread crumbs, fresh: 2 eggs: 2 oz butter:
1 Tbs finely shredded onion: 1 Tbs fresh and finely chopped or
1 tsp dried herbs: seasoning

Gently fry onion in butter, blend in with beaten eggs, crumbs and
milled nuts with onion, herbs and seasoning and, if necessary, a
little hot milk to help bind. Press out on a floured sheet of kitchen
paper, then make stuffing as follows:

4 oz breadcrumbs: 2 oz nut suet: egg to bind: 1 Tbs finely
chopped parsley: 1 tsp thyme and sage

Mix all together and spread on roast. Roll up with the aid of
paper, and pat firm.

Heat 2 oz. nut suet in baking dish, roll roast in this to coat well,
then press on or stick with pine kernels along top to decorate.

Roast in remaining fat in dish at 400°F or Mark 5 for about
an hour or until a good and appetizing golden brown.

When cooked, blend a little flour and some apple or tomato
juice in roasting dish and heat to boiling.

Pineapple slices warmed through in the oven are delicious
served with this roast.

UNCOOKED NUT SAVOURY – No. 49

1 cup milled nut kernels, walnuts, hazels or almonds: 1 cup whole-wheat crumbs, fresh: 1 small shallot finely grated: ½ Tbs olive oil: fresh chopped or dried herbs for seasoning: a large tomato

Blanch and peel tomato and either liquidize it in an electric liquidizer or pass through a sieve into a mixing bowl. Add oil and shallot, then crumbs, and thoroughly mix to moisten them, then nuts and herbs, and really well blend.

Have a small basin well greased with butter or margarine, press in the mixture and smooth down level. Cover and weight down, leave to firm for a few hours if possible, when it will easily cut into slices for serving with salad.

Tomato juice may be used if no fresh tomato available. The savoury will look very small but it is concentrated nourishment and very satisfying.

If liked it can be decorated with piped whipped cream.

I am indebted to Bridget Amies for the first such savoury I tasted. Made with almonds and tomato juice and quite delicious.

STEAMED NUT CROQUETTES – No. 50

½ cup milled hazels: ½ oz margarine: 4 small mushrooms: ½ cup breadcrumbs: hot stock, or hot water and Yeastrel: seasoning and herbs

Four dariole tins well greased. Mushrooms in bottom, underside down. Press down mixture and steam for 25 minutes, with greased paper over all four tins, and corners tucked down towards water.

Half inch water in pan is sufficient, and cover pan with fitting lid. Serve with mushroom sauce No. 363.

WALNUT, VEGETABLE AND NOODLE PUDDING – No. 51

½ cup shelled walnuts: 1 cup noodles, cooked: selection of vegetables to make ¾ lb when prepared (suggest peas, diced carrot, flowerets of cauliflower, diced celery, finely chopped leek and mushroom): 1 Tbs chopped parsley: 2 eggs beaten: a nut of butter: seasoning

Cook vegetables together until nearly tender, in a little water and the butter. Save any liquid from vegetables for sauce. Blend noodles, vegetables, parsley and egg in pan – then add walnuts, and pack into a well greased basin. Cover with greased paper and steam for about $1\frac{1}{2}$-2 hours. Serve with a selection of carefully cooked and arranged vegetables.

GLOBE ARTICHOKES STUFFED – No. 52

4 artichokes of equal size: $\frac{1}{4}$ lb mushrooms: 1 minced shallot: $\frac{1}{2}$ clove of garlic finely chopped: 1 yolk of egg: 2 oz butter: 1 Tbs cashew nuts: 1 cup stock or hot water: 1 cup apple juice: potatoes, carrots and onions

Remove the coarsest of outside leaves from artichokes and trim the tops of remaining leaves with scissors where necessary. Leave the artichokes in a covered pan with enough boiling water to cover them, for 10 minutes to blanch. No heat is necessary under pan. Drain artichokes, handling carefully. Turn back leaves around centre and remove the choke from beneath them.

Make stuffing as follows: In a little stock and with $\frac{1}{2}$ oz. of butter gently stew minced mushrooms, minced shallot, garlic and cashews for 10 minutes. Do not swamp with liquid – only keep from drying. When tender remove pan from heat and stir in egg yolk, mixing well and seasoning to taste.

Now fill centres of artichokes with this mixture and then turn leaves back into natural position.

Arrange artichokes steadily on the bed of vegetables and cover with lid. If pan lid does not fit too well, cover with buttered paper first and then lid. Bring slowly to boil, reduce heat to just simmering and leave for one hour when artichokes should be tender. Remove carefully, arranging vegetables on a hot dish with artichokes in centre, and pour over liquor. If liked this can be thickened with vegetable gelatin or wholewheat flour. In the latter case it will need only a little, and should be brought to boil after adding, and before pouring over each artichoke.

STUFFED AUBERGINES – No. 53

2 large aubergines, split lengthwise: 1 green pepper: 2 medium mushrooms: 2 tomatoes: 1 Tbs cashew nuts: $\frac{1}{2}$ cup warm stock or water: 1 tsp cider vinegar: 2 oz butter or margarine: 1 tsp chopped onion

These can either be grilled or cooked in the oven. If grilling, then into grill pan melt half margarine and in this put thinly sliced pepper, tomatoes, mushrooms with nuts, onion and water or stock. Grill until tender, at maximum heat for a minute and then low for about 10 minutes, and turning about frequently. Spread remaining butter on cut sides of aubergines, place on grid cooking stuffing in pan and grill gently about 5-7 minutes, when aubergines will be tender.

Place on a hot fireproof dish, add cider vinegar to stuffing and blend well, seasoning as desired.

Pile on aubergines, sprinkle with breadcrumbs – if liked fry the breadcrumbs in butter and then sprinkle – otherwise dot with a little butter and either heat through again in oven or under grill.

If cooking wholly by oven, then blanch aubergine halves for 2 minutes only in pan of boiling water before putting in greased dish, and cook stuffing in separate saucepan.

AUBERGINE DISH – No. 54

1 *aubergine:* 1 *medium onion:* 1 *clove of garlic:* 1 *green pepper:* 1 *small or 2 inch thick slices, of vegetable marrow:* ½ *lb tomatoes:* 6 *dates:* 2 *oz cashew nuts:* 1 *oz butter: a little apple juice*

Melt butter in a thick saucepan, add sliced onion and, covering with lid, let these gently "sweat" over low heat, turning them about occasionally, and not letting them brown. Next add finely sliced mushrooms with stalk, finely shredded garlic and thinly sliced pepper. Dice aubergine and marrow into inch-sized squares and slice tomatoes and add, giving a good stir and keeping heat low. When a juicy mass results, add cashews and chopped dates and a little apple juice, only sufficient to prevent the mass becoming stodgy. If liked a very little salt can be added, or a very little yeast extract. The flavour should be good without either, and the savoury can be served on a bed of rice, corn, or large slices of fried wholewheat bread.

AUBERGINES WITH CHEESE AND VEGETABLE SAUCE – No. 55

2 *aubergines:* 1 *pepper:* 1 *carrot:* 1 *clove of garlic: A little marjoram:* 1 *cup wholewheat crumbs:* 1 *oz butter:* 1 *lb tomatoes:* 1 *small onion or shallot: Parsley:* 4 *Tbs grated cheddar*

Halve aubergines lengthwise and boil for 2 minutes only. Grease an oven dish, large enough to take aubergines side by side, or in two pairs. Take aubergines from pan and place in dish, and keep all warm. Empty water from pan, and into the hot pan put butter over gentle heat, and adding sliced pepper, garlic and onion, stir about but do not brown. Add sliced tomatoes, marjoram and parsley stalks and very thinly sliced carrot, stir about and continue to cook over very gentle heat, the tomato making liquid, till carrot is almost tender.

Purée mixture and then pour over aubergines in dish. Blend crumbs and grated cheese, and sprinkle over aubergines. Cook at 350°F or Mark 3 for about 30 minutes, then garnish with finely chopped parsley.

This dish can be served cold, in which case, garnish when ready to serve, adding slices of tomato and surrounding with fresh salad.

AUBERGINE AND CHEESE DISH – No. 56

2 large or 3 smaller aubergines: 1 oz wholewheat flour: 1 egg: ½ pt milk: 1 oz butter: 2 oz grated Gruyere cheese: ½ cup cashew nut cream: a little oil or margarine: some chopped parsley

Into a grill pan put a little oil or margarine, and having halved the aubergines lengthwise, lay them in the pan cut side down and then turn the other way up. Grill for two minutes at maximum heat and then reduce heat to low for about five or six minutes, the same for each side, when it will be soft. Remove from pan, peel off skins, and chop coarsely, then keep warming in an oven-ware dish.

Stir flour into melting butter over gentle heat then gradually add milk whilst stirring. Remove from heat, stir in beaten egg, cashew cream and grated cheese.

Pour sauce over aubergines, garnish with chopped parsley and serve hot.

White stock may be used instead of milk if liked.

ONIONS STUFFED – No. 57

4 large onions: 1 Tbs tomato purée: 2 Tbs grated cheese: ½ tsp marjoram: 1 oz butter

Steam or boil onions whole for ½ hour, then remove from pan, take a thin slice off the top and scoop out enough centre to fill. Chop centres, blend with cheese, marjoram and purée, fill up cavity and pile above. Melt fat in pan that will just hold onions and has a fitting lid. Before putting onions into pan, pour a little hot fat over tops, then arrange upright, cover with lid and braize over gentle heat for about 30 minutes. Serve on spring cabbage or spinach or with young broad beans cooked in the pod, or french beans.

Onions may be steamed or cooked in casserole in oven if preferred.

NUTMEAT AND BEAN DISH – No. 58

1 lb runner or French beans: ½ lb tinned nutmeat: ¼ tsp powdered ginger: 1 oz margarine or butter: Seasoning

Wash beans, remove stringy sides, if necessary, break into inch long pieces and gently cook for 7 minutes and keep hot. In a grill pan melt fat, and add diced nutmeat, sprinkle with ginger and stir about. Grill gently to warm through, then add strained beans, stir about and warm again, then pile onto a hot dish to serve with fruit chutney.

STUFFED CABBAGE – No. 59

1 sound young cabbage with good round heart: stuffing as for No. 49

Skin cabbage, leaving perfect heart. Soak this for 5 minutes, in a covered pan of boiling water, but not overheat. Drain. Turn back leaves, about two layers all round, and with a curved saw-edged knife cut out a hollow in centre, large enough to take a clenched fist. Chop some of this and add to stuffing, fill centre and pile above, gently replace folded back leaves, and either tie round, or wrap the whole in buttered parchment paper. Gently steam for 1½–2 hours.

CURRIED CAULIFLOWER – No. 60

One cauliflower cooked as either No. 182 or No. 183 according to your needs. Curry sauce No. 354 poured over cooked cauliflower after placing in a hot dish.

GREEN PEPPERS STUFFED WITH CHEESE, NUT FILLING – No. 61

Well wash peppers, cut off top and remove seeds. Fill with cheese nut mixture No. 113 and chill before serving.

CORN AND HAZEL NUT FRITTERS – No. 62

Fritter batter No. 2

Cooked corn on the cob No. 194 or tinned and drained corn, ready cooked.

Add 1 tablespoon milled hazels to a cup of corn. Season and

blend well, then blend with batter. Cook 1 tablespoon at a time in hot fat until golden, drain on kitchen paper and serve hot.

ELDER FRITTERS – No. 63

Washed sprigs of fresh picked elder flowers: Fritter batter No. 2

Well drain sprigs, dip in batter and deep fry till golden brown. A delightful accompaniment to soup or savoury dishes, curries, stews, etc.

SPINACH AND SAGE FRITTERS – No. 64

Washed spinach and sage leaves: Batter No. 1 or 2

Well drain leaves, fold a sage leaf inside one of spinach, pinch close with finger, or tweezers, and dip into batter then deep fry till golden. Drain on kitchen paper and serve hot.

YOUNG MARROWS AU GRATIN – No. 65

1 marrow per person, or more if very tiny: 1 egg: 2 oz grated cheese: 2 oz butter or margarine: seasoning, paprika, marjoram: ½ cup top milk: ½ oz butter

Wash marrows and slice ½ inch thick into a basin. Cover with boiling water for a few minutes. Grease an ovenware dish. Blend beaten egg with milk and pour in dish. Strain marrow and pile pieces into dish, sprinkling with grated cheese, a little paprika and marjoram. Dot with butter and cook for 30 minutes at 350°F or Mark 3, when marrow should be tender. Serve hot.

STUFFED MARROW RINGS – No. 66

4 slices of marrow 1½ ins thick: 2 oz butter or margarine: 1 cup milled nuts: a few whole nut kernels: 1½ cups wholewheat crumbs: 1 smallish onion, shredded: herbs, seasoning: 1 egg: ¼ pt milk

Remove seeds and pith from centre of marrow slices but leave on rind. Heat 1 oz. margarine or butter in a baking dish that will hold all four rings flat. Put in rings and turn over, and put in oven to commence cooking whilst preparing stuffing. Blend together nuts, crumbs, herbs and seasoning with egg and enough milk to make soft but not sloppy. Fill centres of rings and heap a little, press on top a few kernels. Top with tiny nuts of butter and bake for 40 minutes at 400°F or Mark 5. If rings are blanched in boiling water without heat, and covered, for 10 minutes, up to 10 minutes can be taken from cooking time.

GRILLED MUSHROOMS WITH SHALLOTS AND GARLIC – No. 67

½ lb mushrooms: 2 shallots: a clove of garlic: butter or oil: chopped parsley to garnish: a little water or apple juice, or white wine

Wash and drain mushrooms, cut stalks off short and slice these rather thinly. Heat oil or butter in grill pan, press each mushroom stalk-side down in oil then turn other way up. Between mushrooms sprinkle chopped shallots, garlic and stalk slices and add liquid, about ½ cup. Grill for 5 minutes at maximum heat, looking at mushrooms occasionally to see if any need dabbing with melted oil on pastry brush. Turn low and leave to gently cook for 10 minutes. Remove mushrooms to hot dish. Stir mixture in pan and cook a little longer and add a little flour to thicken, if necessary. Finally pour over mushrooms and garnish with parsley. Can be served on rounds of hot wholewheat toast or on a bed of mashed potatoes or rice.

BOILED RICE – No. 68

1 cup long grain rice: 1½ cups water

Wash rice for a long while in a sieve under running water to remove starch. Place rice and water in top half of double cooker with lid on, and boil water in lower half for ¾ hour when rice will be perfectly cooked. No water should remain in top pan, and each grain of rice should be easily separated. Shake onto a large dish and fork over to lightly separate, then dry in warm oven. Rice can then be fried if wished, or used for curries or any rice dishes.

CASHEW KEDGEREE – No. 69

1 cup boiled rice No. 68: 1 cup cashews: 1 oz butter: 1 finely minced shallot (or a few spring onions): parsley: 1 hard-boiled egg No. 127: 1½ cups water

Simmer cashews in water with shallot for 15 minutes, with lid on, season if liked. When tender, add rice, butter and finely chopped egg, blending gently. Warm through in greased fireproof dish in oven, or over a pan if oven not in use, and sprinkle with chopped parsley before serving with triangles of toast. A level tablespoon of E.M. soup powder, cream of celery, improves this dish.

CURRY WITH RICE – No. 70

Press hot boiled rice No. 68 into oiled ring mould and immediately turn onto large dish. Fill centre with curry sauce No. 354 and if liked, quartered hard-boiled eggs No. 127. Serve with sliced bananas, and plenty of green salad, and triangles of toast or crisp bread.

SAFFRON RICE – No. 71

1 lb rice, long grain: 2 hard-boiled eggs, finely chopped: 1 medium onion, sliced and chopped: 2 cloves of garlic, finely chopped: 1 cup sultanas: ½ tsp saffron: 2 oz butter or 2 Tbs oil: 1 green pepper: seasoning: Parmesan cheese

Cook rice as No. 68 with saffron. Have a warm oven and when cooked shake rice into large dish and fork lightly to separate and dry.

Whilst drying fry onion and garlic with pepper in strips till onion is a delicate golden colour. Remove vegetable to a hot dish and keep hot, whilst heating sultanas in remaining fat in pan, covered with a lid, and over lowest possible heat so as not to burn, and shaking pan frequently. When sultanas are swollen, blend these with oil, fried onion, pepper, rice and chopped egg. Return again to warm oven for a few moments before serving with Parmesan cheese to shake over as required.

If a main meal dish is required, serve with either fresh sliced or baked bananas No. 424, yellow tomato halves, if available, and crisp lettuce or watercress.

RICE FRIED WITH MUSHROOMS AND DRIED FRUIT – No. 72

2 Tbs rice, preferably brown and unpolished: 2 oz mushrooms finely chopped: 1 Tbs currants: olive oil: seasoning

Warm a little oil in a thick frying pan, sprinkle rice in pan and gently fry for 5 minutes whilst finely chopping mushrooms. Add mushrooms and continue gently frying, and just before mushrooms are tender, add currants and stir about until they swell. Season with a little powdered ginger or paprika. Rice should not be soft but crispish, a little like popcorn. Delicious sprinkled over a mixed salad.

RISOTTO – No.73

2 cups boiled rice No. 68: 2 oz butter: 2 shallots or a medium onion: 2 carrots: 1 cup green peas: ½ large or 1 small cauliflower: 2 oz mushrooms, fresh chopped: herbs: seasoning: 2 oz grated cheese: 1 wineglass apple juice or cider or white wine

Cook finely sliced onions and mushrooms in butter and keep hot. Cook diced carrots, peas and flowerets of cauliflower in minimum of water, covering pan to preserve colour, Tip rice on large dish and separate lightly with fork to dry in warm oven. Blend vegetables with onion and very little vegetable water–a couple of tablespoonsful–also herbs and rice, juice or wine. If a more moist dish is required, add rice to vegetables without drying it. Add cheese to pan and stir to blend. Serve with triangles of crisp wholewheat toast, or pulled bread. Crisp radishes or celery make a good accompaniment to the more moist dish.

SAVOURY RICE CROQUETTES – No. 74

2 cups boiled rice No. 68: 2 eggs: ¾ cup milk: 2 tsp wholewheat flour: 1 oz butter or margarine: 1 tsp finely chopped parsley: 1 cup chopped mushrooms: salt and paprika: wholewheat crumbs for coating No. 699: fat for grilling, about 2 oz

Stew mushrooms in 1 oz. fat with lid on pan, over very gentle heat for 3 minutes, add flour, stirring, and milk to make a sauce, cook for half a minute.

Remove from heat and stir in one beaten egg, parsley, seasoning and rice. Blend well, then turn out onto a large dish to cool. When cool shape into croquettes, brush these with second egg, beaten, then roll in crumbs to coat. Melt 2 oz. fat in grill pan, roll each croquette in fat before grilling them till golden. Drain on paper before serving hot or cold.

SALSIFY FRITTERS – No. 75

1 lb salsify: lemon juice: Fritter batter No. 2 or 1: 1 Tbs grated cheese: 1 Tbs chopped parsley: deep fat for frying

After cleaning and scraping salsify, blanch in boiling water for 15 minutes. Place in a hot dish, sprinkle with lemon juice and parsley, cover and keep hot for 15 minutes. Cut into pieces about 2½ inches by ⅓ of an inch thick, coat with batter and deep fry till golden.

Drain well and sprinkle with grated cheese to serve. Garnish with parsley.

STUFFED VINE LEAVES – No. 76

12 vine leaves: 1 shredded small shallot: 2 cups cooked rice No. 68: 2 oz pine kernels: 1 Tbs sultanas: 1 Tbs olive oil: 1 tsp lemon juice: a pinch of nutmeg

Blanch vine leaves in boiling water without heat under, for 2 or 3 minutes, then remove and drain them and place on board underside up. Blend other ingredients in bowl and season, if liked. Place a spoonful of mixture on each leaf and roll up leaf outside. Place each roll nicely filled in bottom of large pan as finished, and pack close to prevent unrolling. If you have to make two layers, place second layer at right angles to first for ease in removing them. Cover with a plate to prevent unrolling, then add a little water, not quite enough to cover plate, place lid on pan and simmer for 20 minutes, remove lid of pan but not plate, and stand aside till quite cold before removing. Carefully drain and chill. Serve cold as hors d'œuvres or part of luncheon or supper meal. May be served hot if liked, and experiment with herb flavouring.

TOMATOES STUFFED WITH
CHEESE NUT FILLING – No. 77

Allow 1 large and firm ripe tomato per person. Well wash and wipe and remove a slice from the top. Scoop out core and seeds, well chop and blend with cheese nut filling No. 113. Chill and serve on salad.

TOMATO BOUCHES – No. 78

½ pkt prepared nutmeal: 2 oz margarine: 4 large tomatoes: Baked crumb dressing

Prepare nutmeal with cold water as directed on packet for rissoles. Divide into four and wrap each tomato in the rolled out paste. Seal by damping joins and roll with the hand on a board, to smooth, and finally roll in crumb dressing.

Melt fat in an ovenware dish large enough to hold the Bouches. Roll them about in fat to baste, then bake for 30 minutes at about 400°F or Mark 6. Serve hot with vegetables.

This recipe was sent to me some years ago anonymously. If the donor sees this, may I say "Thank you"?

BUTTER BEAN LOAF – No. 79

½ lb butter beans cooked No. 80: 2 eggs: Curry sauce No. 354, ½ pt or Tomato sauce No. 371, ½ pt: a cup of crushed breakfast cereal

Mash beans thoroughly and blend with the sauce chosen, and lightly beaten eggs, add cereal and then pack into fireproof dish, well greased, before baking at moderate heat–350°F or Mark 4 for about 40 minutes.

Turn out and serve with sprouts or spinach and carrots, garnished with watercress and tomato slices, pimento strips, or serve cold with salad.

BUTTER OR HARICOT BEANS – No. 80

Wash well in hot water then soak overnight in a basin that will hold a good 2 inches of water – boiling – over top of beans. Next day, drain beans, then cook in boiling water for about 2 hours. If salting, leave this till the end as it hardens the skins, and beans will take longer to cook. When tender, drain and use as desired, as an accompanying vegetable with tomato No. 371 or parsley sauce No. 366 or curry sauce No. 354, or use mashed as base for vegetable loaf, etc.

CASHEW NUT AND MUSHROOM CASSEROLE – No. 81

1 cup cashew nuts: 2 or 3 medium-sized mushrooms: 1 small onion: ½ a clove of garlic, finely chopped: 1 tsp yeast extract: ½ cup wholewheat breadcrumbs: 2½-3 cups vegetable stock or hot water: ½ cup apple juice: herbs and seasoning: 1 oz vegetarian margarine.

Melt margarine in casserole whilst oven is heating. Meanwhile finely slice onion and mushrooms. Add these to fat and turn about, add crumbs, herbs, seasoning, stock, juice and yeast extract, and stir well. Add cashews, cover, and bring to simmering in fairly hot oven, then reduce heat. Cook about 35 minutes, stir before serving.

CARROT, ONION, POTATO CASSEROLE – No. 82

Prepare young carrots and new potatoes and young onions for cooking. Well grease a casserole, inside of lid as well. Arrange vegetables in casserole and add milk to come barely to the top of them, and dot with bits of butter or margarine. Cover with lid and gently cook in oven at 350°F or Mark 4 for an hour. If possible add a handful of shelled garden peas and some chopped mint for the last 10 minutes.

A sprinkling of cheese will make a meal of this dish.

CARROT, ONION, POTATO AND NOODLE CASSEROLE – No. 83

As for No. 82 only adding half a cup of noodles and rather more milk, to swell the noodles.

HARICOT AND SWEDE CASSEROLE – No. 84

Soak ½ lb. haricot beans overnight. When soaked alternating soaked haricots with pieces of sliced swede, chopped parsley and a finely chopped clove of garlic. Barely cover with milk and cook slowly, with lid on, for about 2½ hours at 300°F or Mark 2. Ten minutes before serving, the dish will be improved by a liberal layer of thickly sliced tomatoes added, and covered for remaining time to warm them through.

A sprinkling of cheese will make a complete meal of this dish.

VEGETABLE HOT POT – No. 85

2 medium carrots: 1 cup soaked haricot beans: 1 large onion: 4 medium potatoes: 2 oz butter: 1 pt stock or hot water and yeast extract: 1 Tbs cider vinegar: 3 Tbs tomato purée: 2 chopped mushrooms: 2 or 3 tomatoes as available: seasoning

Grease a casserole (and inside of lid) adequate for 4 persons. Wash and prepare vegetables and vary according to season – say leeks or a handful of spring onions and peas or broad beans, as available. Gently cook onions in butter till golden and almost tender. Remove to plate, then pour purée and stock into the pan and heat together, and season to taste.

In the casserole place first the onions and tomatoes, if available, (tinned or bottled tomatoes may be used), then soaked beans, then chopped mushrooms, then sliced carrots and lastly sliced potatoes – overlapping these to make a "crust" for the hot pot. Lastly pour in the liquor letting it stop short of the top by about an inch so as not to waste over the sides. Cover with lid, and if no lid, then an ovenware plate or a piece of foil, and place in oven at 200°F or nearly Mark 2 and leave for about 2½-3 hours, remove lid for last 15 minutes. When cooked the potatoes should be an appetizing golden colour and the outside ones slightly crisp. Serve in casserole. The purpose of greasing lid inside is to make it more easy to wash up.

LENTIL HOT POT – No. 86

As for vegetable hot pot No. 85 substituting ½ lb. lentils – not soaked – for haricot beans.

Cook same time.

MARROW AND TOMATO CASSEROLE – No. 87

½ lb tomatoes: 3 cups inch-sized marrow cubes: 1 cup cooked rice No. 68: 1 cup grated cheese: a few spring onions: ½ cup milk: ½ oz butter

Pour boiling water over marrow and cover with lid whilst peeling tomatoes and chopping spring onions, green as well as white, and grating cheese. Well grease a casserole, and make a bed of sliced tomatoes in the bottom. Next place marrow cubes and sprinkle these with chopped onion. Blend cheese and rice and then place over vegetables, pour over milk and cover with greased lid. Cook in moderate oven 400°F or Mark 5 for 1 hour, removing lid for last 10 minutes.

Serve with wholewheat toast or buttered wholewheat rolls and crisp raw cabbage shredded, or watercress.

CORNISH PASTIES 1 – No. 88

Using pastry No. 529 roll out to ¼ inch thick and mark out saucer shapes. Moisten outer edge all round with a pastry brush and water. Into centre put heaps of mixture of vegetables in season, cooked and sliced small (a packet of "Swell" mixed vegetables will give an excellent result). Add diced nut meat in an interesting proportion and keep the whole moist. Take up both sides of round pastry and pressing together above heap of filling continue to press both sides together until it is sealed right across. With thumb and finger pinch centre of sealed edge into a wavy ridge after the fashion of the traditional Cornish pasty. Bake 15-20 minutes at 425°F or Mark 6. Serve hot or cold.

CORNISH PASTY 2 – No. 89

As No. 88 but one large pasty, which can contain larger quantity of filling and from which a family can be served. This will need to be cooked at a lower temperature after the first 15 minutes, when reduce it to 375°F or Mark 4. Roll pastry thicker too, and use raw potato and onions, etc., and sprinkle them with stock before sealing. Brush outside with egg and milk to glaze and cook for about 2 hours.

INDIVIDUAL CASHEW AND
MUSHROOM PIES – No. 90

Using short pastry No. 529 and filling No. 92. Make as for mince pies, using a not too shallow patty tin with spaces for little cakes. Fill pies with mixture – hot – and bake 20-25 minutes in hot oven 450°F or Mark 7. Serve hot with accompanying vegetables and sauce, or cold with salad.

CASHEW NUT AND MUSHROOM FLAN – No. 91

Flan pastry No. 530 for flan case: Filling No. 92

Line flan ring or cover the outside of a sponge sandwich tin. Bake then turn onto a hot dish and fill with nut and mushroom mixture. If using a flan ring on a baking sheet, place a piece of kitchen parchment on bottom and on this a few beans as weight. Keep these by you for other "blind" bakings. If using a sponge tin cook upside down, of course.

CASHEW NUT AND MUSHROOM FILLING
FOR FLANS, ETC. – No. 92

1 cup chopped mushrooms: 1 cup cashew nuts (broken ones will do): a small onion, finely chopped or grated: 1 Tbs butter or margarine: 2 cups vegetable stock or 1½ cups hot water and 1 level tsp yeast extract, and ½ cup apple juice: seasoning to taste: a pinch of powdered sage: 2 level tsp sago

Melt margarine in pan, add onion and cook ½ minute over gentle heat. Add mushrooms and stir well, add sago then hot stock. Add cashews, herbs and seasoning, stir gently till boiling then reduce heat and cover pan, allowing contents to simmer very gently indeed for 15 minutes.

Use as filling for flans or plate pies, when some peas, chopped mint and button onions can be added.

CHEESE AND ONION FLAN – No. 93

Flan pastry No. 530: 1 medium onion thinly sliced: 2 cups white stock: 1 Tbs butter: 1 Tbs wholewheat flour or ground rice: ¼ tsp fresh chopped or dried herbs, mixed, sage or marjoram: ¾ cup grated cheese: ½ tsp made mustard

Make flan case as No. 530 and from spare pastry cut crescents, about 12, to decorate top. Cook flan case and cook crescents on a separate tin.

Cook onion in stock with herbs till tender for about 10 minutes, add mustard and either rice or flour blended with a little milk. Bring again to boil and simmer, stirring for 2 minutes. Add cheese, stir, then pour into flan case, arrange crescents in circle, points to centre.

CHEESE, EGG AND LEEK FLAN – No. 94

As No. 93 but using puff pastry No. 527, slices of white of leek, and when sauce is made, add a finely chopped hard-boiled egg No. 127.

CREAM CHEESE VOL-AU-VENT – No. 95

Recipe No. 527 for *vol-au-vent* and cream cheese filling No. 675 heated before filling unless using *vol-au-vent* cold, when use cold.

MUSHROOM VOL-AU-VENT – No. 96

Vol-au-vent recipe No. 95 and filling No. 92.

VEGETABLE PIE – No. 97

Short crust pastry No. 529

A selection of choice vegetables such as peas, tiny carrots or diced carrots, tiny onions, button mushrooms or sliced mushrooms, a few nut kernels such as cashews, pine or walnut. Hard boiled eggs instead of nuts, halved and carefully placed. Some hot vegetable stock or tomato juice, or hot water and yeast extract. Seasoning with herbs, or vegetable salts. Make either a plate or dish pie. Line plate as well as making cover, but if a deep dish, only line edge of dish and cover with pastry. If vegetables are uncooked the pie will need 20 minutes at 450°F or Mark 7, and then with heat reduced to 300°F for another 20 minutes. With electric cooker heat could be reset after first 10 minutes.

This pie can be as plain or as fancy as you like. I personally like to decorate top with "leaves" of pastry; it takes a very short time and looks gay. A pie funnel in centre helps to keep shape and saves liquid boiling over. Brush pie over with a little beaten egg and milk to "highlight" decorations and edges.

TOAD-IN-THE-HOLE – No. 98

Using batter No. 541 and either "sausages" made from prepared nut meal or tinned "sausalatas", or tinned nut meat, mashed and shaped. Melt 1 oz. cooking fat in a baking dish and in this arrange "sausages" with space between, and heat again till fat is beginning to smoke. Pour on batter and return to hot oven cooking at 425°F or Mark 6 for about 30 minutes till golden brown. Serve hot with vegetables and a sauce.

VEGETARIAN SAUSAGE ROLLS – No. 99

Using shortcrust pastry No. 529 and either "sausages" made from a prepared nut meal or tinned "sausalatas", or mashed and shaped tinned nut meat. Roll out paste to ¼ inch thickness and cut pieces 4 inches by the length of pastry. Along pastry lay sausage mixture, or "sausalatas" touching all the way. Fold pastry over sausage. Damp along length with water and pastry brush, fold over remaining pastry and seal along length. Now you have one long sausage roll. Cut through in about 2 inch lengths or as long as required, and cook in hot oven on baking sheet at 450°F or Mark 7 for 15 minutes. Serve hot or cold.

LEEK FLAN – No. 100

As onion and cheese flan No. 93 but using leeks, well washed and carefully cut into ½ inch thick pieces, and using white part of leek only. (The green can be used for soup).

BAKED CHEESE SOUFFLÉ – No. 101

2 oz wholewheat flour: 2 oz butter or margarine: ½ pt hot milk: ¼ tsp made mustard: 4 oz grated cheese: 2-4 eggs

Melt butter over low heat and when it begins to bubble add flour and stir well, then hot milk and keep stirring to make a panada which is the basis for most soufflés.

Remove from heat and cool a little before adding mustard and beaten egg yolks and cheese, blending well. Lastly, fold in stiffly beaten whites (prepared as instructed in No. 510) very gently, then pile into well greased straight sided soufflé dish with a greased band of kitchen parchment pinned round dish firmly so that it stands above the edge for 2 inches. Gently smooth over then bake at 35° F or Mark 3 for 30-40 minutes.

It is essential that everyone is ready to eat when the soufflé is taken from the oven for it begins to subside as soon as removed from heat.

CAULIFLOWER SOUFFLÉ – No. 102

2 oz wholewheat flour: 2 oz butter or margarine: ½ pt hot milk: 2-4 eggs: 1 small cauliflower cooked and sieved: seasoning

In a large pan heat butter till it bubbles when stir in flour, then hot milk stirring briskly. Remove from heat, season, and allow to cool. Beat in egg yolks and sieved cauliflower. Lastly and gently fold in stiffly beaten whites and pile into straight sided dish with paper well greased and pinned around dish. Bake at 350°F or Mark 3 for 30-40 minutes, and as with all soufflés serve immediately.

MUSHROOM SOUFFLÉ – No. 103
Make as for cheese soufflé No. 101 but use 3 oz. very finely shredded mushrooms, heated in the milk, instead of cheese, and omitting mustard.

MARROW SOUFFLÉ – No. 104
Make as for cheese soufflé No. 101 but with only half the quantity of cheese, and add, before the egg yolk, $\frac{1}{2}$ lb. marrow, preferably young, peeled and steamed in parchment for 30 minutes, and sieved to a purée. Sprinkle a little cheese on top before cooking, but not a strong cheese–the more delicate in flavour the better.

SUMMER SAVOURY JELLIES – No. 105
1 pt tomato juice: 2 tsp agar-agar: 1 cup cooked peas: 1 cup diced cooked carrot: $\frac{1}{3}$ cup tiny pearl onions: $\frac{1}{3}$ cup tiny balls of cream cheese: 1 hard-boiled egg No. 127 sliced

Make the jellies in dariole tins or small individual moulds or small cups. Have a double cooker ready, with water boiling in lower half – blend agar-agar with a little tomato juice in top half and then stir whilst adding the rest of juice. Stir for a few moments then cover and leave to simmer for 10–15 minutes more.

Cool liquid a little, then pour a little in each mould and turn it about so as to coat whole of inside with jelly. Next arrange on bottom of mould, a few pieces of vegetable or egg slices, daintily – remembering that this will be the top when turned out.

Decorate sides of mould also, filling up with vegetables, cheese balls, egg etc, as you go, and filling with jelly liquid as you place each layer. As soon as they are really cold they will be ready to serve, but do not turn them out until you are ready to serve – leaving until the last minute. Serve on salad, after dipping mould in lukewarm water to free jelly.

SUMMER GALANTINE – No. 106

> $\frac{1}{2}$ pt tomato juice: 1 tsp vegetable gelatin: 2 hard-boiled eggs:
> a cup of cooked new peas: a cup of cooked tiny carrots: a few
> button mushrooms, stewed: a few broad beans, cooked: about
> 8 asparagus tips, cooked: or any summer vegetables available

Add gelatin to juice and let stand for a few minutes before heating in double saucepan, and stirring frequently. Let water in lower
pan simmer for 15 minutes when gelatin and juice should be well
blended. Pour into basin measure with lip, and cool. Whilst cooling select and leave ready vegetables. Select a large and shallow
glass dish and cover bottom with jellying juice – thinly. On this
arrange carefully and artistically, peas and beans, quartered eggs,
tiny carrots and asparagus, mushrooms, etc., adding a little jelly
at a time and aiming at making a picture with the vegetables. If
jelly sets, warm, stir and then cool only enough to be sure it isn't
steaming hot, or vegetables will get tired looking. The picture will
be enhanced by the addition of some brightly coloured "relief"
with radishes No. 264, olives or cucumber slices in halves, arranged around edge of dish. Chill well and serve with salad.

Tiny individual dishes are very charming and although fiddling
to prepare are so rewarding.

NUTMEAL DUMPLINGS – No. 107

> $\frac{1}{2}$ cup wholemeal flour: $\frac{1}{2}$ cup prepared nutmeal: 1 oz butter or
> margarine: water or stock to mix

Blend fat with flour and meal and make a soft dough with water
or stock. Roll into tiny balls and add to stews, savoury casseroles,
or soups. Liquid must keep simmering for 15 minutes.

PARSLEY DUMPLINGS – No. 108

As for cheese dumplings No. 122 substituting a level tablespoon
chopped parsley for cheese.

CHEESE DISHES

CREAM CHEESE BOATS – No. 109

8 oz cream cheese: 1 cup chopped nut kernels: ½ cup chopped ginger: lettuce: carrot: crispbread

Blend cream cheese, kernels and ginger together and fill crisp lettuce heart leaves. Make a mast with a strip of raw carrot, and large and small sails with thin Primula crispbread in triangles. Serve as salad.

CHEDDAR MOUSSE – No. 110

¼ lb finely grated cheddar cheese: ½ cup wholewheat breadcrumbs: 4 egg whites: 1 pinch of marjoram: (reserve a little cheese for dressing later)

Whisk whites till they will stand in dry peaks. Add cheese, crumbs and marjoram, and do not be alarmed when the result seems to lessen. Pile in a well greased soufflé dish or a basin that will fit into a steamer or over a basin of boiling water. Leave with water gently boiling for about 20 minutes, and finally sprinkle with cheese and gently brown either under grill on low or a warm oven, 350°F at most, for a few minutes before serving.

CHEESE CREAMS – No. 111

1 Tbs grated Parmesan cheese: 1 Tbs cream: 3 egg whites

Beat egg whites till stiff, add cheese and cream and blend. Have ready 4 well greased tiny individual casseroles standing in a tin of hot water. Spoon mixture into dishes and cook for 15-20 minutes at 350°F or Mark 3. Creams may be cooked in a steamer, when they should be covered with well greased paper and ends turned down to prevent steam condensing into them.

CREAM CHEESE HORNS – No. 112

Puff pastry No. 527: cream cheese: chopped walnuts: a little paprika

Roll pastry to ⅛ inch thickness and cut it into enough ½ inch strips to cover metal horn shapes. Commence wrapping from the point and damp any necessary joins in order to stick the pastry securely, and taking care not to overlap the open end, otherwise pastry will not come off the shape when cold. Cook in hot oven as for puff pastry and fill when cold. Chop nut kernels, blend with cheese and adding a little paprika, fill horns when they will be ready to serve.

CHEESE NUT ROLL – No. 113

4 oz cream cheese: 1 finely shredded onion, small: 1 cup chopped nut kernels: 1 tsp lemon juice: ¼ tsp paprika: 1 Tbs cream or top milk

Blend together and shape into a roll, place in refrigerator or very cool place to firm. Serve in slices on salad.

CHEESE YORKSHIRE PUDDING – No. 114

Batter No. 541: 1 cup grated cheese: either 1 medium onion sliced or 1 leek, or ½ cup tiny spring onions: 1 oz cooking fat: 1 tsp marjoram

Heat fat in baking dish with either onion or leek slices or tiny onions in bottom of dish. When quite hot, blend ¾ of cheese with batter, add marjoram and pour mixture over onions. Sprinkle rest of cheese on top and bake for 20 minutes or until you have a good golden top, at 400°F or Mark 4. Serve hot with vegetables and tomato sauce No. 371.

INDIVIDUAL CHEESE PIES – No. 115
CHEESE PASTRY – No. 532

For filling:
2 cups grated Cheddar: 1 oz butter or margarine: 1 egg: 1 cup milk: a pinch of garlic salt: 1 Tbs wholewheat flour: ½ tsp paprika: 1 tsp cider vinegar

Melt fat in milk in pan over gentle heat. Stir in flour, paprika, cider vinegar and garlic salt, and cook for 2 minutes. Remove from heat and allow to cool a little. Beat in egg and then cheddar.

Fill tarts, press on cover as for mince pies No. 418. Serve hot or cold.

CHEESE AND EGG FRITTERS – No. 116

2 eggs: 1 oz margarine: 2 oz finely grated cheese: ½ cup milk: 1 Tbs wholewheat flour: 1 tsp finely chopped onion or shallot: chopped parsley for serving: seasoning

Boil together margarine, milk and flour, cool, beat in eggs, grated cheese and onion and seasoning, with half a teaspoonful of made mustard, a pinch each of salt and paprika. Deep fry spoonsful till golden and serve hot, sprinkled with chopped parsley.

CHEESE TRELLIS – No. 117

1 cup grated cheese: ¼ pt milk: 1 heaped Tbs flour: 1 oz margarine: 2 tomatoes: seasoning: 1 small onion, shredded: ¼ lb pastry – short No. 529

Well grease dish and blend cheese and onion in bottom. Mix flour, milk and seasoning, and pour over. Add sliced tomatoes and nuts of margarine. Roll pastry thinly, make a trellis of fine strips over tomatoes. Bake for 25 minutes in hot oven, 425°F or Mark 6. Serve hot or cold.

CHEESE AND POTATO CAKES – No. 118

2 lb potatoes: 4 oz margarine or butter: 8 oz grated cheese: a cup of top milk

Well scrub and boil or steam potatoes, removing skins when tender. Into a large warm pan pour top milk and half margarine or butter and finely sieved potatoes. Season and stir well, adding cheese. Blend really well, then form into cakes and, melting remaining fat in grill pan, dip in cakes and turn over till all are ready, then grill till golden.

CHEESE MONKEY – No. 119

4 slices wholewheat bread, toasted: 1 cup wholewheat crumbs: 1 cup milk: 1 cup grated cheese: a nut of butter: 2 eggs, lightly beaten: seasoning: chopped parsley to garnish

Soak crumbs in milk whilst making toast. Keep toast hot after buttering. Melt butter in pan, stir in cheese and heat, but do not boil. Add crumbs, egg and seasoning, stir gently over heat until about to boil, then, pour over toast and garnish with parsley, serve immediately.

My mother gave me this recipe many years since. I do not know its origin.

CHEESE AND POTATO SAVOURY – No. 120

2 lb potatoes: 6 oz grated Cheddar or Cheshire cheese: 2 shallots: celery salt: ¼ pt milk

Steam potatoes in jackets, skin and dice. Chop shallots finely into a greased casserole, sprinkle layers of diced potato, shallots and celery salt, add milk and top with cheese. Heat in oven with lid on at 400°F or Mark 6, removing lid to brown for last 10 of 30 minutes.

CHEESE AND POTATO DISH – No. 121

2 thick slices wholewheat bread: 1 cup milk: 1 large onion: 4 large well scrubbed potatoes: 2 large eggs: 2 oz melted margarine: 2 oz coarsely grated cheese: ½ level tsp marjoram: a pinch of garlic salt: seasoning as required

Into a mixing bowl grate raw potatoes and onion, whilst bread soaks in milk. Mash bread and add to mixture with margarine, herbs and garlic salt, most of cheese, and well beaten eggs. Add salt and pepper, if liked, but remember that cheese is salty and allow for this. Well grease an ovenware dish and fill with mixture, topping with remainder of cheese.

Bake at 350°F or Mark 3 for one hour. Before serving decorate with strips of red and/or green peppers or tomato quarters and parsley.

CHEESE DUMPLINGS – No. 122

Using suet crust recipe No. 531 use half quantity, and to flour and suet add 1 oz grated cheese, 1 level tsp baking powder and 1 egg

Roll into tiny balls. Add to stews and savoury casseroles which must be kept simmering once these are added, for 15 minutes.

EGG DISHES

EGGS BOILED – No. 123

If you have an electric stove with a solid plate, choose your pan to equal size of hot plate. Put just two tablespoons cold water in pan, add eggs, cook with fitting lid and switch to full heat. You will see when water boils by steam escaping from lid. Switch off heat but do not remove pan or lid. Depending upon how well or little you like eggs cooked, they will be ready after 6 minutes from switching on hot plate, and will be gently and digestibly cooked.

EGGS CODDLED – No. 124

For gas or other stoves when a thick based saucepan may not be available, use a pan with a fitting lid. Put eggs in pan, on lowest heat, cover eggs with boiling water, cover and leave for 10 minutes. Do not boil the eggs. This method of "coddling" the eggs is by far superior to fast boiling.

EGGS GRILLED – No. 125

After making toast under grill, remove grid from grill pan and wipe out crumbs from toast, and putting in a little butter, return pan under grill to get hot. Break eggs into saucer and tip carefully into tilted grill pan, and return to heat, basting frequently, when it will quickly be lightly cooked. Remove with "slice" to hot toast.

EGGS FRIED – No. 126

Have a really hot frying pan with a very little fat and heat reduced before sliding in the eggs which have been broken into a saucer, one at a time. Tilt pan to keep egg compact, and when all eggs are in pan – without touching – cover with a fitting lid. This cooks the top of the egg without having to turn it or using a lot of fat. About $1\frac{1}{2}$ minutes will usually be long enough, but it does depend upon individual taste. Of course, do turn the egg and fry on other side if preferred, but the covered way looks better, is more easily digested, and saves risk of breaking eggs. Remove with "slice" to hot dish.

HARD-BOILED EGGS – No. 127

For hard-boiled eggs to have the perfect crumbly yolk rather than waxy or rubbery ones, they should be cooked for 20 minutes. Put them into cold water–it is not necessary to cover the eggs with water, so long as there is enough water to last the 20 minutes cooking. A large pan with a fitting lid is best, and $\frac{1}{4}$ inch of water should then be sufficient, or even less. Bring to boil, reduce heat so that water barely boils. After 20 minutes remove to a bowl of cold water–cracking each shell before leaving the egg in the water to cool. Cooked this way the eggs will be more easily digested and easier to handle. A little salt in the water will prevent eggs boiling out if cracked.

EGGS POACHED – No. 128

Properly, an egg is poached directly in boiling and slightly salted water, but in the main they are cooked over water in a special pan with individual sections–usually four, which are buttered and the egg broken into them. The pan is then covered and water boils until eggs are set – a few minutes only. Covering is very important, it more quickly cooks the white over the yolk and so the egg is more tender.

For poaching proper, have an inch or so of boiling water in a large pan. This is important for separate cooking of eggs, and also to enable the removal of egg with a saucer.

Break eggs one at a time into a saucer, and slide gently into the water, repeat if more than one egg is being cooked, and place second egg well away from first. The water should not be boiling madly, or egg white will "fray" and be wasted. Cooking takes a very short time, about two minutes, and it is important to remove the first egg first, unless someone likes their egg well set. Remove with saucer, then with a "slice" remove egg to hot buttered toast.

Have two rounds of toast with a hole stamped in the top of one, large enough to take the egg. The egg is slipped into the hole and circle of toast placed on top after having been cut into four triangles. Garnish with finely chopped parsley.

EGGS SCRAMBLED – No. 129

It is wisest not to scramble more than two at a time or some of the egg will be overcooked before the rest is cooked at all. Break eggs into a small basin and if seasoning is used, add now. It is most usual to add a little liquid, either milk or water, to beaten egg– about 2 tablespoons for two eggs. Beat only slightly, enough to blend yolk and white. Melt fat in pan and whilst having pan quite hot, reduce heat before adding fat and eggs. Melt fat, pour in eggs and gently stir till lightly set but not dry. Pile onto hot buttered toast and serve immediately. Vary with finely chopped parsley or chives, shredded or finely chopped onion. Spring onions are good –using some green also.

EGGS SCRAMBLED IN GRILL PAN – No. 130

After making toast, remove grid and wiping free of crumbs, melt fat in grill pan as for No. 129. If eggs are whisked whilst toast is cooking, heat can be switched off and grill pan over grill warm from toast will be sufficiently hot to cook eggs, scrambling as for No. 129. Serve on toast that has been keeping hot under switched off grill.

ASPARAGUS EGGS – No. 131

4 rounds wholewheat toast, buttered: 4 eggs: 3 Tbs cream or top milk: 1 tsp chopped parsley: 12 young asparagus tips, cooked till tender and cut into ½ inch pieces

Prepare as for Scotch Rarebit No. 138 using whole eggs, lightly beaten, and adding asparagus whilst gently cooking.

If using whole eggs cook in two lots, since scrambling more than two eggs at a time is seldom satisfactory.

EGGS CURRIED – No. 132

1 egg per person, hard-boiled as No. 127: Boiled rice No. 68: Curry sauce No. 354

Shell eggs when cooked, cut into halves across and then length-wise, and arrange most of these pieces of egg in a circle on a hot serving dish. Chop some egg roughly and stir into curry sauce, then pile this into circle of egg on dish. Surround eggs with a border of hot rice and either serve with salad, or a further border of green peas.

EGG YOLK AND ORANGE – No. 133

For a sick person, or a young child, or for easy digestion and quick recuperation, egg yolk with orange juice is without equal. Squeeze a ripe orange into a cup, remove the yolk from a fresh egg and stir it into the juice. Cover and leave for half an hour, then serve with a teaspoon; to be eaten as it is.

GRILLED EGG CUTLETS – No. 134

> *3 hard-boiled eggs, No. 127: 1 raw egg: 1 lemon: ½ oz butter: barely ⅓ cup milk or tomato juice: 1 level Tbs flour: ½ level tsp curry powder: seasoning if required: ½ cup wholewheat breadcrumbs: 1 oz butter or margarine for grilling cutlets*

Add curry powder and flour to melted butter in small saucepan, and stir till well blended, over gentle heat. Gradually add milk or tomato juice and stir well until mixture leaves sides of pan and does not stick. Remove from heat and add chopped hard-boiled eggs and 1 teaspoon lemon juice, and blend. Spread on plate and when cool shape into cutlets, then brush with beaten raw egg and coat with crumbs. Melt fat in grill pan, lay in cutlets and immediately turn them over. Grill for a short time on top heat, then finish with low heat. Serve with slices of lemon.

SPINACH AND POACHED EGGS ON TOAST – No. 135

Spinach No. 269 on neat rounds of buttered wholewheat toast. Make hollows in centres of spinach heaps and add poached eggs No. 128.

EGGS, SAVOURY – No. 136

> *4 hard-boiled eggs No. 127: 1 heaped Tbs cashew nuts: ½ oz butter: 2 tsp chopped parsley: 1 tsp chopped apple: 1 tsp chopped sultanas or raisins: ½ tsp curry powder: 1 tsp cider vinegar: 1 Tbs fresh or cashew cream No. 557: 1 cup cooked rice No. 68: toast to garnish*

Poach cashews gently for 10 minutes with enough water to cover, and lid on pan.

Cut hard-boiled eggs in half making little cups that will stand with the thinnest slice removed from end. Remove yolks to another dish and keep white "cups" hot. Chop cooked cashews and pound with butter, egg yolk, fruit, cider vinegar and parsley. Heat mixture carefully by standing dish over hot water and covering, then pile into egg whites, roundly and working quickly to keep the food hot.

Serve on bed of rice and with triangles of wholewheat toast to garnish. Add a few sprigs of parsley before sending to table.

SCOTCH EGGS – No. 137

2 hard-boiled eggs No. 127 ($\frac{1}{2}$ per person.): $\frac{1}{2}$ lb prepared nut-
meal such as Savormix, etc: water to mix: deep fat for frying

Shell hard-boiled eggs, dry and flour them. Make nutmeal moist
enough to handle, but dry enough to roll out on floured board.
Roll out, halve paste and wrap each egg, carefully sealing and
rounding so that it will remain firmly fixed. Deep fry till golden
brown, drain and halve for serving.

SCOTCH RAREBIT – No. 138

4 rounds wholewheat toast: Yeast extract: 4 egg yolks: 4 Tbs
cream or top milk: 2 Tbs butter: 1 tsp chopped parsley, 4 sprigs
for garnishing: paprika

Spread toast rounds with yeast extract and keep hot. Melt butter
in pan over gentle heat. Remove from heat and stir in yolks and
cream, again over gentle heat. Stir till creamy. Add parsley and
paprika.

Pour onto toast, garnish with sprigs of parsley and serve very
hot. Use egg whites also if liked, but do not omit cream or top
milk.

OMELET, PLAIN – No. 139

3 or 4 eggs: 1 Tbs top milk, or cream to each egg: seasoning if
desired

Beat eggs and milk until well mixed but not frothing. Have buttered omelet pan good and hot. Pour in half of mixture, lift edges
as it cooks underneath with a palette knife, letting raw egg mixture get to heated pan. When still soft on top, fold in half and
carefully slide onto hot dish. Repeat with other half mixture.

It is advisable to cook this quantity in two omelets. It is too
tricky to lift a larger omelet without breaking it.

OMELET, SAVOURY – No. 140

3-4 eggs: 1 Tbs top milk per egg: butter to grease pan: 1 tsp
finely chopped parsley: 1 tsp finely chopped chives: 1 little pow-
dered sage or thyme or a pinch of marjoram: $\frac{1}{2}$ tsp grated onion:
seasoning

Prepare pan and mix egg, milk and herbs, onion and season. Pour
into hot pan and cook as No. 139. Serve immediately.

MUSHROOM OMELET – No. 141

Make as for plain omelet No. 139 and before folding, pile mushroom filling No. 227 on to half, fold over and slide onto a hot dish.

OMELET, SWEET – No. 142

> *3 eggs: 1 level Tbs each of butter and warmed honey: a few drops of vanilla essence: some jam or sliced fresh or tinned apricots, skinned and warmed but not cooked: butter for cooking – enough to grease pan*

Prepare pan. Mix honey, eggs and vanilla. Cook as for No. 139 but before folding place warmed jam or fruit on half and fold other half over. Lift or slide onto hot dish and serve immediately.

SPANISH OMELET – No. 143

> *1 or 2 eggs: 1 Dstsp hot water to each egg*

Make omelet as instructed in No. 139 but have prepared some small and dainty cooked vegetables, or slices of vegetable, or tiny flowerets of cooked cauliflower, golden fried onion rings, cooked peas or slices of french beans.

Add a handful of vegetables to omelet immediately on pouring it into the pan.

SWEET OMELET SOUFFLÉ – No. 144

> *3 eggs: ½ oz butter: 1 Tbs honey: 1 Tbs cornflour: a few drops vanilla essence: 2 Tbs warmed jam or some warmed half apricots, and 1 Tbs apricot jam, warmed*

Well butter a soufflé dish. Beat egg yolks and honey together with cornflour and vanilla. Beat whites separately, and blend together with mixture. Pour half mixture into dish, add fruit and jam, or jam only, and pour on rest of mixture. Stand dish in pan of boiling water in oven and cook 15-25 minutes at 400°F or Mark 5.

POTATO DISHES

POTATO AND TURNIP CREAM – No. 145

½ lb cooked young turnips: ½ lb cooked floury potatoes: 1 oz butter: ½ cup hot milk: 1 egg, beaten

Mash vegetables into hot milk and butter in large pan over gentle heat. Using a good potato masher pound and mix until a perfect blend is achieved. Add egg, then beat with a rubber squeegee till light and fluffy – still keeping it hot – then serve hot with either croutons of fried wholewheat bread, or elder fritters.

GRILLED POTATO CAKES – No. 146

1 lb mashed potatoes: 1 egg: 1 cup hot milk: a finely shredded shallot or a few spring onions, and using some green: 1 Tbs chopped parsley: breadcrumbs for coating No. 699: 2 oz margarine for grilling

Blend potatoes, milk, onion and parsley, any seasoning required and shape into small round cakes. Brush over with egg and coat with crumbs.

Have fat hot in pan under grill – lay cakes and turn each one over immediately to ensure browning. Grill with high heat for 2 minutes each side, or until golden brown.

POTATO CAKES – No. 147

8 oz hot sieved potatoes: 8 oz wholewheat flour: 2½ oz butter or margarine

Mix to soft dough and roll out to ¾ inch thickness. Cut into rounds and bake in moderate oven till golden, or on girdle or solid hot plate, lightly greased. Turn over, if cooking on girdle or hot Plate, and cook other side.

For oven cooking, 400°F or Mark 5, for about 20 minutes or until a good colour.

POTATO NOODLES – No. 148

Make as potato cake mixture No. 147 but add a beaten egg and omit butter. Knead on a well floured board, and roll into finger-thick rolls. Cut off 1 inch lengths and lay these over bottom of large and well greased baking dish.

Pour over a cup of top milk and dot with butter or margarine and bake in moderate oven 400°F or Mark 5 for about 20 minutes.

Serve with fried wholewheat crumbs No. 697 and chopped parsley or chives.

POTATO DUMPLINGS – No. 149

Mixture as for Potato Cakes but a little more dry, and flavoured with either herbs or a pinch of nutmeg, or the smallest amount of shredded onion, or onion or celery salt. Roll into little balls and cook in boiling stock or soup until they rise to surface, about 10 to 15 minutes. Make small and dainty and they will keep separate.

See also cheese and potato dishes in Cheese section.

VEGETABLES

ARTICHOKES, JERUSALEM – No. 150

Cook as for potatoes, either boil, steam or roast. Do not bother to peel around all the knobs – scrub really scrupulously clean, then skin when cooked if boiling or steaming, as one skins a beetroot after boiling.

If liked they may be part boiled then roasted after skinning, in a dish with a little butter.

ARTICHOKES, JERUSALEM IN CASSEROLE – No. 151

Boil and skin artichokes as in No. 150.

2 lb artichokes in thick slices: 4 shallots or 1 onion – medium: 1 clove of garlic: 1½ cups white stock: ½ cup cider or apple juice No. 746: 1 oz butter or margarine

Well grease a large casserole and after frying onion with garlic in butter till translucent, blend with artichokes in casserole. Sprinkle with a little marjoram and pour over stock and cider. Cover with greased lid and bake in gentle oven at 350°F or Mark 4 for about 30 minutes.

ARTICHOKES, STUFFED – No. 152

See Savouries section.

ASPARAGUS, BOILED – No. 153

A bundle of asparagus: boiling water: salt if needed: lemon juice

Wash, cut stalks to one length and scrape any white ends that need it, being careful not to break tender green points. Tie into small bundles with clean tape. Add a few drops of lemon juice to boiling water. Gently place asparagus bundles in water to cover only. Bring up to boil and keep boiling for about half an hour or till tender.

Remove very carefully and serve with melted butter with lemon juice added to taste.

Alternatively the asparagus can be left in a large bundle, and stood on end with points out of water and a lid on – till tender, keeping water simmering.

AUBERGINES – No. 154
   (*or Egg Plant*)
Recipes given in Savouries section.

BEANS, FRENCH – No. 155
Wash and trim off ends and boil with lid on in only enough water
to cover for 8-10 minutes.
   Either drain and serve, or drain and adding a little butter shake
about in pan with lid on till all buttered, then serve. Pieces of
young beans may be used in salads.

BEANS, FRENCH – No. 156
   "Haricots Vertes Sautes"
It seems a pity not to include French beans as they are served in
France although I personally feel the process serves to spoil them
of their freshness.
   Cook as usual, drain, then fry in butter till slightly browned–
season and serve.

BEANS, RUNNER – No. 157
Boil as for French beans but according to tenderness and thinly
sliced. Use only sufficient water to cook without burning.

BEANS, RUNNER (UNCOOKED) – No. 158
Young beans are delightful in salads, carefully selected for tenderness.

BEANS, SPROUTED – No. 159
Small green Chinese beans smaller than peas, are sprouted in the
same way as corn No. 199 and used in the same way. These are
easily obtainable from any store that sells oriental and continen-
tal foodstuffs. Sprouted beans are a vital health food, they can be
used in salads, dropped into soups only a minute or two before
soups are served, or served as an hors d'œuvres, see No. 667.

BEETS, RAW AND SHREDDED – No. 160
Wash and peel beets and finely shred. If liked hot, warm between
two plates over hot water for 10 minutes, otherwise serve with
salad, separately, dressed with a little oil and lemon juice No. 335
and garnished with parsley, watercress or mustard and cress.

BEET TOPS BOILED – No. 161
Cook as spinach No. 269. Thick stalks serve as a separate dish with parsley sauce.

BEETS BOILED – No. 162
Wash carefully and leave several inches of stalks when trimming. Beets bleed if cut so leave any other trimming until cooked. Boil according to size, tiny new ones cooking in as little as 20 minutes and larger or older ones for an hour or even 1½ hours. Leave old ones to cool in pan. Skins will slip off easily hot or cold. Serve as hot vegetables or dice cold for salads.

BROCCOLI, PURPLE SPROUTING – No. 163
This delectable green makes a very welcome appearance in early spring. Use raw for salads, the young tender sproutings, and if cooking, cook with lid on in only sufficient water to float it. Cook up to 7 minutes, drain – do not waste the water – and adding a little butter replace lid and shake pan, to butter evenly before serving.

BROCCOLI BOILED – No. 164
Cook as for cauliflower, the white broccoli resembling cauliflower. small flowerets may be happily used in a salad.

BRUSSELS SPROUTS – No. 165
Well wash and trim sprouts, cook as for cabbage but of course leaving sprouts whole unless they are very large, when halve. Cook with a fitting lid, only enough water to float the sprouts, and finish cooking whilst they are still a little firm, and do not let them get waterlogged.

SPROUTS WITH CHOPPED NUTS – No. 166
As for cabbage No. 170.

CABBAGE – No. 167
There are many and varied cabbages–from white to dark blue, green and even red. All can be eaten raw as well as cooked and should be frequently presented.

When cooking, use a pan with a fitting lid and keep it covered. Less water will be needed then and the cabbage tenderized in a matter of minutes. Never waste the liquor–never add soda to make it green–if cooked as recommended it will be really green.

When serving raw, finely shred, dress with oil and lemon and add chopped ripe apple to aid digestion.

Use red cabbage raw as well as cooked, it will provide colour for a salad when there is not a wide range of salad available.

CABBAGE, PLAIN BOILED – No. 168
Well wash and coarsely shred. Cook fast from 5-7 minutes just covered with water and with close fitting lid on pan.

CABBAGE, BOILED AND TOSSED IN BUTTER – No. 169
As No. 168 but after straining add a nut of butter and shake pan well before dishing up.

CABBAGE, BOILED WITH CHESTNUTS – No. 170
As for No. 168 but add cooked chestnuts No. 662 chopped or minced, for last 2 minutes of cooking.

CABBAGE, BOILED WITH WALNUTS – No. 171
As for No. 170 but do not pre-cook nut kernels. Chop walnuts before adding.

CABBAGE, BOILED WITH ONION – No. 172
When cabbage is not at its best, or for a child who does not find it easy to eat, a small finely shredded onion will make a good addition if cooked with it.

CABBAGE FRIED – No. 173
Wash and shred cabbage then fry with a little butter or oil, with sufficient to cover the bottom of the pan. Cover with fitting lid and fry gently till tender, shaking the pan frequently. About 10-15 minutes should be sufficient. Serve hot.

CABBAGE STUFFED – No. 174
See recipes given in Savouries section.

CABBAGE, RED, IN CASSEROLE – No. 175
Red cabbage: 1 *Tbs lemon juice:* 1 *Tbs wholewheat flour:* 1 *Tbs butter* (*rounded*): *seasoning if desired*

Prepare and shred, then cook for 5 minutes in a little water and with fitting lid on pan. Drain and keep liquor. Place cabbage in a greased casserole and make a sauce with cabbage stock – making it up to ¾ pt. with hot water if necessary – butter, lemon juice and flour – mixed with a little cold water, boil together for about a minute then pour over cabbage in casserole, cover and heat through in a slow oven for about 20-30 minutes. 300°F or Mark 2.

Apple juice in a larger quantity, i.e. half the ¾ pt. needed for sauce, may be used instead of lemon.

CARROTS – No. 176

Both carrots and carrot tops are really health giving foods. Use raw carrots wherever possible, make carrot juice to drink No. 749 and give finely shredded carrot warmed over hot water to tiny children and invalids – not cooking but just warming. Serve carrots often, as an appetizing pre-meal drink, in soups, salads, hot with main hot dishes, or as part of savouries or even in sweet puddings.

Carrot tops can be made into a delectable and health-giving drink with the aid of an electric liquidizer. Failing this, bring to boil, then pass through *Moulilegume* sieve.

CARROTS BOILED – No. 177

Unless really new, wash and peel carrots as they are selected by grubs and infected by them. Peeling reveals any grubs and they can be removed. Very new carrots will be free of grubs as a rule.

Having trimmed carrots, if small boil whole, if large split down centre and again if necessary.

Cook in ½ inch of water with lid on pan, and simmer once boiling. They are best a little less than quite soft. From 10 minutes according to age, and drink the liquor, or use for sauce.

CARROTS BUTTERED – No. 178

Preferably baby carrots, boiled as in No. 177, drained, and then gently heated again with an ounce of butter, a squeeze of lemon juice and a teaspoon of honey. Toss about with lid on pan.

A sprinkling of chopped parsley is a delicious addition, before shaking.

CARROTS STEAMED – No. 179

Prepare as for boiling and cook about 45 minutes.

CARROTS CREAMED – No. 180

Boil as in No. 177, drain and, unless very small, slice ¼ inch thick slices.

Keep hot whilst making a sauce with 1 oz. butter in pan, 1 level tablespoon corn flour stirred in over gentle heat, and a cup of half milk and half carrot liquor added a little at a time whilst stirring continuously.

When smooth and boiling remove from heat, add carrots and coat thoroughly, leave a minute or two to re-heat, then serve.

CARROTS WITH PEAS – No. 181
As for boiled carrots No. 177 and preferably very young carrots and very new peas.

Cook with only $\frac{1}{2}$ inch of water, a good nut of butter, $\frac{1}{2}$ teaspoon sugar; the carrots alone for about 7 minutes, then add peas and cook for about 3 or 4 minutes. When both are tender strain, saving liquor. Keep hot whilst boiling liquor again without lid till reduced to half its bulk, add 1 tablespoon finely chopped mint, stir, then pour over carrots and serve.

CAULIFLOWER 1 – No. 182
Trim and wash well, leaving deep in running water a while to wash out any insects or caterpillars. Cut stalk near to flower and make a deep cut criss-cross in it, so that heat will penetrate and more quickly cook.

Cauliflowers are ruined if over cooked so take every care of this lovely vegetable. Place it stalk uppermost in a deep pan of water, cover and bring to boil. Start to test through centre with a steel knitting pin for least damage, and remove it carefully whilst it is still nutty. Cook from 7 minutes according to size.

CAULIFLOWER 2 – No. 183
Wash and trim as for No. 182 then carefully cut each section off at base of its stalk and cook separately with centre stem. If liked it can be re-assembled in dish to look like a whole cauliflower, or it can be served as pieces individually. Cook less time than for the whole cauliflower and dish up carefully whilst still nutty.

CAULIFLOWER CURRIED – No. 184
See Savouries.

CAULIFLOWER FLOWERETS DEEP FRIED – No. 185
Cook cauliflower after dividing the flowerets (the natural branches of the flower, cut into equally sized pieces about 2-3 inches in length).

Drain carefully, and cool before handling further. Dip cold

flowerets into raw beaten egg and then into fine breadcrumbs. then deep fry till golden, using a deep fryer with basket if possible. Drain on paper keeping hot if wished to serve hot. May be served hot or cold.

CELERIAC BOILED – No. 186

Scrub and peel, cut in $\frac{1}{2}$ inch slices and then in fingers or cubes. Boil in a little water with fitting lid on pan, until tender. Exact time to tenderize will be determined by its age and this must be decided by the cook. If young and small, $\frac{1}{2}$ inch cubes should be cooked gently for 20 minutes. Older celeriac may need an hour.

CELERIAC FRITTERS – No. 187

As for boiled celeriac, cutting into fingers $\frac{1}{4}$ inch thick. When cold coat with egg and crumbs and deep fry. Serve hot or cold.

CELERY – No. 188

Cannot be too often used for health. Use scrupulously clean, crisp and raw in salads with cheese, with jacket potatoes and cheese – or cook as vegetable with hot meal, make into soups or soufflés, – it is a great boon to those with creaking joints.

When boiled never throw away the liquor – drink as it is or use as stock.

CELERY BOILED – No. 189

Divide prepared celery into even lengths and boil in about an inch of water and with fitting lid on pan. Gently boil for about 25 minutes, adding a little lemon juice to keep celery a good colour.

Serve hot as a vegetable or use to purée for sauces or soufflés. On no account waste the water celery is cooked in – it is invaluable to drink, or for broths or soups.

CELERY BRAISED WITH ONIONS – No. 190

Celery: 1 large or 2 good-sized onions: 1 oz butter: 1 cup apple juice: 1 Tbs flour: bay leaf or marjoram

Cut prepared celery into evenly sized pieces. Slice onions and fry them till beginning to get tender in butter. Place in buttered casserole and arrange celery on onions. Pour over most of apple juice, add bay leaf or marjoram, cover well, and bake in slow oven, 300°F or Mark 2 for 45 minutes. Blend flour with remaining apple juice, add and return to oven for a few moments before serving.

CELERY BRAISED WITH TOMATOES – No. 191
As No. 190 but making a bed of peeled and sliced tomatoes without first cooking them.

CELERY STEAMED – No. 192
Wash, trim and quarter celery and steam for about an hour. Use as vegetable, or purée for sauces or soufflés.

CHERVIL – No. 193
See herbs.

CORN-ON-THE-COB – No. 194
Only young cobs of sweet corn can be eaten, and these are usually sold at the right stage. If you are growing them they must be cut whilst the corn is tender if they are to be eaten as corn from the cob. Trim off silky strands and outer leaves and cut stalk close. Allowing one per person cook gently in boiling water with lid on pan for 10-15 minutes, testing for tenderness. If not really young it may take up to 30 minutes. Drain when tender and serve with pats of butter. They are easiest to eat straight from the cobs, held in the hands.

CHICORY – No. 195
By chicory I mean the blanched silvery white plant mainly found with pale green tipped leaves, but sometimes with mauvish tips. Slightly bitter in taste, it is, however, a firm favourite where it is tried.

With an elegant head of chicory one can use small shoots of whatever is available in the garden and achieve a magnificent salad. A ripe pear, some soaked dried fruits and nut kernels go well with chicory.

CHICORY IN CASSEROLE – No. 196
Wash and trim and gently boil in sufficient water to just float chicory, and a squeeze of lemon juice, for 10 minutes with lid on pan. Drain partially cooked chicory then place in buttered casserole and cover with cheese sauce No. 351. Gently cook in oven for about 30 minutes at 350°F or Mark 3. The sauce may be sprinkled with wholewheat crumbs fried in a little butter, No. 697.

CHICORY BRAISED – No. 197

4 heads chicory: 1 large onion: 1 oz butter or margarine: a little white stock: 1 Tbs wholewheat flour

Cook chicory in boiling water for 5 minutes. Gently fry onions in bottom of a large pan till golden, add enough stock to make them secure from burning, to make about ½ inch with onions, in bottom of pan. Arrange the drained chicory on onions, cover with lid and cook over lowest possible heat till tender, according to size of chicory, about 30 minutes.

Remove chicory when tender to a hot dish, blend flour with a little milk or water and adding to onions, bring to boil and simmer for one minute. Pour sauce over chicory and serve. I have not mentioned seasoning – there is much flavour in the dish – only add seasoning if you cannot bear it without!

CHIVES – No. 198

See herbs.

CORN SPROUTED – No. 199

If you are lucky enough to be able to come by some good compost grown wheat, do try sprouting some. It is considered to be a very highly nutritious and vital food and is easy to prepare. The whole takes about five days to a week during which time very little attention is needed. You need some butter muslin – double thickness, a cake-cooler, or similar rustproof rest for the muslin, with plenty of airholes. Underneath the cake-cooler, a dish to catch water drippings. Thoroughly damp the muslin, lay half the double thickness over the cooler, sprinkle corn on muslin almost touching, and fold other half of muslin over the corn. Each day pour fresh cold water over the muslin, having removed any drippings from dish, and leave alone. Not in direct sun, but in normal pantry conditions. When the sprouts are about an inch or so long the corn is ready for use.

Serve raw or cooked and cold in salads. Add to soups, curries, risottos.

Do not cook for long–only a few minutes so that they are still a little crisp and have to be chewed.

(Compost grown wheat now available at Health Stores in this country).

DANDELION LEAVES – No. 200

Well washed they may be used as spinach or in salads and sandwiches.

In order to be enjoyed dandelions should be picked before
flowering or they will be bitter.

ELDERFLOWER FRITTERS – No. 201

Using Fritter Batter No. 1 or 3, trim flowerets to short stalk and of
even size, keeping small. Dip by stalk into batter and deep fry till
golden. Serve hot. Nice with soup or curry.

ENDIVE – No. 202

Well wash and use uncooked in salads dressed with oil and lemon
juice. In some parts of the country, known as chicory, and then
chicory is sold as endive. By endive, I mean the green lettuce-like
plant with fringed leaves.

FENNEL – No. 203

Orthodox eaters use fennel mainly as a sauce for fish, and meat,
and perhaps for flavouring. Vegetarians may enjoy this dish of
fennel with onions and cheese.

FENNEL SAVOURY – No. 204

*5 or 6 fennel plants: 1 leek: 1 large onion: ½ cup chopped parsley:
¾ pt milk and water or white stock: 1 oz butter: ½ cup grated
cheese: ½ cup wholewheat crumbs*

Boil fennel and white part of leek in stock or milk and water till
tender whilst frying onions golden in butter. Place fennel and leek
in ovenware dish and sprinkle with crumbs and parsley. Cover
with onion and heat stock or milk in pan in which it was cooked;
season gently, bearing fennel flavour in mind, then pour over
contents of dish, add grated cheese evenly sprinkled, and heat
through in moderate oven about 15-20 minutes at 400°F or Mark
5. Serve hot.

FENNEL CASSEROLE – No. 205

*4 fennel plants: 1 large or 2 medium onions: 2 good sized carrots:
½ cup chopped parsley: 1 cup green peas: 1 pt white stock or milk
and water: 1½ oz butter or 2 Tbs cream: 1 oz cooking fat*

Wash, trim off inedible outside of fennel and split in 4 length-

wise. Gently fry onion slices in 1 oz butter or margarine. Prepare
carrot and cut into strips. Place fried onions in bottom of casserole, then carrots, fennel and stock, seasoned gently, cover and
cook at 300°F or Mark 1 for 1¼ hours, add peas, if no cream,
butter, cover and return with lid on for further 15 minutes or less
according to age of peas. If cream is used, stir it in last thing before serving, with chopped parsley. Cheese dumplings No. 122
may be added to this dish 15 minutes before end of cooking.
Serve very hot.

FENNEL SALAD HOT – No. 206
Boil fennel till tender. Cut to neat smallish pieces and dress with
1 oz. butter melted and juice of half a lemon added.

FENNEL SALAD COLD – No. 207
Boil fennel as in No. 204 and allow to cool. Serve small pieces
tossed in mayonnaise No. 332.

GARLIC – No. 208
Made up of small "cloves" the garlic is the most healthgiving of
all the wonderful onion family. I am told that it is being used in
the east for healing wounds etc. that are slow to heal. A vital food
and powerful aid to health.

A very small amount is used in most dishes to flavour. The cut
half of a small clove rubbed round a salad bowl will give it a fine
flavour and bouquet, and half or a very small whole clove will
finely flavour a pan of soup.

Garlic salt and powder can be obtained for flavouring. A cut
clove held in the cheek will cleanse and heal unhealthy throat or
mouth. Chewing raw parsley will remove odour of garlic.

GARLIC ROASTED – No. 209
Cloves of garlic roasted on a tin or ovenware dish, a little oiled
first, and cooked till slightly golden, has a wonderful flavour and
makes a welcome addition to a roast meal.

HOPS – No. 210
Some uninvited hops grow in my London garden and are most
healthy and persistent. After trying to get rid of them, saving only
one or two for the decorativeness of the green hop flowers and
their distinctive perfume – I made the best of a bad job by trying

to eat them. The shoots are rather like asparagus and can be cooked in the same way and served hot or left to cool and served with a mixed salad.

HORSERADISH – No. 211

The well scrubbed and finely shredded root, shredded down its length by the way, leaving the woody core, will add piquancy to a winter salad. Use very little. The skinned root – kept in a polythene bag in the fridge – is invaluable to migraine and headache sufferers. A piece held in the almost closed fist and its aroma inhaled has a wonderful effect.

A little may be added to the rich cream cheese filling for a sandwich.

KALE – No. 212

If you are lucky enough to be able to collect curly kale shoots in winter and early spring you may enjoy them either uncooked in salads or cooked as cabbage. Take every care with them as greens are indeed precious at the time kale shoots are to be found.

KOHLRABI – No. 213

Cook the green leaves as for Spinach Beet No. 270 and the root – which develops above ground, unpeeled and steamed when it may be peeled if liked. In my youth I ate many a dozen raw, peel and all, and have pleasant memories of the flavour. Use cooked or raw in salads. Serve in small cubes and dressed with a little lemon juice and oil. Excellent for hors-d'œuvre, or for soup.

LEEKS – No. 214

Leeks are available during several months and I am always sad when they reach the end of their season.

In winter of 1947, one of the worst for shopping I have known, I was able to use leeks with apples for salads and discovered how delicate and delicious they are. In fact, if you have only one leek, one apple and one tomato you can make a delicious salad, with oil and lemon dressing. Use all of the white part and the best of the green near the white. Use the rest of the green in the stock pot.

For a delicate vegetable, for soups, stews and salads, the leek is invaluable.

I find cleaning simpler if the leek is halved lengthwise and soil carefully removed under a running tap. Do not disturb the shape, hold firmly and replace leaves moved for cleaning – then if cooking, cut to even size and lay carefully in pan, to serve them daintily.

LETTUCE – No. 215

There are many kinds of lettuce and many ways of serving, including cooked dishes. Apart from using the coarsest leaves in soups and stocks and an occasional small one cooked with green peas, I personally do not feel happy cooking it. The main function seems to me to be as salad food, being so easy to prepare, serve and eat. Those who cannot possibly digest it may find it easier with raw apple added. If even then it is not possible and I have had personal experience of this, then take as much as possible liquidized with the help of an electric food mixer.

If you are tired of eating uncooked lettuce and really want to cook it I am sure there are excellent recipes in other books. Wash lettuce really well under running water with one of the cheap sprinkler attachments for the cold tap. Eat the dark leaves as well as the heart – they are the vital leaves. Dress the lettuce with one part lemon juice to two olive oil, well blended for about 30 seconds, and of course, add your fresh chopped green herbs as fresh and green and as varied as possible. With the addition of mint, parsley, tarragon, chervil, chives, spring onions, green and white, sliced leek and a little help from a clove of garlic – either very finely chopped or cut and rubbed around the bowl – some sliced hard-boiled eggs, tomatoes, grated cheese or milled nuts, a feast can be prepared in a matter of minutes. Lettuce blends well with fruit and vegetables, left over really fresh, carrots, peas, potatoes, cauliflower, as well as oranges, grapefruit, bananas, soaked prunes or figs, dates, raisins, etc., etc., help to turn lettuce into a perfect meal.

LETTUCE FRITTERS – No. 216

Just one lettuce recipe then.

Using fritter batter No. 1 or 2. Wash and dry lettuce leaves, if large break in evenly sized pieces about 2 inches each way, put two together and dip in batter then deep fry till golden and serve with soups, *au gratin* dishes, curries or rice dishes.

MARROWS – No. 217

The marrow is in season for many weeks, beginning with the baby marrows, or courgettes, which are cooked whole without remov-

ing skin or pips, and going on to the large firm and ripe marrows
that are mainly used for making preserves.

Without much flavour, it is however valuable as are vegetables
for mineral salts and lends itself to being blended with sauces, or
herbs and other vegetables.

MARROW BOILED OR STEAMED – No. 218

Courgettes, or marrows up to the length to one's hand, are
cooked whole either steamed or boiled in about an inch of water
and lid on pan.

Larger marrows may be peeled or not as desired, after cutting
into conveniently sized pieces for serving, and removing seeds.
Either steamed or boiled as above, with lid on pan. Serve with a
white or freshly made tomato sauce.

MARROWS FRIED – No. 219

Steam or boil as for No. 218 and cool. When cool dip in beaten
egg, then crumbs and then deep fry till golden. Serve hot or cold.

MARROW RAISED WITH TOMATOES – No. 220

Make a bed of sliced tomatoes in a buttered casserole and arrange
thin slices of marrow on this, cover with lid or foil and gently
cook in oven at 300°F or Mark 2 for about 40 minutes.

MARROW BRAISED – No. 221

Cook as for marrow braised with tomatoes No. 220 but substituting a bed of golden fried onions and adding $\frac{1}{2}$ cup of cider or
apple juice and a dash of paprika.

Blend before serving, without mashing marrow, and thicken,
if preferred, by adding a little flour to some of the apple juice,
about 1 level tablespoon and be sure it boils again after adding
to the casserole.

MARROW – No. 222

For other marrow dishes see Savouries.

MUSHROOMS – No. 223

When using the oven mushrooms can be cooked in a dish on a tin
easily. Wash and drain, remove stalks level with centre of mushrooms. Warm a little margarine in the dish in the oven whilst it is
heating. Place each mushroom underside down in fat then turn
other way up. Slice stalks to evenly sized slices and toss these also

in fat before arranging them between mushrooms. A squeeze of lemon juice gives a delicious flavour, or a small glass of apple juice, cider or white wine can be added for special occasions. Oven 350°F or Mark 3 for 15–20 minutes.

MUSHROOMS GRILLED – No. 224
Prepare as in No. 223. Use grill pan without grid. Into this put a small wineglass of either water, apple juice or white wine, and an ounce of margarine or butter. Put pan under heat to melt and stir to blend. Place mushrooms in pan, underside down and turn over again – see that all are coated in liquor. Grill.

MUSHROOM PURÉE – No. 225
Cook finely chopped mushrooms and then stalks in very little water or milk in covered pan for 3 or 4 minutes, then purée. Use for soufflés or sauces.

MUSHROOMS STEWED – No. 226
Small or sliced mushrooms and their stalks sliced also, may be stewed, with water, milk and water, all milk, wine and water or cider and water, and in any case, a little butter and a squeeze of lemon if wine is not used. Cover the pan, cook very gently and only long enough to make mushrooms tender. They need very little cooking – say from 5 to 10 minutes.

MUSHROOMS CREAMED – No. 227
Finely shred 2 oz washed mushrooms, using either a sharp knife or a coarse grater and gently heat in ½ pt of bechamel sauce No. 345. Use for filling *vol-au-vent* or as addition to cooked aubergines, peppers, french beans, spinach, etc.

MUSTARD AND CRESS – No. 228
Always use raw and fresh after washing and floating away any seeds sticking to the stalks. These can be avoided when growing in the home by growing on flannel and turning it upside down as soon as they show signs of growth. Seeds then remain underneath and can be scraped off after soaking and flannel used again. Use for salads or sandwiches.

NASTURTIUM LEAVES AND SEEDS – No. 229
These, washed, and especially examined on undersides for grubs and eggs, and sound young ones used for salads and sandwiches.

Seeds may be pickled for a few days in lemon juice and used as capers.

NETTLES – No. 230
The tips of young nettles may be cooked as spinach No. 269 either by themselves or with some spinach added. Use every drop of the liquor when cooked, it is a valuable drink and if found too strong in flavour can be diluted with a little top milk.

ONIONS BOILED – No. 231
Wash, trim and slice very thickly, then slowly simmer in a little water in a covered pan, till tender. When tender add some top milk or, if liked, thicken with a little flour blended with the top milk and simmer for a few minutes. Season to taste. An old and tried remedy for a state of cold or chill, or a pleasant sauce. If a brown sauce desired see No. 347.

ONIONS, BRAISED – No. 232
Have a large pan and onions of even size. Skin or merely trim, as you fancy, then melt a little fat in about $\frac{1}{4}$ inch of hot water or stock in the pan, then stand onions carefully in pan, allowing several per person if smallish, and onions about 2 inches high are about the right size. Sprinkle with powdered sage and cover with fitting lid. Gently simmer for about 30–45 minutes according to size. Served on a bed of spring greens they make a delicious meal. Sliced tomatoes may be used for a bed on which to braise onions if liked.

ONIONS, FRIED – No. 233
Slice onions fairly thickly and fry in oil or vegetable fat. If you wish them to be soft, cover with lid and cook slowly, examining every little while so as not to over-brown them. If crisp onions are needed slice thinly and separate the slices into rings, and turn them about in seasoned flour on kitchen paper till all are coated. Cook carefully for they can very suddenly become too dark to be edible.

ONION PURÉE – No. 234
Either steam or boil or cook slowly in covered casserole with a little water. When tender purée and use as desired.

ONIONS, ROASTED – No. 235

Large English or Spanish onions, golden and ripe, and washed and trimmed but not peeled are right for roasting. Place one per person on an ovenware dish well greased. Rub over onions with a butter paper, then roast in a moderate oven for quite a long while – according to size, from 1½ to 2 hours. Serve with green vegetables and savory and with generous pats of parsley butter No. 339.

SPRING ONIONS – No. 236

Use mainly in raw salads after washing and trimming, and also for delicate onion flavouring in cooked dishes. Tiny spring onions are used also for pickling in white wine vinegar.

ONIONS, STUFFED – No. 237

See Savouries section.

PARSNIPS – No. 238

Scrub till they look like old parchment, then halve lengthwise, and if very large, quarter. Either boil for about 20 minutes, or steam for 40 minutes or roast in a shallow tin with a little margarine for 30 minutes.

Save liquor, if boiling, for soup or sauce to accompany the meal.

Parsnips may also be prepared as for turnips or swedes, as a delicious frothy dish that can be served very hot covered with fried wholewheat crumbs.

PARSNIP PATTIES – No. 239

Tender boiled or steamed parsnips mashed with a little butter, shaped into patties, rolled in crumbs and grilled both sides in a little margarine.

Left over cooked parsnips may be used – bring them to the boil again before mashing, for ease.

PEAS, GREEN – No. 240

Fresh green peas are such a treat they need very careful cooking. When shelled, wash, then cook in only sufficient water to float them, adding a saltspoon of sugar and some mint leaves. Cook very new peas for three minutes only, and add on a minute or so as the season progresses. Do not overcook, leaving the peas some "life" and not letting them get soggy. Strain and use the water for sauces or for drinking with some yeast extract or on its own.

Use peas hot or cold, either are delicious, and use young uncooked in salads.

PEAS, DRIED, GREEN–No. 241
See pulses No. 263.

GREEN PEAS FRENCH STYLE – No. 242
Cooked in either a casserole or thick saucepan over very gentle heat.

> 2 lb shelled peas: 1 lettuce: a small bunch of spring onions: 1 tsp sugar: 2 Tbs water: $\frac{1}{2}$ oz margarine or butter

First melt butter in pan or casserole, and in this partially cook sliced onions, add water and sugar, shredded lettuce and peas. Cover securely then cook in saucepan for about 15 minutes or in casserole for 20–30 minutes at about 350°F or Mark 3.

SWEET PEPPERS – No. 243
These may be green, yellow or red and may be used cooked or uncooked. They are very flavoursome and tangy, and a great gift to the table. Use raw in strips in a salad, or as colour and flavour giving additions to open sandwiches, canapés, etc. Use sliced in stews, savoury flans, curries, etc. To slice, halve and remove core and seeds. Do not waste these but use them in stocks or gravies.

STUFFED COOKED PEPPERS – No. 244
If large halve first, or slice top off smaller ones. Stuff with mixture of minced tinned nutmeat, onions and rice or any of the savoury nut dishes in this book.

Arrange in casserole on a bed of sliced tomatoes dotted with margarine and cooked for about 30 minutes in moderate oven – 400°F or Mark 6.

STUFFED RAW PEPPERS – No. 245
If large halve, if small slice off top and remove seeds. Stuff with either cream cheese, the cheese with chopped nuts added, with any of the uncooked nut savouries or a mixture of cooked rice, chopped hard-boiled egg and golden fried onions, cooled.

POTATOES – No. 246

The potato is almost despised in this age of slimming. Potatoes
fatten as well as nourish when they are ruined as a balanced food
by peeling and boiling in a lot of water which is thrown away.
Potatoes, like beets, skin so easily after cooking that the job takes
almost no time at all if you have a thick folded cloth in one hand,
or kitchen paper folded, and a vegetable knife in the other. Eyes
lift out easily too, and the vegetable is a *whole* food, and not an
unbalanced food. Eaten thus, they digest more thoroughly and
are not stowed away round the body to be used in a cold and lean
season. Few of us know cold and lean seasons nowadays so do
not need to carry around an extra blanket of fat against emer-
gencies.

To be logical, if you peel the potato you should peel it a quarter
of an inch thick and throw the potato away. If you do the oppo-
site, you are laying up unwanted material. Always scrub scrupulously clean – I use a nylon pot cleaner and hot water and achieve
a wonderful complexion for the potato – boil or steam whole or
boil in halves with only a very little water in a thick pan with a
fitted lid.

Roast whenever possible, just greasing the skin a little. In
short – give the potato a *chance*!

POTATOES, BAKED – No. 247

Scrub scrupulously clean evenly sized potatoes, dry and rub over
with oiled paper – margarine or cooking oil. Bake in hot oven 45
minutes when they will be golden and appetizing. Hold in cloth
and crack one side by bending a little, keep hot and covered by
napkin till ready to serve when they will be floury. Jackets may be
eaten. Serve whole, or opened and buttered then closed again, or
add cheese and close, or scoop out holes and break in an egg in
the halves and return to oven to cook, a few minutes only for
this.

POTATOES BOILED – No. 248

Scrub scrupulously clean, evenly sized potatoes. Place in large pan
with half cup of water and well fitting lid. If electric cooker is
used, switch on to full till boiling and then off – leaving on hot
plate for 20 minutes when potatoes will be cooked. If gas stove is
used, then more water must be added, but not enough to cover,
and simmer 20 minutes after coming to the boil. Add fresh chopped mint or parsley before serving.

POTATO CASSEROLE – No. 249

1½ lb potatoes: ½ lb tomatoes: 2 cloves of garlic: 1 good sized onion: 1 oz margarine: ½ pt hot white stock, or hot milk: a pinch of marjoram

Slice and cube potatoes in 1 inch cubes. Slice and chop onions and garlic, and slice tomatoes. Melt fat in stock or milk. Blend vegetables and herbs in casserole and pour over stock or milk. Season to taste, cover with lid, greased paper or foil and cook slowly in oven at 325°F or Mark 2 for about an hour. If liked, when cooked, grated cheese may be thickly sprinkled over and allowed to heat through under lid, forming a main dish for supper.

CHIPPED POTATOES – No. 250

Choose evenly sized potatoes. Scrub potatoes thoroughly. Cut square each side – so that you have evenly shaped *blocks* of raw potato. Next cut blocks same length then make long chips ½ inch square. Do not waste cuttings which can be used for soup or purée. Have a deep pan of hot oil, with wire basket fitted inside preferably. Dry chips with a cloth then fry in hot oil till a light golden colour. If you have carefully made chips of a like size they will be done together. Remove and lay on tissue paper on a hot dish in hot oven till ready to serve.

MATCH STICK CHIPS – No. 251

As No. 250 but very, very finely cut, and needing careful handling. It is wise to use a deep fryer and basket.

DUCHESSE POTATOES – No. 252

1 lb potatoes steamed in jackets and peeled hot: 1 oz butter: ½ cup hot milk: 1 beaten egg: seasoning if required: a pinch of nutmeg or any favoured flavouring

Finely mash hot potatoes, add milk and ½ beaten egg and seasoning and put all into forcing bag with large star nozzle, and force into either heaps, or any desired shape, directly onto greased baking dish. Brush with rest of egg and bake in hot oven – 400°F or Mark 5, or near heat. As accompaniment to savoury or as a flan-ring shape for savoury filling.

POTATOES LYONNAISE – No. 253

To each 1 lb potatoes allow ¼ lb chopped shallots or onions. Butter or margarine. Chopped parsley to garnish. Boil or steam potatoes and when tender remove skins and cut into thin slices and fry in hot fat. When all are done fry thinly sliced shallots or onions till golden. Blend all together seasoning if liked, whilst blending, and adding parsley at the same time.

POTATOES MASHED – No. 254

Steam or boil in skins, remove skins and mash with masher. Heat some milk, about ⅔ cup to 1 lb potatoes, and in it some butter or margarine, pour into pan of hot potato and mash well together. This may be forced with a forcing bag and large nozzle, into servings and browned under grill. Used for bordering a flan – again with bag and nozzle, or may be served with the addition of any of the following.

> *Finely chopped spring onion: finely shredded onion: finely chopped chives: finely chopped raw carrot: finely chopped celery: finely chopped mint: finely chopped parsley: sliced cooked carrot: cooked new green peas: carraway seeds: grated parmesan or other cheese*

and can have cream, top milk, and beaten eggs whipped up in it.

POTATO PURÉE – No. 255

> *2 lb potatoes: ½ pt top milk: 2 oz butter: seasoning*

Boil or steam well scrubbed potatoes whole. Remove skins and sieve finely into a bowl. Season, stir in butter and mash well, add milk gradually and beat well till fluffy. Heat again – in ovenware dish, covered either in hot oven or over a pan of boiling water.

POTATOES, ROAST, BIRCHER-BENNER METHOD – No. 256

As served in the famous Bircher-Benner clinic in Zurich. Quarter-inched sliced scrubbed potatoes, oil for baking as above, then sprinkle top side with salt and carraway seed. Cook 30–40 minutes in hot oven when they will be crisp and brown and very easily digested. These have to be well chewed so are better digested and the carraway helps too.

SAUTÉ POTATOES – No. 257

Potatoes boiled or steamed in jackets No. 248 and peeled hot. Slice about ¼ inch thick and fry till golden brown both sides. Or grill, melting fat in pan and turning over carefully, each slice as placed in pan. Grill both sides.

POTATOES ROAST – No. 258

Well scrub large potatoes and cut up to evenly sized pieces – say quarters. Have an ounce of fat in pan heating in oven. Put in pieces of potato and turn them about to oil all over, fill tin, sprinkle with salt, herbs (sage or marjoram, thyme or mint), and bake in hot oven for 40 minutes.

POTATOES ROAST IN JACKETS – No. 259

Choose sound evenly sized potatoes – scrub scrupulously clean. Rub over outside with a butter paper. Roast on oven shelf at 400°F or Mark 5 for 45 minutes or at a lower temperature if slow cooking another dish, for longer.

When tender hold in cloth and slightly bend to crack one side in the centre, cover with cloth for a few moments on serving dish, and the potatoes will be floury when served.

Skins can be eaten and enjoyed if care is taken in preparation. If any trimming is necessary the result will still be good.

POTATOES STEAMED – No. 260

Well scrub with warm water and stiff brush, having potatoes of even size or cut to even sized pieces. Place in steamer over boiling water for 40–50 minutes. Have well fitting lid and allow about an inch of water in container.

SWEET POTATOES – No. 261

Sweet potatoes: butter: seasoning

Well scrub and roast in oven at 350°F till soft all through – an hour. Peel off skin and slice into hot dish – dab with bits of butter and sprinkle with celery salt or season with salt and chopped parsley.

PUMPKIN – No. 262

Preferably ripe, cut into suitably sized portions leaving on the skin for decorative value. Roast in ovenware dish for 30 minutes in a moderate oven 400°F or Mark 6. Serve as hot vegetable.

PULSES – No. 263

Beans, butter and haricot: peas, green and dried: peas, split yellow: peas, split brown: peas, split green: lentils, split yellow: lentils, split white

These are valuable foods to vegetarians as builders and nourishers.

The beans usally need soaking overnight. Wash in cold water, then put to soak in hot, allowing plenty of room for swelling, cover and leave till next day.

Dried green peas are best put to soak after breakfast, if needed for lunch, or after lunch for evening meal. If soaked too long they break up most unattractively.

Cook beans for 1½–2 hours after soaking, or for about 25 minutes in a pressure cooker, or according to instructions or your particular pressure cooker.

Green Peas No. 241 may vary in time needed for cooking according to age. I have had them tender in 20 minutes or still hard after 2½ hours. Round about 2 hours unless you find them tender sooner, but each lot you buy may be different. Use mint and a little sugar with dried peas, and onion if liked. Peas dried the moden way such as SWEL, are wonderful. These need soaking only for an hour or less, and when soaked cannot be distinguished from fresh garden peas. These are soaked with enough boiling water to cover by about an inch and cooked in the same water. Soak them in saucepan and save a little washing up.

For pressure cooking dried peas old style, see own instructions. Split peas need soaking for about 3 hours, then boiling for 2 hours. Unless again, a pressure cooker is being used, when again, follow own instructions. For pease pudding, after boiling till tender, purée peas, add butter and some hot stock or milk, beat in an egg or two, if liked, and finish cooking slowly in a well greased casserole, and covered with greased lid, for an hour at moderate temperature. Onion, carrot, tomato and herbs turn this dish into a main meal and if using these, add them decoratively to the purée after part-boiling and slicing. Dot with butter or margarine and cook together for the last hour.

Lentils do not need soaking and will be tender by boiling for ½ hour or cooking in casserole for an hour slowly.

I personally find that a little rice added – 1 tablespoon to ½ lb lentils, lightens the dish and renders it less stodgy. A lentil casserole is easy and takes care of itself. Use plenty of tomatoes, a goodly share of onion or shallots, and try the recipe for lentil hot-pot No. 86.

RADISHES – No. 264

Serve uncooked, well washed and trimmed. If liked they may be crisped up in cold water for a few minutes before serving – just cutting from bottom nearly to the stalk, four or more times, when they will open like flowers.

In salads or for hors-d'œuvres the opened radish may have a little wedge of cheese pushed into the centre.

Old and overgrown radishes may be used as small turnips for flavouring a stew or soup.

SAGE FRITTERS – No. 265

Using Fritter Batter No. 1 or 2 and about 30 sage leaves. Wash and well dry leaves. Hold by stalk, dip into batter to coat, and drop into hot deep fat. Cook till golden and well drain. Serve hot especially with any *au gratin* dish or with soup.

SALSIFY – No. 266
(or Oyster Plant)

Scrub and scrape roots and boil or steam as for parsnips, placing each one as soon as scraped into a bowl of water in which is a lemon skin, or a little lemon juice – to keep it white. Add a little lemon to the boiling water in which salsify is cooked also. When tender, drain and serve either plain, or cut into neat pieces and tossed in butter over heat for a minute or two. Fritters may be made with salsify pieces.

SEAKALE – No. 267

1 lb seakale: boiling water: butter: salt if needed

Seakale, like leeks and celery, needs most careful washing. Trim neatly until only enough stump remains to hold it together. Tie in bunches of several pieces with clean tape to make easier handling and boil for about 20 minutes, testing for tenderness with a fine skewer or steel knitting pin. Remove carefully from pan to a hot dish and serve with melted butter. If any over, serve in salad with either whipped cream or a light fresh cream cheese, chilled well, of course.

SORREL PURÉE – No. 268

3 lb sorrel: 3 Tbs butter: ½ cup cream: seasoning

Cook as for spinach No. 269, sieve and blend in saucepan over gentle heat till well heated – 5 minutes or so – add butter and cream – blend and serve. This needs very careful blending and stirring, but is well worthwhile. Serve with croutons.

SPINACH, BOILED – No. 269

2 *lb spinach*

Remove stalks and carefully select. Stalks take longer to cook than leaves and can either be put into pan sooner or cooked for another meal and served with parsley sauce. Wash spinach several times. Rinse out a large pan and put in spinach very wet but add no other water. Boil quickly till soft, stirring occasionally. When tender – after a few minutes of cooking, either purée or strain and chop and re-heat with butter. Do not waste liquor.

SPINACH BEET – No. 270

The large leaved spinach with thick white stalks is easy to grow and will grow for some years once planted.

When preparing, separate stalk from leaf and cook leaves as for spinach No. 269.

Cut stalks into inch long pieces and cook in a little water for about 25 minutes or until tender. It depends on age of stalk and may take a shorter time. When cooked, strain and keep hot, then use liquor with milk to make parsley sauce No. 368 and pour this over stalks.

If liked this can be used in separate meal from spinach green, of course.

SPINACH FRITTERS – No. 271

Using fritter batter No. 1 or 2 make as for lettuce fritters No. 216 only using two or three leaves together.

SHALLOTS – No. 272

Use as onions, either cooked, shredded or pickled.

TOMATOES – No. 273

Best used raw, either as a second vegetable, as part of a salad or stuffed raw.

In their natural state these are a wonderful alkaline food – cooked they become an acid food. Alkaline foods are of inestimable value to health – so in the main it is wisest to eat more raw than cooked tomatoes.

TOMATOES, GRILLED – No. 274

If you wish to serve cooked tomatoes they are best grilled. Wipe well, cut in half and place cut side up in a grill pan under gentle heat. Do not scorch, but just soften them. If serving on toast, a little margarine in the pan first will make a welcome addition if poured over tomatoes when cooked. Garnish with parsley.

STUFFED TOMATOES – No. 275
See Savouries section.

TURNIPS, BOILED OR STEAMED – No. 276
Wash and remove skin, then slice unless very small, when cook whole. Boil in about ½ inch of water for 20 minutes with lid on. Do not waste liquor when straining cooked turnips. Mash with a little butter when strained, and serve hot.

Allow 30–45 minutes for steaming after preparing as for boiling.

TURNIP TOPS – No. 277
Well pick over and wash and cook in ½ inch of water with lid on pan, shaking about at intervals in order to cook all evenly. When straining before serving, save liquor for drinking or for stock. Chop greens with a little butter in hot pan before placing in hot dish.

WATERCRESS – No. 278
Cannot be used too often for health. It has to be well chewed which helps it on the way to digestion. Its lovely colouring and crisp, decorative appearance to say nothing of its health and nutritive value, recommend it to every kitchen as often as possible.

Take every care when washing and trimming. If you stick the trimmed off stalks into a flowerpot of sandy soil that is standing in a dish kept filled with fresh water, you can have pretty little posies of it to deck salads when variety is difficult.

WATERCRESS, BOILED – No. 279
(Hot or cold)
Cook as spinach No. 269, drain well, conserving liquor, chop finely with butter and a pinch of nutmeg, serve hot with hot meal or cold with salad.

WINTER SALADS

JERUSALEM ARTICHOKE, CAULIFLOWER AND SPROUTS – No. 280
Cook artichokes as No. 150 and cool. When cold shred and blend with a very little shredded onion or leek and oil and wine dressing No. 337.

Serve on a bed of shredded raw sprouts, decorate with tiny cauliflower flowerets and garnish with chopped olives and milled roasted peanuts.

Serve with yoghourt, cream cheese or grated cheese.

FRESH RAW BEET – No. 281
Small new beets or an older beet. Well wash, peel, and finely shred. Dress with oil and lemon No. 335 and garnish with chopped parsley.

RAW BEET AND HORSERADISH – No. 282
Shred peeled beet finely and scrape and shred some horseradish. Blend in a bowl with dressing as advised in mixed summer salad No. 314.

COOKED BEET SALAD – No. 283
Cold cooked beets skinned and diced small and dressed with oil and lemon dressing No. 335 and garnished with spring onions and then strips of celery curled by laying in chilled water for a few minutes, and quartered hard-boiled eggs No. 127.

BEAN AND VEGETABLE – No. 284
Cold cooked butter beans No. 80 – thinly sliced white of leek, and chopped dates blended with oil and wine dressing No. 337 and served on a bed of shredded brussels sprouts or chopped broccoli sprouts.

CABBAGE, CARROT AND OLIVE – No. 285
½ lb fresh cabbage heart: 2 carrots: 6 olives: 1 small onion, finely shredded: olive oil

Finely shred cabbage and stir in bowl with onion and a little oil.
Pile on dish and arrange strips of carrot from outside to centre,
with olives between toward centre.

RED CABBAGE AND BEET – No. 286
Finely shred red cabbage and blend with chopped celery, apple
and cold cooked beet.

Blend in oil and apple juice dressing No. 334 and surround
with watercress or mustard and cress.

COLESLAW – No. 287
Prepare bowl and dressing as for No. 314 summer salad – but
blend thinly shredded cabbage heart and apple slices. Dress as
directed.

CAULIFLOWER – No. 288
Carefully cook a small and perfect cauliflower, removing it from
pan whilst it still has a slightly crisp condition but is just cooked.
Chill. When cold take very carefully apart and coating stems
thickly with cream cheese, build up again. If flowerets are laid in
general position and shape on table they can easily be built up
with the cheese to hold pieces in place.

Serve on a bed of potato salad No. 303 arranged with green
salad around dish, and garnish with sliced tomatoes overlapping
and sprigs of watercress or parsley on thinly sliced green or red
peppers.

CELERY, APPLE AND WALNUT – No. 289
Diced celery and apple dressed with oil and orange dressing No.
336 piled on lettuce endive and garnished with coarsely chopped
walnut kernels.

CELERY AND APPLE – No. 290
Dice crisp celery and dessert apples and blend with whipped
cream No. 670 or yoghourt dressing No. 341.

CELERY AND CREAM CHEESE – No. 291
Carefully take to pieces the best of a head of celery. Wash well,
dry, then fill hollow sides of sticks with cream cheese, then build

up again, wrap tightly in damp cloth or foil and chill well for
some time. Before serving cut into slices with a sharp knife and
serve slices on a bed of green salad.

CELERY, APPLE AND WATERCRESS – No. 292
Dice celery and dessert apple and dress with oil and lemon No.
335. Serve on a bed of watercress.

CELERY, RAW – No. 293
Dice crisp celery and blend with diced potato, carrot and cooked
peas. Dress with oil and apple juice dressing No. 334 and serve
on a bed of lettuce garnished with celery green and sliced radishes.

CELERY, COOKED – No. 294
Cook a head of celery with a shallot, after dividing it into quarters. Leave to cool in liquor. When cold drain and dry then arrange on a bed of finely shredded sprouts and coat with whipped
cream, white or green coloured.

CELERY AND HORSERADISH JELLIED
SALAD – No. 295
Using chopped celery blended with grated horseradish set as for
jellied vegetables No. 300 and serve on a green salad base.

CELERIAC – No. 296
Boil celeriac whole until tender – about an hour or according to
size. Drain and skin whilst hot, then set aside to cool. When cold
dice and blend with shredded onion – a little only, or thin leek
slices, cold cooked peas, the SWEL variety are excellent for winter
use.
   Dress with oil and lemon No. 335 and garnish with olives and
quarters of hard-boiled egg No. 127 or thinly sliced peppers and
grated cheese.

CREAM CHEESE, PRUNE AND WALNUT – No. 297
Soak washed prunes overnight when the stone will come out,
replace prune with walnut kernel half. Make a bed of endive or
lettuce and on this pipe rounds of cream cheese, placing a stuffed
prune on top of each.

COTTAGE CHEESE AND ORANGE – No. 298

On a bed of lettuce or shredded cabbage place slices of orange, carefully peeled and seeded.

Top with piped cottage cheese, garnish with carrot strips and parsley.

GRAPEFRUIT SALAD – No. 299

Peel grapefruit, remove pith and divide into segments. Dress some lettuce and watercress with a little olive oil and arrange on platter. Make a heap of milled nut kernels in centre, arrange segments coming out from this like curved flower petals and serve.

JELLIED VEGETABLES – No. 300

Following instructions on packet of vegetable gelatin and using a deliciously flavoured consommé, make enough jellied consommé to one third fill mould, either large ring mould, shaped mould, or individuals. Pour jelly into moulds and turn about to coat sides. Return jelly to measure and keep it warm.

Half fill moulds with a prepared selection of diced vegetables – very small – cooked peas, tiny pearl onions, chopped olive, cucumber, etc. Fill up with jelly and set really cold. These jellies will set very quickly but must only be turned out at the last minute unless they can be turned out and kept in salad section of fridge.

Serve on bed of mixed green salad and if a ring mould is used, fill centre with whipped cream No. 671 or cottage cheese. Dressing could be piped on top of individual moulds, or in a circle round base.

LEEK, APPLE AND TOMATO – No. 301

Carefully split and clean white and pale green of leek, then keeping halves in shape, slice thinly. Dice apple and quarter tomatoes, then blend all gently with oil and lemon No. 335. I saw Bridget Amies, then Bridget Milton, demonstrate this salad at the Country Life Vegetarian Restaurant in Ludgate Hill many years ago. It has been a firm favourite ever since and has earned my gratitude.

PARSNIP SALAD – No. 302

Scrub parsnip till it looks like old parchment then shred it finely. Dice apple and celery and blend with parsnip and oil and lemon dressing No. 335.

Surround with mustard and cress and garnish with sliced tomatoes overlapping round the mixture.

POTATO SALAD – No. 303

2 cups cold cooked potatoes, new if possible: an apple: a leek or spring onions: ½ cup raisins: ½ cup cooked peas: 1 cup tomato juice: parsley or chopped mint to garnish

Dice potatoes and apple – split and clean leek – keeping halves neat, thinly slice. Blend all together with peas and raisins adding a cup of tomato juice. Garnish with mint or parsley sprigs.

SUMMER SALADS

APPLE, RAISIN AND WALNUT – No. 303a
Prepare bowl and dressing as for mixed summer salad No. 314. Add shredded white cabbage, diced apple, seeded raisins and chopped walnuts.

ARTICHOKE – No. 304
Carefully cook globe artichokes till tender, chill till really cold. Cut in halves downwards, remove halves of choke, turn halves about gently in oil and lemon No. 335 until coated, and serve on a little mustard and cress.

BEAN SPROUT SALAD – No. 305
Prepare salad bowl and dressing as for mixed summer salad No. 314. To a broken crisp lettuce, add a cup of bean sprouts No. 159, $\frac{1}{2}$ cup sweet chutney, $\frac{1}{4}$ cucumber diced and 1 cup halved pineapple cubes. Blend well together and garnish with sliced tomatoes overlapping round edge of bowl and halved hard-boiled eggs decorated with colourful strips of red or yellow peppers.

BANANA, DATE AND GINGER – No. 306
On a bed of lettuce or shredded sprouts, arrange bananas quartered lengthwise, stoned dates, and dress with whipped cream No. 670. Sprinkle dressing with shredded preserved ginger.

CARROT, APPLE AND NUT – No. 307
Shred raw carrots, dice apples and blend with chopped or coarsely milled nuts and a cream or mayonnaise dressing.

CREAM CHEESE AND PINEAPPLE – No. 308
Arrange pineapple slices on a bed of green salad and on the pineapple heap cream cheese. Sprinkle with finely milled nuts.

CHICORY SALAD – No. 309
As for mixed summer vegetable salad but using chicory instead of lettuce and blending as directed.

CHICORY, PEAR AND PEPPER – No. 310
Prepare salad bowl as for mixed summer salad, and blend chicory pieces, thin strips of pepper and quarters of ripe pear.

CHICORY, APPLE AND TOMATO – No. 311
Prepare bowl as for mixed summer salad No. 314 and toss chicory pieces, diced apple and quartered peeled tomato till well blended.

CUCUMBER NUT – No. 312
On a bed of lettuce heap diced cucumber with chopped nut kernels or pine kernels. Garnish with watercress and radish roses No. 264. Serve with oil and lemon dressing No. 335.

DANDELION SALAD – No. 313
As for mixed summer vegetable salad No. 314 but using young dandelions before they have bloomed, breaking leaves and blending as directed.

MIXED SUMMER SALAD – No. 314
Rub round salad bowl with a cut clove of garlic or a saltspoon of garlic salt, and a wooden spoon. Add 1 teaspoon of made mustard – preferably French – and stir, 1 tablespoon of olive oil and stir, and lastly 2 tablespoons of lemon juice till all well blended.

Gradually add and toss and turn about, quartered lettuce hearts and larger leaves shredded, uncooked new garden peas, tiny carrots in strips, spring onions, watercress and skinned quartered tomatoes. Dress with quartered hard-boiled eggs No. 127.

MARROW AND GREEN BEAN – No. 315
Diced cooked marrow – not watery or squashy but still firm, please – with cooked and cut up French or runner beans. Blend with oil and apple juice No. 334 and serve with watercress or mustard and cress surround.

SORREL SALAD – No. 316
As for mixed summer vegetable salad No. 314 but using sorrel leaves instead of lettuce and blending as directed.

SPINACH SALAD – No. 317
As for mixed summer salad No. 314 but using shredded spinach instead of lettuce.

ROLLED SALAD FOR YOUNG CHILDREN – No. 318
Mince raisins and grate carrot and place on lettuce leaf. Fold in one end of leaf and roll up, cutting across unfolded end to disclose filling.

Placed in a youngster's fist with open end to eat from, it will be much enjoyed and is rarely put down till eaten.

Fillings may be varied, but should only contain small and finely shredded food such as raw finely shredded root vegetables, grated cheese or chopped hard-boiled egg.

STUFFED EGG SALAD – No. 319
Hard-boiled eggs No. 127 one per person. Slice off top and remove yolk carefully.

Pound yolks with a wooden spoon in a basin, adding a nut of butter, a little paprika and finely grated cheese and a small quantity of tomato purée. Blend till smooth, then pipe back into egg whites, a little more than filling, and placing top on so that it appears hinged on one side. Serve on green salad.

TOMATO AND CUCUMBER JELLIED – No. 320
Make as jellied vegetables No. 300 but using diced cucumber and sliced skinned tomatoes. Serve on green salad base and pipe with cream or cream cheese. To skin tomatoes easily pour boiling water over them in a bowl, leave 1 minute, then drain and skins will slip off easily if cut.

TOMATO BASKETS – No. 321
Carefully leaving a band across round end of tomato cut out sides so that band forms a handle, scoop out pulp and seeds. Fill baskets with grated cheese blended with whipped cream and a little purée from sieved pulp. Place tiny sprigs of parsley or watercress between tomatoes on a bed of green salad.

TOMATO HEALTH SALAD – No. 322

   1 *cup chopped celery:* 1 *cup leek slices:* ½ *cup chopped parsley:*
   4 *large firm tomatoes, sliced:* 1 *head endive*

Blend all in bowl with oil and lemon dressing No. 335.

TOMATO AND ONION – No. 323
Peel and slice tomatoes, and very thinly slice onion, having more tomato than onion. Carefully blend with apple juice and oil No. 334 – very little – and serve in bowl to hand round.

CUCUMBER AND TOMATO – No. 324
As for tomato and onion but using cucumber slices, rather thin, and with rind left on to assist chewing.

TOMATO AND RICE – No. 325
Half cup cooked whole rice No. 68 to 3 good firm tomatoes. Skin tomatoes and slice, then blend together with rice and either cream No. 670 or oil and lemon dressing No. 335.

STUFFED TOMATOES – No. 326
Cut off top and scoop out centre pulp and blend it with chopped or creamed mushrooms, and hard-boiled egg No. 127. Or fill with uncooked nut-meat mixture No. 49. Or fill with uncooked nut-meals sold ready prepared and made into a soft mixture with tomato juice. Or fill with cream cheese and chopped nuts and a little chutney. Add finely chopped parsley to fillings for extra nourishment.

TOMATO, ENDIVE AND CASHEW NUT – No. 327
Prepare bowl as for mixed summer salad No. 314 and use endive, sliced tomatoes and whole or chopped cashew nuts.

If liked cashews may be simmered whole and cooled before blending with vegetables.

VEGETABLE SALAD – No. 328
Dice new potatoes, French beans, carrots and with cauliflower flowerets – all cooked, add fresh diced cucumber, radish slices, spring onions and diced apple. Blend with a cup of tomato chutney No. 612 and serve on crisp lettuce garnished with sliced tomatoes and coarsely grated cheese.

SAUCES AND DRESSINGS

INTRODUCTION
This section may seem over-large, but since vegetables will be used cooked and raw, for most of all the days of the week, and sauces, quite apart from their nourishment, do provide scope for varying meals and allowing for an element of surprise, I think it will be found useful.

I do advise experiment with the many herbs to be obtained.

AVOCADO DRESSING – No. 329
Thinly peel ripe avocado and quarter, removing stone. Mash pulp and gradually add zest and juice of lemon. Beat till creamy and use for salad dressing.

Orange zest and juice make an interesting alternative. A cut clove of garlic may be rubbed around bowl before mixing, if liked.

FRENCH DRESSING – No. 330
1 Tbs lemon juice: 1 Tbs olive oil: ¼ tsp french mustard: a pinch of sugar: a pinch of salt, if liked: a pinch of pepper

Place dry ingredients in a small bowl, add lemon juice gradually and beat with wooden spoon, add oil, drop by drop, and beat till sauce thickens, and serve at once.

HONEY MINT SAUCE – No. 331
2 Tbs lemon juice (juice of 1 lemon): 2 Tbs honey: 2 Tbs boiling water: 2 Tbs level, chopped mint

Pour boiling water onto mint, add honey and blend, and finally lemon juice when it will be ready to serve. Delicious with summer vegetables.

MAYONNAISE – No. 332
¼ pt olive oil: 1 egg yolk: 2 Tbs lemon juice (1 lemon): ½ tsp french mustard: a pinch of salt: a pinch of pepper: 1 tsp tarragon vinegar

Mix egg yolk, pepper and salt, vinegar and oil, drop by drop, and continuously stirring and finally lemon juice, very gradually.

Should mayonnaise curdle, break another egg yolk into a bowl, and add curdled mayonnaise drop by drop and stirring continuously.

MINT BUTTER – No. 333
As parsley butter, but substituting chopped mint.

OIL AND APPLE JUICE – No. 334
Half cup apple juice No. 746 to an egg cup of olive oil, shaken or beaten together.

OIL AND LEMON JUICE DRESSING – No. 335
½ *cup lemon juice*: 1 *egg cup olive oil*: 1 *tsp honey*

Shake or beat together and use for dressing salads cooked or uncooked.

A cut clove of garlic may be rubbed around the bowl before blending. Use wherever vinaigrette is recommended if vinegar is not favoured.

OIL AND ORANGE DRESSING – No. 336
One egg cup of olive oil and 1 teaspoon honey to ½ cup of orange juice and the zest of the orange. Blend well together and dress salad. A cut clove of garlic rubbed round bowl before blending, if desired.

OIL AND WHITE WINE DRESSING – No. 337
½ *cup white wine*: 1 *egg cup olive oil*: 1 *tsp honey*

Shake or beat together and use for dressing salads cooked or uncooked.

A cut clove of garlic may be rubbed around bowl before blending if liked.

PEANUT AND HONEY DRESSING – No. 338
1 *round Tbs finely milled and roasted peanuts*: 1 *Tbs lemon juice*:
1 *tsp honey*: 1 *tsp almond oil or olive oil*

Blend well then beat till creamy and use for salad dressing.

PARSLEY BUTTER – No. 339
1 *Tbs butter*: 1 *Tbs finely chopped parsley*: 1 *tsp lemon juice*

Blend on a plate with palette knife, shape into neat pats, the size

of a shilling, ¼ inch thick. Chill and serve with hot savouries and
vegetables where sauce not being served.

ROQUEFORT CHEESE DRESSING – No. 340

½ cup crumbled roquefort cheese: 2 egg cups olive oil: ½ cup lemon juice

Rub cheese through sieve and gradually add oil and lemon,
beating all the while till a cream results.

YOGHOURT DRESSING – No. 341

Add to yoghourt finely chopped green herbs to make a health-
giving and interesting dressing for green salads.

SALAD DRESSING – No. 342

4 eggs: 3 Tbs milk: 1 cup lemon juice: 1 rounded Tbs honey: salt and pepper, if liked – ¼ tsp each: 1 tsp mustard

Beat eggs with milk and lemon, any seasoning, mustard and
honey.

In double saucepan cook over gentle heat till thick, stirring
continuously with wooden spoon.

Will keep indefinitely in fridge, or several weeks in cool pantry.
Keep corked.

WATERCRESS BUTTER – No. 343

As parsley butter, using finely chopped watercress instead of
parsley.

SAUCES, SAVOURY

APPLE SAUCE – No. 344

1 cooking apple: lemon juice: 1 tsp honey or sugar

Peel and grate apple finely, blend with a little lemon juice and sugar. If needed warm, beat in basin over hot water without cooking.

BECHAMEL SAUCE – No. 345

½ pt white stock No. 35 or light vegetable liquor, boiling: ½ pt milk, boiling: 1 oz butter: parsley, a good large sprig, or several small, tied with thread to pan handle for retrieving: ¼ tsp nutmeg: a little salt: 1 Tbs sieved wholewheat flour or 1 Tbs cornflour

Melt butter in pan, add flour and stir whilst cooking for ½ minute, then stir continuously whilst adding hot stock and milk very gradually. Add parsley bunch, salt and nutmeg – taste for flavour before serving. Strain and re-heat.

BREAD SAUCE – No. 346

1 cup wholewheat crumbs: 1 Tbs margarine: 1 small shallot: 1 tsp tarragon or cider vinegar: ½ tsp sage and thyme: 1½ cups vegetable stock or 1½ cups hot water and 1 tsp yeast or vegetable extract: seasoning

Finely chop shallot and simmer in stock or hot water with herbs and seasoning. When tender add crumbs and margarine and stir, add vinegar.

If no shallots a pickled onion may be used, when omit vinegar.

BROWN SAUCE – No. 347

As for white sauce No. 372 with addition of 2 tablespoons tomato purée and 1 teaspoon of yeast extract or Vecon or other nourishing vegetable extract.

A little onion or garlic salt or celery salt will improve flavour and nourishment.

MELTED BUTTER SAUCE – No. 348

Melt butter over gentle heat without boiling and stir in a squeeze of lemon juice.

CAPER SAUCE – No. 349

As for white sauce No. 372 adding chopped capers to taste, and 1 tablespoon lemon juice.

CASHEW NUT SAUCE (SAVOURY) – No. 350

A rounded tablespoon cashew cream to a cup of white stock or vegetable liquor, i.e. onion, carrot, celery, pea or potato. Stirred over gentle heat.

CHEESE SAUCE – No. 351

Making white sauce No. 372 and adding ⅔ cup of grated cheese.

One teaspoon of made mustard may be added, or a pinch of garlic salt, or a good pinch of marjoram.

CHEESE AND TOMATO SAUCE – No. 352

1 cup tomato after sieving to purée: 1 cup finely grated cheddar: 1 Tbs olive oil: ½ tsp mustard: 1 tsp tarragon or cider vinegar

Warm together oil, purée and mustard but do not boil. Add cheese and stir well, heat but not to boiling, lastly add vinegar.

CELERY SAUCE – No. 353

Celery outside sticks, as required: 1 tsp celery seeds: making about 2 oz shredded: 1 cup hot milk: 1 tsp sieved wholewheat flour: 2 tsp butter: seasoning as required

Shred celery finely and drop into pan with melted butter and cook for a moment without browning. Stir in flour and then gradually hot milk and season to taste; simmering for a few minutes.

CURRY SAUCE – No. 354

1 oz butter: 1 onion: 1 apple: a few chopped dates: 1 level tsp herbs: 1 tsp lemon juice: 2 rounded tsp good curry powder: 2 tsp wholewheat flour: seasoning: 1 pt hot stock or hot water and a tsp of vegetable extract: 1 clove garlic (½ water and ½ apple juice may be used instead of stock)

Fry onion and chopped garlic slowly until tender but not brown. Add curry powder and flour and stir, then cook for a few minutes, stirring. Add herbs, chopped apple, dates and seasoning. Boil, simmer till apple is tender, sieve, add lemon juice, re-heat if necessary.

EGG SAUCE – No. 355

1 *hard-boiled egg No.* 127: 1 *Tbs butter:* 1 *cup milk: lemon juice*

Rub egg through grater or chop finely, add to milk and boil together. Cool a little, stir in butter and a squeeze of lemon juice and serve immediately.

FENNEL SAUCE 1 – No. 356
Finely chop fennel and simmer in a little water for 10 minutes, add a nut of butter and heat till melted.

FENNEL SAUCE 2 – No. 357
As parsley sauce No. 368 but using chopped fennel instead of parsley.

If making a salad, save the stalks of the fennel to add to it – first peeling them.

HORSERADISH SAUCE 1 (COOKED) – No. 358
Make white sauce No. 372 and when cooked add finely shredded horseradish, previously washed and peeled, about 2 tablespoons 2 tablespoons lemon juice, 1 teaspoon brown sugar and, if liked, a little salt and 1 teaspoon made mustard.

Blend well and chill before serving. May be used with rich nut roasts, or made thicker, chilled and small pieces shaped into tiny balls for appetizers. Roll the balls in milled cashew nuts.

HORSERADISH SAUCE 2 (UNCOOKED) – No. 359

A finger sized stick of horseradish: $\frac{1}{2}$ *tsp made or french mustard:* 1 *tsp sugar:* 1 *tsp lemon juice:* 1 *cup cream or top milk: a pinch of salt, if liked*

Well wash and soak horseradish for a while to make grating easier. Peel and grate really finely. Add mustard, sugar, salt, if needed, and lemon juice.

Finally whip cream and add very gradually. Keep very cold till required.

If using top milk make thicker with vegetable gelatin according to instructions, and cool before using for sauce.

MAYONNAISE – No. 360

1 *egg yolk:* 1 *tsp made mustard:* 1 *tsp honey:* 2 *Tbs lemon juice:* $\frac{3}{4}$ *cup olive oil*

Over hot water warm honey in basin and with wooden spoon gradually blend in mustard and egg, then leave till cold and add oil and finally lemon, drop by drop.

MINT SAUCE – No. 361

1 Tbs finely chopped mint: 1½ Tbs boiling water: 1 level tsp honey: 2 Tbs lemon juice (1 lemon)

Place mint in sauceboat, pour on boiling water and stir till all green (boiling water will tenderize the mint and bring out the colour). Add honey and stir, then lemon juice, and it is ready to serve.

This way it is delicious, and without vinegar it does become mint sauce, not mint flavoured vinegar.

MINT AND PINEAPPLE SAUCE – No. 362

Chop a slice of pineapple and with half the quantity of water and 1 tablespoon honey, simmer till honey is blended and remove from heat. Stir in two heaped teaspoons chopped mint and 1 teaspoon cider vinegar.

Serve hot with savouries, or cold with cooked vegetable salads.

MUSHROOM SAUCE – No. 363

Using ½ pt Béchamel sauce with 2 oz finely chopped mushrooms and stalks, and 1 tsp finely shredded onion

Make thicker with flour for filling *vol-au-vent* with 3 oz mushroom rather than two. Adding 1 tablespoon flour. Use also for filling savoury pancakes. For spreading on croutons etc. Add stock or milk to make a mushroom soup.

Dried mushrooms, soaked first, may be used.

MUSHROOM HERB SAUCE – No. 364

¼ lb mushrooms: ¼ tsp green or dried herbs: 1½ cups milk or top milk: ¼ tsp salt if required: 2 Tbs butter or margarine: 1 Tbs each wholewheat flour and soya flour

Wash and chop mushrooms and stalks finely. Heat butter in pan, add flour and soya and stir well over gentle heat till a ball of paste leaves sides of pan. Gradually add milk in small quantities, stirring briskly, till a smooth sauce results. Add mushrooms and simmer for 10–15 minutes.

ONION SAUCE – No. 365
Béchamel sauce No. 345

With an onion simmered in minimum liquid till tender, well mashed and added with liquor. A little nutmeg should be added. If preferred, add onion to brown sauce No. 347.

PARSLEY SAUCE 1 – No. 366
1 cup tomato juice: $\frac{1}{2}$ cup finely chopped parsley: 1 tsp finely chopped onion: $\frac{1}{2}$ oz butter: 1 tsp honey

Combine over gentle heat for 10 minutes. Serve hot with hot meal or use cold to coat cooked vegetables for salad.

PARSLEY SAUCE 2 – No. 367
$\frac{1}{2}$ cup chopped parsley: 2 tsp cider vinegar: juice of half a lemon: 2 oz butter

Melt butter in lemon juice and vinegar over very low heat, then add parsley. Serve hot with hot vegetables, or cold with cooked vegetable salad.

PARSLEY SAUCE 3 – No. 368
Make white sauce No. 372 and add $\frac{1}{2}$ cup chopped parsley, when cooked, and before serving.

PEANUT SAUCE – No. 369
As cashew nut sauce No. 374 substituting peanut butter.

TARTARE SAUCE – No. 370
1 cup mayonnaise No. 332: 1 Tbs chopped capers: $\frac{1}{2}$ tsp or one tiny pickled onion finely chopped

Blend and serve.

TOMATO SAUCE – No. 371
2 good sized tomatoes ($\frac{1}{2}$ lb): $\frac{1}{2}$ oz butter: seasoning: 1 tsp finely shredded shallot: 1 level tsp yeast extract: 1 tsp flour: 1 cup vegetable stock or hot water: 1 tsp tarragon vinegar

Melt butter in pan, add onion and cook for a minute gently. Add sliced tomatoes, stir well, and simmer for another minute, then add yeast extract, water and flour blended together, a shake of pepper and pinch of salt and stir well till it has boiled for two minutes. Sieve and serve.

Two tablespoons – level – tomato purée or a small tin of tomatoes may be used.

WHITE SAUCE – No. 372

½ pt white vegetable stock or milk: 1 oz butter or margarine: 3 level Tbs wholewheat flour after sieving (do not throw sieved-out bran away, use it for breakfast cereal or in scones etc.): a pinch of grated nutmeg: salt, if wished: a little paprika

Melt butter over gentle heat, add flour and stir to blend well, cook for a minute, then gradually add stock or milk whilst stirring vigorously till a smooth blend is achieved. Season and stir again. Use this as basis of any sauce such as mushroom, caper, horseradish or parsley, etc.

SAUCES, SWEET

MELTED BUTTER AND HONEY SAUCE – No. 373

3 oz butter: 2 Tbs honey

Melt butter, stir in honey and blend over minimum heat – keep warm to serve, stirring before pouring. A little lemon juice may be added if liked.

CASHEW NUT SAUCE – No. 374
(CASHEW NUT CREAM)

Either 1 rounded tablespoon cashew nut cream to $\frac{1}{2}$ cup of water blended warm, and served either warm or cold, or $\frac{1}{2}$ cup cashew nuts to 1 cup water blended in electric liquidizer till smooth.

CHOCOLATE SAUCE – No. 375

2 oz chocolate grated: 1 oz cornflour: 2 oz sugar or honey, or 2 oz vanilla sugar No. 564: a few drops vanilla essence, if no vanilla sugar: 1 cup hot water or milk

Blend chocolate, cornflour and sugar or honey with a little cold water. Boil water in pan and pour on mixture, return to pan and bring to boil, stirring, and simmer for ten minutes. Remove from heat, add vanilla, if necessary.

HARD SAUCE – No. 376
(FOR XMAS PUDDING)

2 oz butter: 2 oz soft brown sugar: $\frac{1}{4}$ tsp nutmeg: either 1 Tbs brandy or juice and grated zest of $\frac{1}{2}$ lemon

Beat sugar and butter till fluffy then gradually add brandy, or juice, when it is ready to serve. Sherry may be used with excellent results.

LEMON SAUCE 1 – No. 377

2 Tbs butter: 1 Tbs lemon juice: grated zest of half lemon: 1 tsp honey

Melt butter, add juice, honey and zest. Do not boil.

LEMON SAUCE 2 – No. 378

*1 cup milk : 1 Tbs butter : 2 tsp cornflour : juice and grated zest
of half a lemon : 2 tsp sugar*

Heat milk, blend cornflour, lemon juice, zest and sugar, pour on
milk when boiling, return to pan and bring again to boil.

ORANGE SAUCE – No. 379

As lemon sauce No. 378 using orange juice and zest instead of
lemon.

VANILLA SAUCE – No. 380

As lemon sauce No. 377 but substituting a vanilla pod for lemon.
This should be heated in the milk and left to stand a while. Later
remove pod – (wash, dry and store this for further use) – and
make sauce as directed.

BAKED APPLES 1 – No. 381

1 cooking apple per person: a little cold water: honey or sugar

Wash apples and after peeling a thin strip around each one, near the top, stand them with about ¼ cup water on an ovenware plate. If honey is to be used, put only a small spoonful on top of each apple before cooking; if sugar, sprinkle a little on wet apples before putting in oven.

Cook at 375°F or Mark 4 for about 30 minutes, although the exact time will depend on size of apples. Test for softness through centre, if uncertain.

Serve with a spoonful of the glaze on the plate over each, and pass honey or sugar to taste, and dairy or cashew cream.

BAKED APPLES 2 – No. 382

Wash evenly sized apples, remove stalk and flower, and carefully core without breaking skin at bottom. Peel one inch down from top. Stew peel and core for a few minutes, mash, and strain juice into centre of each of the cored apples. Add to each centre a nut of butter.

Bake as for No. 381, and serve with honey, sugar, or if you are lucky enough to have some, maple syrup.

(Since writing this I have seen maple syrup on sale.)

BAKED APPLES 3 – No. 383

Stuff centres of cored apples with dates, figs or raisins and serve with honey and cashew cream.

APPLE CHARLOTTE 1 – No. 384

½ lb wholewheat crumbs: 1 lb cooking apples: 1½ oz butter or margarine: a little lemon zest: 1 cup of brown sugar

Have ready a greased ovenware dish, warm fat in medium sized pan, drop crumbs into warmed fat and stir them about till all fat is absorbed and crumbs equally buttered.

Wash apples, halve, remove stalk and skin around it and flower and skin around that, and remove any blemishes. Grate down apple, medium to fine, and stir in lemon zest and sugar and blend. Sprinkle some crumbs on bottom of dish, then some apple mixture, then crumbs, and so on finishing with crumbs.

Bake at 350°F or Mark 3 for about 30 minutes.

APPLE CHARLOTTE 2 – No. 385

4 cups of corn flakes, or other crushed cereal: 1 oz butter: 2 large cooking apples: 2 Tbs brown sugar: pinch cinnamon, clove or ginger

Grease a fireproof dish. Wash, trim and grate apples, melt butter and pour over flakes in bowl, add apples and blend all together with chosen flavouring. Bake in gentle oven at 350°F or Mark 4 for 30 minutes.

BAKED APPLE MERINGUE – No. 386

Baked Apples No. 381, and when cooked cover with meringue, No. 556 and sprinkle with demerara sugar; lightly brown in oven or under grill.

APPLE BATTER – No. 387

Using batter No. 541, and allowing it to stand for an hour or so. Into a greased dish put some fat to heat in oven, and prepare slices of apple quarters, enough to lay in rows all over dish. When fat is hot, pour in batter, then arrange apples neatly and quickly, sprinkling with demerara sugar. Bake at 400°F or Mark 5 for 30 minutes.

APPLE BATTER WITH GINGER – No. 388

As No. 387, but adding small slices of preserved ginger with apples.

APPLE MERINGUE – No. 389

Place 4 cups of purée No. 392, in an ovenware dish and cover with meringue No. 556, then put into a cool oven 250°F or Mark ¼ to set and lightly brown, for about 25 minutes. Serve hot or cold. Some milled nuts sprinkled over when meringue has set, but not quite finished, and/or a few halved glacé cherries and pieces of angelica added for festive occasions.

APPLE PANCAKES – No. 390

Make a batter with:

¼ pt milk: ¼ pt water: ¼ lb flour: 1 Tbs olive oil: 2 eggs: pinch salt

Cut 2 peeled apples into very thin slices. Pour some batter into greased pan, add some apple slices. Cook both sides till apple is tender. Serve hot on plate with sugar and cinnamon.

APPLE PURÉE – No. 391

Peel, core and quarter apples, windfalls or any damaged apples will serve (after removing damaged parts, of course). Cook slowly with very little water, and with grated lemon rind added. Sweeten with demerara sugar to taste.

UNCOOKED APPLE PURÉE – No. 392

Wash, halve and remove stalk and flower dints of matured cooking apples, such as Bramley Seedlings, or ripe windfall eating apples. Remove any damaged parts, then grate into bowl. Remove any large pieces of skin or core, and use as sauce, cold, or for making dishes where purée is needed.

APPLE SNOW – No. 393

4 large cooking apples: honey to sweeten: 1 or 2 egg whites

Wash the apples and remove a thin strip of peel from round top. Bake on a dish in a moderate oven till tender. When cool, remove skin and finely mash pulp, sweetening with honey to taste. Stiffly whisk eggs till all dry to the bottom of bowl, and lightly fold into purée. Pile into glasses and chill. Decorate with crystallized violets and some chopped nuts.

APRICOT DUMPLINGS – No. 394

Potato pastry No. 533: whole apricots

Roll out pastry and cut into circles of convenient size to wrap each fruit. Moisten edges with water and press well together to seal.

Have a large pan of boiling water with fitting lid, drop in dumplings singly and cook for 30 minutes, gently boiling. Test one with a steel needle for tenderness of fruit. Serve with melted butter and honey sauce No. 373.

APRICOTS, DRIED AND SOAKED – No. 395

Dried apricots need no cooking. Wash in boiling water and soak in cold for 36 hours. Do not soak in a lot of water, use the minimum and turn them about to absorb it all. The fruit will be tender and well flavoured and should not need more than a little honey, if any, to sweeten it.

Use as stewed fruit, but do not cook, it is unnecessary and spoils it. Serve with custard or cream.

APPLE CREAM CROWDIE – No. 396

*3 large Cox's orange pippins: ¼ pt thick whipped cream No. 670:
2 breakfast cups raw rolled oats*

Lightly roast oats in a shallow tin in oven and allow to cool. Wash
and top and tail apples, remove any blemishes before coarsely
grating.

Keeping all very cold, blend apples, oats and thick cream
lightly, then pile into glasses, individual waxed paper cases or a
large dish. Decorate with either crystallized flowers or fruits in
small pieces. Will make 25–30 small servings in cases for a party.
Keep very cold till served.

(I cannot recall to whom I am indebted for my first "Crowdie"
recipe. Should this meet the donor's eye – many thanks indeed.)

APPLE AND ALMOND CREAM – No. 397

*3 sweet dessert apples: 2 oz milled almonds: ¼ pt thick fresh
whipped cream No. 670*

Wash and trim and grate apples, blend with nuts and cream, pile
into individual glasses and decorate with praline No. 589.

BANANA AND HAZEL CREAM – No. 398

*2 bananas: 2 oz milled hazel kernels: ¼ pt thick fresh whipped
cream No. 670: cherry or angelica for decorations*

Peel, trim and mash bananas, blend with hazels and lightly with
cream. Pile into individual glasses or force in with forcing bag
and a mashed potato nozzle. Decorate with tiny pieces of cherry
or angelica.

RASPBERRY CREAM – No. 399

*2 cups mashed raspberries: 2 Tbs honey, or light pieces sugar:
¼ pt thick fresh whipped cream No. 670*

Blend lightly and freeze in refrigerator tray, removing and stirring
frequently.

STRAWBERRY CREAM – No. 400

As No. 399 but using ripe strawberries.

PINEAPPLE CREAM – No. 401

As No. 399 but using mashed ripe pineapple.

FIG CREAM – No. 402

1 *cup soaked figs:* 1 *cup nut kernels:* ¼ *pt thick fresh whipped cream No.* 670

Figs should have been washed in hot water and soaked in cold for 36 hours.

Mince figs and nuts, or finely chop if no mincer, and lightly blend with cream. Serve in individual glasses, very cold.

FRUIT CRUMBLE 1 – No. 403

1 *lb fruit as available:* 4–6 *oz demerara sugar, according to tartness of fruit*

For Crumble:

4 *oz wholewheat flour:* 2 *oz butter or margarine:* 1 *oz sugar*

Well grease a fireproof dish, and into it put cleaned and prepared fruit, evenly sized or in evenly sized pieces. If fresh fruit such as blackberries or apples, or a combination of both, some water will be needed, but not much, only sufficient to make a little juice and not boil over. Sprinkle sugar over fruit before adding water. If a 1 lb bottle of fruit is used its liquid will be about right if it is well packed. Melt butter, cool a little, then add sugar and flour and blend well. Tip all onto fruit and spread over. It looks impossible, but a nice nutty top will be achieved by baking at 400°F or Mark 5 for about 25–30 minutes. Serve with cream or custard.

My favourite is blackberry and apple, and it delights my family during the winter months, for luscious blackberries abound in our London garden, and I fill many 1 lb bottles. One bottle to a large cooking apple is a good mixture.

An apple crumble with the berries from 2 large heads of ripe elderberries is delicious too.

FRUIT CRUMBLE 2 – No. 404

As for No. 403 but cooked in a close lidded pan on top of stove. Use fresh or bottled fruit and sweeten to taste. When simmering in pan about 6–8 inches, and no wider. Sprinkle crumbs on top. Cover with lid and cook on low heat for about 20 minutes. Do not have a lot of liquid. If using bottled fruit the amount of fruit and liquid in a 1 lb bottle is right for 4 people. This dish can be cooked over a grill whilst grilling main course, but be careful not to boil too hard. It needs very little heat to cook it once simmering.

BREAD AND BUTTER PUDDING – No. 405

2 cups dry bread cubes: 2 pts milk: 1 oz butter: 2 Tbs sugar: ¾ cup sultanas: 2 Tbs demerara sugar: 2 eggs: a little lemon zest and sprinkle of nutmeg

Into a well buttered fireproof dish place bread cubes and sultanas, well mixed. Heat milk in a pan, adding butter and sugar, stirring until all is blended. Remove from heat and stir in beaten eggs and lemon zest. Pour over bread and sultanas and push down all bread leaving none dry on top. Sprinkle nutmeg and slowly cook. 45 minutes at 300°F or Mark 1. The top should be browned golden but pudding must not race, or it will curdle and be unpleasant.

ORANGE BREAD AND BUTTER PUDDING – No. 406

1 pt milk: 1 egg: 1 cup dry bread cubes: nut of butter: zest of one orange: 1 Tbs sugar

Place bread cubes in fireproof dish – greased. Heat milk, sugar and butter and allow to cool a little. Add grated rind of orange and beaten egg. Pour over bread and push down all cubes till wetted. Bake in moderate oven about 30 minutes. 350°F or Mark 3.

WHOLEWHEAT BREAD PUDDING – No. 407

2 cups wholewheat crumbs: 1 pt milk, hot: 1 beaten egg: 1 cup raisins or sultanas or a mixture of both: a pinch of spice: 1 oz margarine: 1 Tbs Barbados sugar

Combine all and bake in a buttered dish for 30 minutes at 375°F or Mark 4. Serve hot or cold.

DATE PUDDING – No. 408

3 cups wholewheat crumbs: 1 cup dates (stoned): 1 cup water: 1 pt hot milk: a little lemon

Boil together dates and water for a few minutes only, add lemon and stir well and mash.

Have a greased dish, and make a layer of half the breadcrumbs, then add date mixture dotted over crumbs, and cover with remainder of crumbs. Pour hot milk over, and bake at 375°F or Mark 4 for about 30 minutes. Serve with cashew cream No. 374.

FIG PUDDING – No. 409

As for date pudding No. 408, but using figs instead of dates, and chopping them in mincer before cooking.

FRUIT AND CARROT PUDDING – No. 410

3 cups grated carrots: ½ cup milled nut kernels: 1 cup stoned and minced dates: 1 cup stoned and minced raisins: ½ cup honey or soft brown sugar: ½ cup melted butter or margarine

Blend all together and packing in a greased dish bake in a moderate oven – 375°F or Mark 4 for 30 minutes.

QUICK FRUIT PUDDING – No. 411

Fruit puddings need not be cooked for hours. I cook mine whilst the vegetables are cooking, and they take the same time as potatoes. Have a smallish pan – 6 inches across say, and with a close fitting lid. Put prepared fresh or 1 lb jar bottled fruit in pan with necessary sugar and set it to boil whilst making dumpling dough No. 531. Do not make it into dumplings, but shape roughly to fit inside pan on top of fruit. Place on fruit, put on lid and let it just boil for about 20 minutes. Turn carefully onto a hot dish for serving, and have warmed plates. Serve with cream or custard. The fruit will still taste fresh and not be cooked to death.

SPONGE PUDDINGS – No. 412

4 oz wholewheat self-raising flour (or plain and baking powder): 1 egg and 1 extra yolk if possible: 2 oz butter or margarine: milk or water to mix: syrup or jam in bottom of greased mould

Cream butter and sugar, gradually beat in egg and milk and flour alternately till a light soft mixture results.

For quick cooking, have several dariole tins, or discarded cups with no handles, but whole, and well grease inside. If jam or syrup is being used, put a spoonful in bottom of tin before adding mixture, and then a little more than half fill. Stand in pan with ½ inch of water boiling in it. Over puddings spread a piece of greased paper and turn corners and edges down so that steam does not get into cups. Fix on lid – this is essential – and boil for 20 minutes.

Pan will boil over grill and be ready as soon as grill and vegetables.

Puddings will be light and delicious.

GINGER PUDDINGS – No. 413

As No. 412 but blending 1 level teaspoon powdered ginger and 1 tablespoon syrup with mixture and adding a pinch of soda bicarbonate to mixing liquid. A few pieces of home preserved ginger would make all the difference, and a little of its syrup used to flavour in mixing. See No. 584.

ORANGE DATE PUDDING – No. 414

2 breakfast cups fresh wholewheat crumbs: ½ lb minced dates: ¼ lb demerara sugar: 2 oz margarine or butter: 1 egg: 2 Tbs marmalade: juice and zest of an orange

Melt fat and add to dry ingredients, add marmalade and beaten egg. Preferably mix and pile into greased basin or individual cups some hours before they are to be cooked. Cover with foil, sealing by tucking in all round. Cook as one pudding for 1½ hours in covered pan – or as individual ones for 20–30 minutes.

SUMMER PUDDING – No. 415

This delicious pudding needs no cooking and is best made the day before it is used, but needs cooked blackberries and apples, or blackcurrants, or loganberries and raspberries, and with fruit sweetened to taste, and in a pudding basin with slices of crustless, stale, wholewheat bread, fitting pieces together until basin is well lined. Into this pour cooked fruit, leaving room at the top for a covering of fitted slices. When all covered, press down with a plate, and weighting this to keep all firm. Leave till next day when it will turn out a perfect pudding. Serve with cream.

CHRISTMAS PUDDING – No. 416

10 oz wholewheat flour: 4 oz wholewheat crumbs: 8 oz raisins, seeded: 8 oz sultanas: 8 oz currants: 4 oz mixed chopped peel: 8 oz dates, stoned and chopped: 2 oz glacé cherries: 4 oz chopped almonds or cashews: 1 lb shredded nut suet: 5 oz barbados sugar: 1 cup black treacle: 2 good sized cooking apples, grated: 2 good sized carrots, grated: 2 lemons, juice and grated zest: 1 nutmeg, grated: 1 tsp powdered cinnamon: apple juice to mix: 4 eggs, optional

(Make about 6 weeks before Christmas. After cooking remove cloth, not paper, and replace with a clean dry one for storing in a dry and airy pantry. The flavour is enormously improved by keeping.) Prepare fruit and nuts and add to flour and spices. Mix well, then add all other ingredients. Quantity fills two 7 inch basins. Well grease basins, fill and cover with greased paper and a scalded and floured cloth. Tie firmly and securely round, pin up ends neatly on top. Tie under pinned ends a longish loop of string and leave it outside the pan lid. It is very much easier to lift pudding up when you need to see how water is during the 8 hours' boiling. Have boiling water half way up basin. Store in cool dry place until Christmas, when boil again for at least 1 hour.

UNCOOKED CHRISTMAS PUDDING – No. 417

> 1 *cup finely grated carrot: 1 cup seeded raisins: 1 cup currants: ½ cup candied peel: ½ cup milled almonds: 1 cup wholewheat crumbs: 1 cooking apple, medium sized: zest and juice of an orange: a few glacé cherries: 1 piece or two of preserved ginger: a little nutmeg*

Put dried fruit and prepared apple, cherries and ginger through mincer, and blend with carrot, add orange zest and juice, nutmeg, nuts and crumbs. Press firmly into greased basin, cover with a plate, and weight down. Leave overnight if possible, keeping cold. Turn out and serve with fresh dairy cream No. 670, cashew cream No. 557 or coconut cream No. 558.

MINCE PIES – No. 418
Using short pastry No. 529 and a tin for individual cakes or tarts. Roll out pastry to about ⅛ inch thickness and stamp out rounds with a pastry cutter, a little larger than the space in the tin. Cut same number of smaller rounds for lids. Fill with mincemeat, cover with lid.

Cook at 450°F or Mark 7 for 20–25 minutes. When cooked, if liked, pies can be brushed over with a little water, sprinkled with sugar and returned to oven for a few minutes to crisp the surface.

PLUM DUMPLINGS – No. 419
As for apricot dumplings No. 394.

STEWED PEARS – No. 420
Thinly peeled pears are halved and put in a casserole with a little water, sugar and lemon juice. Cover with a lid; they should be slowly cooked but not long enough to darken. They should be

creamy white and only just tender, not flabby. Serve hot or cold with either cream or milled nuts.

PEACHES, BAKED – No. 421

Cook as for pears, without lemon juice. Normally I would consider it a crime to bake peaches, but if you have a tree and you have a lot all ripe at the same time, you need a change in preparation after a few weeks.

PEARS, BAKED – No. 422

Pears: lemon juice: sugar or honey: a pinch of nutmeg

Wash and halve pears and after removing stalk and flower, place cut side down on a fireproof dish with a little water and a sprinkling of lemon juice and nutmeg.

Slowly bake for about 1 hour at 300°F or Mark 1. Put a spoonful of honey or sugar on each pear when almost cooked, and before serving, baste with its own liquor.

Serve hot or cold with cashew No. 374 or dairy cream, or custard. Exact length of cooking time will depend upon pears, of course.

PEARS WITH GINGER – No. 423

Bottled, or fresh stewed pears with a little of syrup of preserved ginger No. 584 poured over, and a few pieces of the ginger chopped and blended.

BAKED BANANAS – No. 424

Very firm bananas that are too hard to eat enjoyably will do admirably for this dish.

Allow one per person, peeled, in a greased ovenware dish, and sprinkle with barbados sugar, and lemon juice, and some small nuts of butter. Bake at 350°F or Mark 3 for 30–40 minutes. If liked desiccated coconut can be sprinkled with sugar and lemon as a change of flavour.

BANANA FRITTERS – No. 425

Using fritter batter No. 1 or 3, peel banana and remove "strings" from sides. Divide into halves lengthwise and divide each into two shorter lengths. Dip first into lemon juice, then soft "pieces" sugar – then into batter. Deep fry in hot fat, drain on paper and serve hot.

BANANA ROYAL – No. 426

Thinly slice bananas into individual dishes, add either 2 table-spoons of orange juice or the same amount of orange juice jelly No. 463. Add a few ripe raspberries or strawberries and garnish with fresh whipped cream No. 670 or serve with cashew cream No. 557.

BANANA DELIGHT – No. 427

Mash bananas and divide into individual dishes or glasses. Pour over fresh or frozen raspberry purée, and top with ice cream or dairy cream.

BOMBE SURPRISE – No. 428

> 1 *large ice cream brick frozen very hard: a piece of firm but light plain cake twice as thick and half as long again as brick: some fresh or bottled or tinned fruit: 5 egg whites: 3 Tbs caster sugar: for decorating, 4 glacé cherries, and strip of angelica and a few chopped nuts*

Have an ovenware dish that will do for serving also, shallow, and longer and wider than ice brick – say at least 4 inches longer and wider. Next, cut the cake into even slices lengthwise, about $\frac{1}{4}$–$\frac{5}{8}$ inch thick, and making 5 slices. Cut one slice in halves across. On the centre of the dish lay one slice of cake, for the bottom of a box of cake that will contain the ice cream and fruit. On each side stand another slice, fitting closely and evenly, do the same at each end. If you are nervous about fit being secure you can brush touching edges with a pastry brush and some honey or warmed syrup. You will probably find the end pieces a little too wide, so cut to fit, and leave the box in the dish whilst you make a meringue, as directed in No. 556 with egg whites and sugar. Lift it and tilt bowl to make certain there is no liquid egg white left, before adding sugar.

Now, into the box, arrange fruits along as a bed for ice cream. Fruits must be drained so as not to wet cake. Sliced peaches or apricots or fresh strawberries or raspberries are excellent as a blend of ripe fruits. Make a level bed, and onto this put the frozen ice cream as it is, in one piece. There should be no space between ice cream and cake "box," so fit well together, and fit on cake "lid," over it. You should now have what looks like a slab of cake, with nothing but cake to be seen. The meringue is piled over and all round – coating the "box" but leaving surface rough and sprinkling with sugar. Make sure that no cake shows before putting dish in a very hot oven, 550°F or Mark 9 for 1½ to 2 minutes only. Put it in the centre of the oven, and stay with it, timing it, and never leaving it. Have the cherries halved, and angelica in tiny pieces, and nuts chopped ready to decorate prettily immediately after taking out of oven, and before serving. The meringue should be palely tinted with a little deeper colour on highest points. The ice cream will still be frozen. Serve by cutting into slices to the bottom, to include fruit and box. It is worth a little care, although one would not wish to take so much trouble often! Everything can be prepared beforehand, and actually when main course is being cleared from table. Final assembly, ice cream brick in place, and meringue over, can be quickly done, the brief cooking and decoration – all need take less than 5 minutes if everything to hand.

A simple "bombe" may be made with sponge fingers closely placed.

ON FLAVOURING CUSTARDS – No. 429

I seem to have been rather tied down to the vanilla bean for the flavouring of custards, but would definitely recommend branching out here – as in flavouring other dishes. For instance, try some elderflowers in the milk, it has to be strained when egg has been added anyway. It gives a delicious flavour, akin to muscats. Use sparingly to give a subtle flavour.

Lime blossoms, available in dried form for making tea, are also delicious for custards.

I have never tried lavender flowers – very few I should think would be delightful. Lavender tea is used and is good for head and nerves. Geranium I should also like to try, but alas this is winter and none available.

BAKED EGG CUSTARD – No. 430

1 pt milk : 2 standard or 3 small eggs : 2 level Tbs sugar : 1 vanilla bean or a few drops of vanilla essence : a little butter

Heat milk and sugar together with vanilla bean if being used. Remove bean, wipe and dry for future use. Beat eggs, add to milk and if not already flavoured now add a few drops of vanilla essence. Butter an ovenware dish and strain custard mixture into this. Next, stand dish in a baking tin, add enough hot water to rise ½ inch up the side of dish. Place in oven and set switch at

250°F or Mark ¼, allowing custard to bake for about 1 hour during which time the water in tin must not boil. Serve hot or cold.

CARAMEL CUSTARD – No. 431

For Caramel:
   4 *oz sugar:* 2 *Tbs water*

For Custard:

   1 *pt hot milk:* 3 *standard or* 4 *small eggs:* ½ *oz sugar or vanilla sugar No.* 564*: vanilla pod in hot milk or a few drops of vanilla essence*

To Make Caramel: Into a small pan put sugar and water and boil without stirring until it is a golden brown and syrupy. Prepare either 1 large dish or several small dariole tins, by tipping in and swirling round caramel and coating whole of inside. Do not grease tins first. Leave tins until custard is prepared.

For Custard: Pour hot milk in which sugar has been dissolved and bean soaked or with flavouring added, on to beaten eggs. Strain and pour into prepared dishes.

   Stand these in a large baking tin holding some hot water, coming about ½ inch up sides, in an oven heated to about 250°F or Mark ¼. Water in pan must not be allowed to boil, and custards will be cooked in about ¾ hour for individual custards, or up to 1¼ hours for one large one. Turn out to serve.

CUSTARD FOAM – No. 432

   1 *pt hot milk:* 2 *eggs:* 1 *Tbs honey*

Heat a large pan of water and when simmering place a dish that will fit over it closely, and butter it lightly. Pour in hot milk and 2 beaten egg yolks, cover closely with a lid and cook for about 30 minutes till set.

   Before serving add spoonsful of the stiffly beaten egg-white in heaps dotted over the custard. Sprinkle with fine sugar and garnish with pieces of cherry or angelica and nut kernels on each heap.

BAKED CUSTARD PIE – No. 433

Short pastry No. 529 lining of pie dish must be *very* well pricked all over before custard is poured in before setting, or pastry will rise and custard will spill over. Bake pastry case for 10 minutes at 450°F or Mark 7 then cool to 350°F, add custard and bake till set.

STEAMED CUSTARD WITH GINGER – No. 434

Make as for steamed custard but omitting vanilla or nutmeg.
When serving sprinkle well with crystallized ginger finely milled
in nut mill.

STEAMED EGG CUSTARD – No. 435

2 *standard or* 3 *small eggs:* 1 *pt new milk:* 2 *level Tbs sugar:*
1 *vanilla bean or nutmeg grated: a little butter*

If cooking vegetables this can be cooked over them if a basin is
found that will fit pan well; otherwise steam over a pan of boiling
water – about 2 inches in the pan of medium size. Well grease
basin and put in the milk, sugar, and vanilla bean or nutmeg.
Cover with lid and whilst heating well beat eggs. When milk is
hot stir very well, and if using vanilla bean remove this and wipe
dry for further use. Then strain in eggs, stir again and cover with
lid. Let water gently boil for about 20–25 minutes when custard
will set and be of a delightful creamy texture.

CHESTNUT CREAM – No. 436

½ *lb chestnuts:* ¼ *pt thick fresh whipped cream No.* 670: 1 *Tbs
clear honey: praline to decorate No.* 589

Boil chestnuts for 10 minutes, shell and skin, then steam till
tender. Sieve and cool, then blend with cream that has been sweetened with honey after whipping. Serve in individual glasses and
top with praline No. 589. Honey may be omitted if too sweet.

CHESTNUT PURÉE – No. 437

1 *lb chestnuts:* 1 *Tbs soft sugar: water*

Slit flat side of each chestnut several times. Bake in moderate oven
15 minutes. Remove shells and peel chestnuts, then boil till tender. Rub through sieve to purée and add sugar.

CHEESECAKE – No. 438

6 *oz cottage cheese: shortcrust pastry No.* 529: *zest of* ½ *a lemon:*
2 *egg yolks: a few currants:* 2 *level Tbs demerara sugar:* 1 *level
Tbs cake crumbs: a pinch of nutmeg*

Melt butter, stir into cottage cheese, add lemon zest, sugar and
currants.
Line shallow dish with pastry and prick over, sprinkle with cake
crumbs, pour on mixture and smooth, sprinkle nutmeg on top

and cook for about 30 minutes at 400°F or Mark 5. Serve hot or cold.

APPLE MERINGUE FLAN – No. 439
As No. 443, but pouring apple purée in flan case No. 530, and adding meringue No. 447 following same procedure as with No. 443.

FRUIT FLANS – No. 440
Use flan pastry No. 530, and either a flan ring on a baking sheet or cover outside of a sponge tin as advised, and bake "blind" or empty. When cold remove from tin and daintily arrange fruit in flan, keeping it neat and making decorative use of fruit colours and shapes. Orange segments, skinned, grapes peeled, thin slices of apple, fresh ripe berries or bottled fruit all can be used to great advantage in a flan case. When filled set some fruit juice with either agar-agar, or by boiling ¼ pt with a level teaspoon of arrowroot or cornflour mixed first with cold juice, until liquid is thickened but will pour over fruit. When set, decorate with fresh whipped cream.

JAM TARTLETS – No. 441
Using short crust pastry No. 529, and stamping out rounds slightly larger than the sections in the patty tin. Press rounds into tin neatly, prick bottom lightly with a fork, place a rounded teaspoon of jam in each tartlet, and smooth over level. On top of jam pour a teaspoon of water or fruit juice before baking. Bake about 425°F or Mark 6 for 10–15 minutes.

FRUIT TARTLETS – No. 442
Using flan pastry No. 530, make as above but bake empty, having pricked bottom several times with a fork. Bake as above, and when cold daintily arrange pieces of fresh fruit or ripe berries in tartlets, and glaze as in fruit flan No. 440.

Pipe fresh or confectioner's cream round edges when cold, or in a criss-cross over fruit, letting the colour of the fruits show, since they are so decorative.

LEMON MERINGUE PIE – No. 443
Using flan pastry No. 530, make a flan, baking at 450°F or Mark 7 for 15 minutes.

For filling:

> 2 *eggs:* 6 *oz demerara sugar:* 2 *oz wholewheat flour:* 1 *oz butter:*
> ½ *pt water:* 2 *lemons if medium sized or* 1½ *if large*

In a saucepan blend sugar with flour and gradually add water.
Bring to boil, whilst stirring, over gentle heat. Remove from heat
and beat in butter and egg yolks and finally grated zest and
strained juice of lemons. Pour into flan case and then cover with
meringue No. 447 half quantity as directed in No. 556. Serve
cold.

LEMON VELVET – No. 444

> 3 *or* 4 *egg yolks, well beaten and strained: juice and zest of* 2
> *lemons:* 1 *good Tbs honey, or more if required:* ¼ *pt whipping*
> *cream No.* 670

Have a double saucepan simmering over heat, blend yolks and
lemon. Melt honey in upper pan, and stirring continuously add
mixture. Continue to stir with under pan simmering, till the mixture thickens. Remove to a large basin, and when cool and nearly
cold, add whipped cream No. 670. Pile into glasses, chill before
serving.

MINT FINGERS – No. 445

> *Short pastry No.* 529: ½ *cup of chopped fresh mint:* ½ *cup brown*
> *sugar:* 1 *cup currants:* 1 *Tbs honey*

Blend mint, sugar, currants and honey. Roll out pastry into large
and thin rectangle. Spread filling over half, fold over other half
and roll out again. Cut into fingers and bake in hot oven as for
pastry.

ORANGE MERINGUE PIE – No. 446

Following instructions for No. 443, and using 2 oranges and 4 oz
sugar, and slightly less water.

MERINGUE FOR PIES – No. 447

Using recipe No. 556 only half quantity, and piling on pie when it
is cooked, and drying out at a slightly higher temperature – 250°F
or Mark ¼ and until meringue is a pale colour, rather, with peaks
a biscuit colour. This will take about 25 minutes.

MUESLI – No. 448

Per person:
  1 *Tbs raw oats or medium oatmeal:* 3 *Tbs cold water: fruit and*
  juice and dried fruit as available: top milk, cream, nut cream or
  evaporated milk

Overnight put oats and water into a basin and after stirring to
wet, cover and leave at room temperature.

In the morning add some grated zest of orange or lemon, and
some of its juice. How much will depend upon how many help-
ings are being prepared. Half orange or lemon for 2 persons is a
guide. Add a washed and grated raw apple, some dried fruits or
whatever fruit is available, and serve with either top milk, fresh
or nut creams and if liked, some milled nuts.

This can be a complete breakfast or supper, or can be served as
a sweet course. Excellent for children and adults alike. It requires
no cooking. Quite tiny children can be given the strained juice
before or after adding nut cream. The value of this food cannot
be over estimated.

PANCAKES – No. 449

Pancake and Yorkshire pudding batter No. 541, but with 2 eggs
and rich top milk if available. Just before cooking add 1 tablespoon of either melted butter or olive oil.

Use a pan from 6–8 inches across preferably. Over gentle heat,
brush pan all over inside with oil and pastry brush. Pour 2–3
tablespoons batter into centre of pan and quickly tilt to distribute
evenly. Either turn with a palette knife or toss pancakes as soon
as underside is golden, and cook other side. When cooked lift
onto a hot plate – if sweet pancakes – sprinkle with lemon juice
and dust with sugar. Then roll up and keep hot on a dish with a
paper d'oyley. Adjust heat so that one side will be cooking whilst
you are rolling previous pancake and so on until all batter is used.
Finally dust neatly rolled and stacked pancakes with sugar, and
garnish with lemon wedges.

CRÊPÉS SUZETTE – No. 450

Follow instructions No. 449 for pancakes, and make required
number in a small pan. Pile flat on dish on crumpled kitchen
paper and keep hot.

With a dozen sugar lumps rub the rinds of oranges – the most delicious are tangerines – to absorb as much of the perfumed oil as possible. Into a large shallow pan – frying pan suitable – pour about ¼ pt orange juice, add sugar lumps and 1 oz of butter. Heat and crush lumps and when quite dissolved and well stirred and leaving only *very* gentle heat, taking one pancake at a time, place it in sauce, turn it over and then fold just in halves and in halves again. Draw it to side of pan and continue till all are done.

If this is a special occasion and you wish to make a show and serve the suzettes flambé it will be necessary to have them arranged on a silver or pottery entrée dish keeping hot, and at the last minute before serving to pour over them a small wine-glass of either brandy or curaçao and set it alight. Serve as flame dies down.

APPLE FRITTERS – No. 451

Batter No. 1 or 3.

Medium sized cooking apples: lemon juice: sugar: deep fat for frying

Peel and core apples and cut into ¼ inch thick slices. When fat is ready, dip each slice of apple first into lemon juice and then in sugar before dipping into batter and coating. Drop into batter, a few at a time, and when golden the apple should be tender. Test though just to make sure and when done, keep hot on a dish with crumpled tissue paper to drain well. Continue, keeping and serving really hot.

DATE FRITTERS – No. 452

Using fritter batter No. 3 and adding 2 tablespoons chopped dates soaked for a while in lemon juice before adding to batter. Fry in flat pan with hot fat, about 1 tablespoon mixture at a time. Turn when underside is golden and cook other side. Serve hot after draining on kitchen paper.

ON STEWING APPLES, GOOSEBERRIES, ETC. – No. 453

These fruits can be so very unappetizing if cooked to a mash. Instead, boil sugar and water together first, allowing only a very little water, say a cup, to a pound of fruit at most, and when syrup has boiled for two minutes add fruit and simmer with lid on, in which case one can use less water for steam cooks the fruit too, only till just tender. Try to serve fruit looking very fresh and appetizing.

Apples should be in large quarters or small halves, pears in halves if ripe, and if tough they will need longer cooking in a casserole in the oven.

Rhubarb should never be cooked in an aluminium pan, cook it in the oven in an ovenware dish, wetted and sprinkled with demerara sugar or a very little sugar and some dates, when it will be delicious and not just shreds floating in water.

CHESTNUT MOUSSE – No. 454

3 Tbs chestnut purée No. 437: vanilla essence: 1 Tbs sugar (not as well as sugar in purée): 2 egg whites: vegetable gelatine

Make purée. Dissolve quantity of gelatine as stated on packet needed for same quantity of purée, delicately flavour with vanilla essence. Finally lightly add stiffly whisked egg whites and chill in well wetted mould.

DATE DESSERT – No. 455

Mince stoned dates and blend 1 cup with 1 cup whipped cream and a little lemon juice. Serve really cold.

FRESH FRUIT MOUSSE – No. 456

Using any plentiful fresh ripe fruit that needs using up, peel and mash and combine with whipped cream, add honey or if you have it, maple syrup – and blend, then chill well before serving in individual dishes.

Suitable fruits – peaches, apricots, bananas, grapes, chopped ripe apples, etc.

GOOSEBERRY FOOL – No. 457

1 lb gooseberries: ⅓ cup water: 4 oz demerara sugar: a few drops of green vegetable colouring: ¼ pt whipped thick cream No. 670: (if liked: 2 stiffly whisked egg whites also)

Gently melt sugar in water over heat then add gooseberries washed, topped and tailed and minced, then bring to boil. Simmer a few minutes till tender then sieve and leave to cool. When cold tint carefully and gently to blend with whipped cream, pile into custard glasses and chill again before serving.

RASPBERRY FOOL – No. 458

Purée fresh raspberries, sweeten a little, if necessary, and blend with whipped cream as in No. 457.

STRAWBERRY FOOL – No. 459
Using ripe strawberries purée and blend with cream as in No. 457.

BLACKCURRANT FOOL – No. 460
Either cook as for gooseberry fool No. 457 or liquidize in electric mixer and sweeten, if necessary, before blending with cream as for No. 457.

APPLE FOOL – No. 461
Cook as for No. 457, using same quantities.

GOOSEBERRY DELIGHT – No. 462
   3 cups gooseberry purée: 1 Tbs butter: 2 eggs: 1 cup sugar: a little icing sugar: green vegetable colouring

Prepare purée as for 457. Stir in egg yolks, butter and sugar and stir over gentle heat until mixture thickens. Cool a little, and add a few drops of green vegetable colouring, then place in individual glasses and decorate with meringue No. 447, made from egg whites and icing sugar. Chill thoroughly.

FRUIT JUICE JELLY – No. 463
   ½ pt fruit juice, fresh, bottled or tinned: 2 cups of water: 1 Tbs of honey or sugar: 1 level tsp agar-agar

Into double saucepan put 1 cup of water and agar-agar, leave to simmer for 15 minutes till a clear liquid results. Stir well, add honey or sugar to hot liquid in pan, then juice and water. Pour into wetted individual moulds and leave in a cool place to set. This jelly sets much more quickly than jelly made with animal gelatine and will be set as soon as cold. Prepared paper cases, as bought, are very useful.

JELLIED FRUIT SALAD – No. 464
As No. 463 placing grapes, pieces of orange, any ripe berries, pieces of apple, pear, or pineapple, soaked prunes, etc. Apple does not lose its colour in this jelly.

APPLE JELLIES – No. 465
As No. 463, adding finely shredded eating apple to individual dishes and pouring jelly over. Make jelly with either home-made or a good bottled apple juice.

FRESH FRUIT SALAD – No. 466

When available use fresh, ripe sound fruits, using berries whole unless very large. Always wash and drain on kitchen paper or a clean cloth, and remove stalks or "top and tail" fruits. If sufficient fresh fruit a blend of fresh and bottled or tinned can be made. Even a few from a garden will give colour and perfume to an otherwise ordinary fruit salad. A handful of ripe red or yellow gooseberries or luscious blackberries, or strawberries will make all the difference.

Oranges peeled, with pithy white inside removed, and either finely sliced or with segments skinned carefully, will release juice and perfume. If in winter, or when no fresh juices are available, use Rose Hip Syrup or Ribena – about 2 tablespoons to a bowl for 4–6 persons. Bananas sliced, ripe pears, and apples. I know it is said that apples are not successful, but I always find them very amenable to helping eke out winter fruits especially. Cut with a stainless knife – as for all fruits, and push well under juice when blending. Serve fruit salads with either fresh whipped dairy cream No. 670, or cashew or other nut creams No. 557, or ice cream, or pass a dish of milled nuts, or serve with a cold custard.

There *is not* a time of year when fresh fruit salads are not available. In 1947 when buying was at its worst, I set out to provide a fresh uncooked sweet for our main meal for every day in the year, and I succeeded. Nowadays we have seasons of luscious pineapples and melons that will feed six persons for 7½p or 10p for several weeks at a time. Use these for breakfasts, giving a really delightful start to the day, as well as for desserts. Many exotic but inexpensive fruits appear suddenly, to bring us the joys of other climates. Delicious Chinese gooseberries and lychees, perfumed and cool, and many others. Use them without cooking of course, but, if you can afford only a few, introduce into a fresh fruit salad, peeled, and for the gooseberries, sliced.

MELON BASKET SALAD 1 – No. 467

Lay melon on its side and with a sharp knife cut the skin only twice across centre for about 6 inches, leaving about 1½ inches between lines, for handle of basket. Then cut around from lines to meet each other at other end of handle. When you have the shape to your satisfaction, cut into melon along lines, removing the two pieces that will disclose handle and open top of basket. Now with a curved knife, remove seeds and pithy lining and tip into sieve over a basin to drip. The basket can now be filled with an assortment of fresh fruit and cubes of melon cut from removed sections. Add, if liked, a little liquid, white wine, or apple juice, and chill before serving. It will be deliciously cool and will make a lovely centre piece for a gala dessert. Serve with cream.

MELON BASKET 2 – No. 468

Instead of making a handle, cut 2 inch diagonal lines making a zig-zag round centre of melon and meeting accurately. You will find that when getting round the melon will be springing apart, but it is a very simple operation.

Now you have two half melons with fancy cut edge, empty these and stand each on a dish, and fill with fruit as in No. 467 or use half for appetizer at commencement of meal and serve fruit salad in the other, or cut up some of second half in cubes to blend with contents of salad.

PEACH MELBA – No. 469

Per 4 persons.

4 peeled fresh or tinned or bottled half peaches: 4 portions ice cream: 2 Tbs raspberry purée for melba sauce: fresh whipped cream to garnish

In individual glasses place ½ portion ice cream, rounded, with large spoon, on this ½ peach, then ½ a tablespoon purée, more ice cream, and garnish with fresh cream.

BREADS

WHOLEWHEAT BREAD 1 – No. 470

3 lb 100 per cent wholewheat flour: 1 Tbs crude molasses: 1–2 oz yeast, fresh or dried: 2 oz vegetable fat: 1 dsp sea or biochemic salt: ½ pt very hot water: ½ pt cold water: ¼ pt warm water: 1 Tbs barbados or demerara sugar

Set the oven at 200°F or less than ¼ if gas, and into this put the whole bag of flour in the centre, as well as two 2 lb and one 1 lb bread tins. Leave these to warm. Have a large mixing bowl ready either in a warm place and covered with a clean cloth, or pour in some very hot water and cover, to warm it thoroughly. Have ready also a small basin, a pint measure, a tablespoon, a dessertspoon and a large wooden spoon. A little extra flour will be needed, some tissue paper, and a knife for dividing the dough. Into the small basin pour the ¼ pt warm water and into this dissolve the sugar. This must not be hot or it will kill the yeast. Next add the yeast . . . either an ounce of fresh, or half a packet of dried yeast, stir about, then cover and leave for 10 minutes. Now take the tins from the oven and really well grease them using the tissue paper, getting well into the corners and along the top edges. When tins are greased thoroughly, sprinkle in some flour and shake it all round the tins till well coated. Shake out the surplus. By this time the yeast should be frothing. Take the bag of flour from the oven and leave oven on low. Into the dry bowl tip the flour, and into a hole in the centre tip the yeast mixture. Into your pint measure put molasses, sea salt and fat and on to this pour the very hot water. Stir well, and when dissolved add cold water. Tip this all into the mixing bowl *and stir until you have a soft dough.* Tip the dough onto your floured table or board and quickly knead for about 30 seconds. Divide into three, leaving one piece smaller for the small tin, and shape these with the hands to fit the tins, press well down in the tins and put to rise, or prove. The perfect place for this is on a folded cloth over the oven and under the hot-plate. Cover with a cloth and leave for ¾ hour or a little more if needed. If there is a drawer under the oven that is also perfect for proving the bread. It will be seen that the bread is rising in the tins, and should reach the top before it is cooked. When the dough has been proving for 15 minutes turn the oven switch to 525°F or 9, (very hot). The oven heat will be right by the time the bread has risen – 30 minutes. The high heat is to stop the dough rising and give the bread a good start. Arrange the tins in the centre of the oven, close the door and if the cooker is electric set it at once to 450°F. If gas reduce the heat to 7 after 10 minutes. The small loaf will be ready in half an hour when you can switch off an electric oven and leave the two larger loaves for another 10 minutes. The loaves should leave the tins very easily if they have been well greased, in case of any difficulty stand the tins for a few moments on a damp dishcloth and then turn out. Cool on a wire tray and do not cut until really cold. Keep bread on a rack on an airy pantry shelf, covered with a clean cloth. Do not keep this bread at room temperature.

WHOLEWHEAT BREAD 2 – No. 471

As No. 470, but omitting crude molasses. If liked a tablespoon malt may be substituted.

FRUIT AND MALT BREAD – No. 472

As No. 470, but with malt instead of molasses, and also raisins or currants. I find it a good plan to make one small loaf and two large from the 3 lb mixture, and make the small one fruit.

NUT BREAD – No. 473

10 oz wholewheat self-raising flour: 3 oz brown sugar: ½ cup chopped dates: ½ cup chopped walnuts: 1 cup milk: 1 egg

Soak walnuts in milk one hour then add well beaten egg and sugar, and lastly flour and dates. Blend to soft dough, shape to tin which must be well greased and floured, and bake at 400°F or Mark 6 for about 45 minutes.

I have cooked this bread in a round tin, for instance a large ovaltine tin with lid on, very successfully. It is really delicious sliced and buttered. Care must be taken to grease tin well, also lid. It is worth the trouble to have evenly browned round smooth slices for a special occasion.

(Recipe given by Doreen Lyle, an Australian friend, many years ago, but made with white flour.)

SOUR MILK BREAD – No. 474

1 lb self-raising wholewheat flour: 1 egg: 3 Tbs melted margarine or olive oil: 2 cups sour milk

Blend beaten egg with sour milk and make a dough that is soft but not sticky. Either cook in greased and floured tin, or better I think, for this "informal" bread, make a shape with the hands and cook on a baking sheet in hot oven 450°F or Mark 7 for about half an hour.

OAT BREAD – No. 475

> 10 *oz fine oatmeal:* 10 *oz wholewheat flour: pinch of salt:* ½ *oz yeast:* 1 *Tbs demerara sugar: warm water*

Melt sugar in cup of hot water and when warm crumble in yeast with a little flour and stir. Cover and leave to froth. Warm flour and oatmeal together with salt, add yeast and sufficient tepid water to make a soft dough that is not sticky. Grease and flour the 2 lb bread tins. Divide dough into two pieces and shape each to fit tins, on floured board, kneading at the same time to remove possible bubbles, for not more than 30 seconds. Press down in tins. Have oven really hot – 525°F or over Mark 9 and when placing bread in centre of oven reduce to 450°F or almost Mark 9. Bake for 45 minutes.

ROLL DOUGH – No. 476

> 1 *lb wholewheat flour:* 1 *egg:* 2 *tsp soft brown sugar:* 2 *Tbs olive oil:* ½ *tsp salt:* 1 *cup hot milk:* ½ *cup warm water:* ½ *oz yeast*

Add oil and salt to hot milk and stir. Let cool a little then add beaten egg. Dissolve sugar in water and then add yeast, cover and allow to froth. When yeast is frothing, add this with other liquid to warmed flour and make a soft dough. Beat for a minute then form into rolls and allow to rise to double the size, before cooking.

CLOVERLEAF ROLLS – No. 477

Roll dough No. 476. After mixing shape small balls of dough with hands and place 3 in each section of a greased and floured patty tin with sections for buns. Allow to rise until size is doubled then bake in hot oven for about 15 minutes.

SALAD STICKS – No. 478

Roll dough No. 476. Break off and roll on a floured board, pieces of dough, till about 6–8 inches long and a little thicker than a pencil. Brush all round with olive oil and place an inch apart on a greased and floured baking sheet. Allow to rise till twice the thickness then bake in hot oven for about 10 minutes.

UNFIRED BREAD – No. 479

½ lb 100 per cent wholewheat flour: 1 oz barbados sugar: 1 oz milled walnuts: 2 oz chopped or minced seeded raisins

Mix ingredients to a soft dough with water and well knead for one minute then turn out on floured board. Roll out thinly and cut into round biscuit shapes. These are put on a wooden board in the sun. The drying-out process will be hastened by having the board well warmed by the sun before placing bread on it. Very early morning on a warm day put the board out to get really hot. I have known April days when this was possible and the bread dried out in about three hours. I made such cakes as a small child, they were not very clean, being made in the garden. They were much enjoyed by my playfellows though!

OATCAKES – No. 480

4 oz fine oatmeal: ½ oz vegetable shortening: a little salt, if liked: saltspoon of soda bicarbonate: tepid water to mix

Rub fat into dry ingredients and then make a soft dough with tepid water. Knead dough for a minute or two then roll it out thinly on a floured board, keeping shape round. Cut into sections toward centre, making triangles.

Heat the oven to about 300°F or Mark 2 and whilst heating start cooking oatcakes on top of grill plate, if electric cooker, at low heat, and in a large thick frying pan over low heat if gas is being used, and of course if you have one, a girdle, or "griddle." When cakes start to curl up remove to floured baking sheet and finish them in the oven. They should not take long to get a very light brown. Cool and store in airtight tins.

CHAPATI – No. 481

Half pound wholewheat flour and enough cold water to make an elastic dough. This may be ½ gill or more or less, depending upon the flour entirely. It must not be dry, nor sticky, but just short of being sticky. On a floured board knead very well, plenty of pummelling will improve the dough. Divide into egg sized pieces and roll out very thinly, keeping shape round. The solid hot plate of an electric cooker is ideal for cooking chapatis, but if cooking by gas a heavy frying pan or a girdle will be needed. Make this really hot but do not grease it. Lay chapati on hot plate made really hot but reduce heat to low. Cook till by lifting with a palette knife you can see a skin formed on underside, then turn and repeat.

Place chapati on a cloth in a warm place and raise heat – return with first cooked side uppermost, and again lowering heat, leave till it suddenly puffs up when remove to warm place again immediately. This sounds troublesome but the routine is quickly learned and it is worth the care taken. I recall seeing Indian dancers performing a chapati making dance. No rolling pins were used, but the (imaginary) dough was patted and shaped by the hands, and thrown gracefully from one hand to the other, all to a jolly air that no doubt helps considerably!

DATE LOAF – No. 482

1 cup wholewheat flour: 1 tsp baking powder: 1 egg: ½ cup sugar: ½ cup chopped dates: ½ cup chopped walnuts: 1 cup milk

Soak walnuts in milk for 1 hour then add egg well beaten, and sugar. Finally add flour and baking powder well blended, and dates. Bake in moderate oven 400°F or Mark 6 for ¾ hour. Best cooked in deep round tin such as 1 lb cocoa tin, and can be steamed equally well for same length of time. Serve cold in thin slices, buttered.

YORKSHIRE TEA CAKES – No. 483

2¾ cups wholewheat flour: 1 rounded Tbs butter: 1½ cups milk: 1 egg: 1 tsp sugar: ½ tsp salt: ½ oz yeast

Well grease two round soufflé or cake tins and, if shallow, tie round 3 inches deep greased paper bands.

Warm milk and butter together slightly. Mix yeast and sugar together until liquid. Add salt to flour and knead well. Make a well in centre of flour and strain in yeast, milk and beaten egg. Stir well and then knead till smooth, soft but not sticky. Turn onto floured board and work together for a minute or two then divide into two flat cakes free from cracks. Place one in each tin and cover in warm place to rise. When dough fills tins bake in very hot oven for 20 minutes. Finish cooking out of tins to brown sides, brushing top with milk to glaze.

BUN DOUGH – No. 484

1 lb wholewheat flour: 2 oz butter: 2 oz soft "pieces" sugar: ¼ pkt dried yeast or ¾ oz fresh yeast: 1 egg: ¾ cup tepid to warm milk: a little warm water

Warm flour and mixing bowl, warm butter in milk. Into a small basin put sugar and yeast and 2 tablespoons warm water – not hot. Blend sugar and yeast for a moment, then cover and stand aside. When yeast mixture froths pour it into centre of flour in large bowl, add tepid milk and make a soft dough.

Use for tea buns, hot cross buns, etc.

HOT CROSS BUNS – No. 485

Using bun dough No. 484 add to flour 2 oz each of currants and chopped peel, and 2 level teaspoons mixed spice.

Turn onto floured board and knead for 30 seconds, quickly. Cut into pieces and shape into buns, allowing for rising to nearly double the size. Place buns on a greased and floured baking sheet as they are shaped. Cut a cross on each and brush over with some raw egg and milk. If a white and well defined cross is desired, make some shortcrust pastry and insert thin rolled strips into the cuts. Cover and allow to rise to nearly double their size, then bake in hot oven at 450°F or Mark 8, for about 15 minutes.

TEA BUNS – No. 486

Using bun dough No. 484, add 3 oz sultanas and 3 oz chopped peel to flour. Shape as for hot cross buns omitting cross. Larger cakes may be made if desired, dividing dough into four pieces, cover and allow to rise to nearly twice their size. Bake at 450°F or Mark 8 for about 15 minutes.

MUFFINS – No. 487

¾ lb wholewheat self-raising flour: ½ tsp salt: 1 Tbs soft brown sugar: 1 egg: 2 Tbs oil: 1 cup milk

Add oil, sugar and salt to milk and stir to blend. Beat egg and add to liquid, then make a soft dough with flour, but do not handle overmuch. Quickly shape into rounds to fit muffin rings on floured baking sheet. Cook for about 20 minutes at 450°F or Mark 8.

BRAN MUFFINS – No. 488

As for muffins No. 487, but using half All Bran and half wholewheat flour. Cook for about 15 minutes.

FRUIT MUFFINS – No. 489

Muffins as No. 487, and adding chopped date or whole raisins.

SCONES

DATE SCONES – No. 490

1 oz butter: 6 oz wholewheat flour: 4 oz demerara sugar: 5 oz rolled oats or coarse oatmeal: 1 tsp baking powder: 1 egg: pinch of salt, if desired: a little milk or water

Cream butter and sugar and add beaten egg gradually, then flour, baking powder and oats, and enough milk to make a soft dough. Roll out on floured board to ¼ inch thickness. Cut out 2 inch circles with pastry cutter, and sandwich with date paste No. 681, before cooking at 425°F or Mark 6 for about 20 minutes.

OAT SCONES – No. 491

Make dough as No. 490, for date scones, cooking without date paste. A few sultanas may be added if liked.

POTATO SCONES – No. 492

2 cups cooked potatoes: wholewheat flour: pinch of salt: milk to mix

Mash potatoes and well mix in as much wholewheat flour as can be held by potato, add salt and a little milk to form a soft dough. Roll out fairly thinly on well floured board. Bake on well greased tin in hot oven, or on greased top of hot plate, turn when browned one side to brown the other. Serve hot. Oven 450°F or Mark 7 for about 20 minutes.

DROP SCONES – No. 493

8 oz wholewheat flour: 1 Tbs soft brown sugar: 1 egg: 1 tsp cream of tartar: 1 saltsp soda bicarbonate: ½ pt milk or milk and water

Blend flour, sugar, soda and cream of tartar, add egg beaten in milk, a little at a time beating well, till a good batter results. Have ready a little margarine and some tissue paper for greasing either the top of the grill plate or the thick frying pan on the girdle on which scones are to be cooked. Also a palette knife, a large warm plate covered with a napkin to receive the scones. Each time you make a fresh batch stir the batter round. Have the grill top or whatever you are baking scones on hot, then reduce heat for cooking. A dessertspoonful is about the right amount to pour on at a time and do not pour them too close together. I put 5 on my grill plate, one at each corner and one in the centre, and that gives me room to turn them over. Very soon after putting on the last one of a batch the first wants turning over. It should be golden, and again the other side – remove each batch to the plate and cover with napkin. Rub over hot plate again with greased tissue and repeat till finished. The scones are so delicious I'm sure you had better make twice as many, and butter them well – to serve immediately, or serve as they are for individual buttering.

GRIDDLE SCONES – No. 494

1 lb wholewheat flour: 1 tsp baking powder: 2 oz currants: a good pinch of salt: enough milk to mix

Blend dry ingredients and then make a soft dough that will be easy to handle. On a floured board roll dough to $\frac{1}{4}$ inch thickness and cut triangles about $2\frac{1}{2}$ inches each way, and bake on a grill plate, greased or on a griddle or a thick large pan over a flame. Grease and flour griddle and turn scone when underside is golden and repeat for second side. Serve hot, split and buttered.

MALTED RUSKS – No. 495

Dip fingers of really stale wholewheat bread into malted milk made as for drinking. Slowly bake on a baking sheet at about 300°F or Mark 2 for about 40 minutes or until light and crisp, turning over halfway through baking. Store in airtight tin.

HONEY RUSKS – No. 496

As for No. 495, but using 1 tablespoon honey to $\frac{1}{2}$ pt warm water, well blended, for dipping fingers of stale bread.

CAKES

WHOLEWHEAT CAKES – No. 497
(Basic mixture)

> 6 *oz veg. margarine or butter:* 12 *oz wholewheat flour:* 2 *tsp baking powder:* 1 *or* 2 *eggs:* 6 *oz demerara sugar: a little milk if only one egg*

For small cakes set oven to 450°F or Mark 7. For large cakes cook at a low heat, 275°F or Mark ¼, in both cases with well greased tins, lightly floured, and if a solid bottomed large tin, with no paper either inside or out, even for a very large Christmas cake. Cook medium sized cakes at about 325°F or Mark 2.

In cold weather partly warm margarine, or warm mixing bowl. Otherwise, beat margarine and sugar together until fluffy. Add beaten eggs or egg and milk and beat till well blended. Add half the flour and the baking powder and blend gently but well, finally fold in the rest of the flour and blend. For small cakes cook as recommended for 15 minutes or until a nice golden colour. For medium sized cakes cook for about 1½ hours. Really large Christmas cakes can be left for four to six hours according to size and will not burn. Vary above recipe with 4 oz desiccated coconut, or juice and grated rind of a fresh lemon or orange, a tablespoon cocoa and a little water in which a vanilla bean has been steeping, or 2 oz currants or sultanas with spice or nutmeg added. Or bake in a Victoria sandwich tin and when spread in tin arrange one stoned date in centre and eight around it. Or bake plain and fill for a layer cake after splitting.

GOLDEN SUNSHINE CAKE – No. 498

> 8 *oz wholewheat flour:* 8 *oz sugar:* 5 *eggs:* 1 *Tbs lemon juice:* ¼ *pt orange juice:* 2 *tsp baking powder*

Beat egg yolks and ½ sugar till sugar is dissolved. Whisk whites till stiff, fold in other half sugar.

To beaten yolks and sugar add gradually flour and baking powder and fruit juice. Finally, fold in lightly, the egg whites, pile in large well greased floured tin and bake for 1 hour at 300°F or Mark 1.

VICTORIA SPONGE – No. 499

2 eggs: the weight of the eggs in butter or margarine, soft light pieces sugar, and wholewheat flour

Place fat in mixing bowl and with either rubber squeegee or the back of a wooden spoon cream it very well indeed. Add sugar and beat till mixture is light and fluffy. Sprinkle over mixture 1 tablespoon flour and beat in one egg really well, then a little more flour and the other egg. Add remaining flour and lightly blend.

Grease two sponge tins and in centre fit round of greased parchment. Flour tins and shake out any remaining loose. Divide mixture and spread in tins. Bake at 370°F or Mark 5 for about 20 minutes. Cool on wire rack and when quite cold spread one with jam, or jam and cream, fruit and cream, etc., and cover with the other.

FRUIT GATEAUX – No. 500

Make two or three sponges No. 499, either round or as desired, and when quite cold sandwich with mashed raspberries or strawberries, pineapple or other suitable fresh fruits. Cover fruit with cream and sandwich. Slice each sponge into three slices.

Using butter icing No. 548, coat with palette knife and decorate with forcing bag and nozzles. I like to use fresh flowers or leaves for these special dishes. If not on top, group round sides, mimosa, jonquils, or narcissi for a yellow cake. Rambler roses and pale green for a summer fruit, etc.

A thin spread of a jam to match fruit will stop it seeping into cake and making it soggy.

The general effect is enhanced by building up the gateaux on a silver paper covered board, and a dab of icing in the centre of the board before the building up commences will fix it securely.

SWISS ROLL – No. 501

2 eggs: 2 rounded Tbs soft pieces sugar: 2 rounded Tbs wholewheat flour: 2 oz butter or margarine: 1 rounded tsp baking powder: 2 Tbs milk: jam for spreading

Line a swiss roll tin with kitchen parchment fitting it neatly, and letting it be a little higher all round than the tin. When fitted, take it out and well grease it with a little fat and some screwed up tissue paper. Put back into tin and fit corners neatly.

Cream butter and sugar and mix as for Victoria Sponge No.

499 adding the milk last. Spread evenly till over tin and bake in a
hot oven 450°F or Mark 8 for 7–10 minutes till a delicate golden
colour. Whilst roll is cooling, warm jam very carefully, then
spread a tea cloth on table and on this a piece of kitchen parchment the size of the tin in which roll is cooling. Spread this liber-
ally with caster sugar. When cooled, turn cake out browned side
down onto sugared paper. Peel off paper from the now upper
side of cake and quickly spread with the jam. With a sharp knife
quickly trim off thinly the four edges of roll. Then holding cloth
with both hands at front edge, roll up the cake and stand on
outside edge to keep folded. It is easy, but you must be
quick.

YULE LOG CAKE – No. 502

Swiss Roll No. 501, coated with chocolate or coffee butter icings
No. 546 and 547.

The roll must be really cold, preferably made the day before.
Coat with a palette knife, all over, including ends, roughing-up
the icing here and there to make it look more log-like. If able, or
adventuresome, pile some icing into a forcing bag with a fine star
nozzle and make slightly irregular lines representing bark, from
end to end, and perhaps the remains of a sawn off branch. A little
chopped or milled pistachio will represent moss and perhaps you
can find a little ornamental robin to stand on the cake. A very
little sieved icing sugar sprinkled over will make the whole look
seasonable.

GINGERBREAD – No. 503

6 oz wholewheat flour: 2 oz demerara sugar: 1 oz sultanas:
1 oz almonds, blanched: 1 oz crystallized ginger: $\frac{1}{2}$ lb golden
syrup: 2 oz butter: 1 rounded tsp ground ginger: 1 level tsp soda
bicarbonate: $\frac{1}{2}$ gill milk: 1 egg

Melt butter and syrup together, add milk and stir to blend, add
beaten egg and soda dissolved in a very little water. Put flour,
powdered ginger and sugar in bowl and gradually add blended
liquid, then sultanas and chopped ginger. Spread in a square or
rectangular tin, well greased and floured. Lay halved almonds on
top to decorate. Bake at 350°F or Mark 3 for about 30–35
minutes.

PINEAPPLE CAKES – No. 504

2 oz butter: 2 eggs: 4 oz soft sugar: 6 oz wholewheat flour: 6 cubes or 1 slice tinned pineapple: 2 oz icing sugar

Have ready paper baking cases. Cream butter and soft sugar, add egg and flour and beat really well. Lightly fold in pineapple cut small, then spoon into paper cases, half filling them.

Bake at 425°F or Mark 6 for about 10 minutes. When cool ice with icing sugar and pineapple juice mixed to icing consistency.

HONEY CAKES – No. 505

1 oz butter: 4 oz wholewheat flour: 2 eggs: 1 Tbs mixed spice: 4 Tbs honey: lemon juice: sugar lumps

Blend butter with flour and spice, add honey and well beaten eggs and if necessary, a very little water to form a stiffish paste. Roll out to ¼ inch thickness on a floured board, and cut out small rounds with a pastry cutter. Soak a sugar lump for each round in lemon juice on a small plate, turning them over to make certain they absorb all juice, then press a lump into centre of each round.

Bake in hot oven 425°F or Mark 6 for about 15 minutes, till a good colour, and serve and split, buttered and very hot.

UNCOOKED CHOCOLATE CAKES – No. 506

4 oz plain chocolate: 1 cup toasted crumbs – pulled bread No. 698 reduced to crumbs with rolling pin, or corn flakes: ¼ cup chopped dates or raisins: 1 Tbs hot water

Have a mixing bowl over a pan on heat, with a little water boiling to heat basin. Into basin grate chocolate and stir till melting. Adding the hot water and continuing to stir, add crumbs or flakes and fruit. Take teaspoonsful and shape with another spoon, place on a dish to set in a cool place, when they will be ready for use.

BUTTER CAKE – No. 507

6 oz wholewheat flour: 1 tsp baking powder: 4 oz butter: 4 oz soft brown sugar (pieces): 1 egg: ½ cup chopped nuts: ⅔ cup sultanas: ½ cup milk

Cream fat and sugar and add egg, beat together. Add flour and baking powder, then nuts and sultanas and finally milk. Mix well, then spread in a greased and floured shallow tin. Then bake in moderate oven, 400°F or Mark 5 for about 25 minutes or till golden.

Ice with 1 cup pieces sugar, boiled for 3 minutes, stirring with 1 oz butter or margarine and 3 tablespoons top milk. Cool a little, heat till it begins to thicken, then spread over cake that has cooled. Leave to set before using.

CHRISTMAS CAKE – No. 508

¾ lb wholewheat self-raising flour: ½ lb barbados sugar: ½ lb butter or margarine: ½ lb currants: ½ lb sultanas: ¼ lb chopped peel: 2 oz glacé cherries: 2 oz cashew nuts coarsely chopped: 2 oz almonds: 1 good sized cooking apple, grated: ¼ nutmeg grated: 1 tsp ground ginger: 1 heaped tsp mixed spice: 1 tsp almond flavouring: grated rind of an orange: grated rind of a lemon: juice of lemon and orange to mix: 2 Tbs black treacle

Well grease a 9 inch cake tin, shake flour into tin and turn about until coated all over. Into a large bowl put 2 oz flour and add sugar, all dried fruits and nuts as they are prepared. Mix well. Into a separate mixing bowl put the rest of the flour and spices and into this, shred the fat. Well blend to breadcrumb consistency. When ready add flour mixture to the large bowl containing the fruit and mix thoroughly.

Next add black treacle, flavouring, grated orange and lemon zest, and grated apple. Very thoroughly mix again and finally add orange and lemon juice and if needed, a little water or apple juice to obtain right consistency. Pile carefully into tin and smooth over flat. Cook in very slow oven Mainstat A, Regulo ¼ or 200°F for six hours. Place low in oven.

You will notice that there are no eggs in this cake. I devised the recipe when eggs were so scarce as to be impossible, and haven't felt the need to revise the recipe. Many people have found the cake really good as it is. If you feel a Christmas cake without eggs is heresy, then add eggs and use less fruit juice.

UNCOOKED CHRISTMAS CAKE – No. 509

1 cup stoned dates: 1 cup soaked and stoned prunes: 1 cup seeded raisins: ½ cup milled almonds: ¼ cup candied peel: a few glacé cherries: a strip of angelica for decoration: ¼ lb coconut cream for icing, or fresh whipped cream

Mince dried fruits and peel, reserving two or three cherries, and blend these with milled almonds in a bowl. Line a flat victoria sandwich tin with rice paper and carefully press in mixture level and cover with rice paper. Leave for a few hours, then grate coconut cream and gently melt without browning. Spread over cake, top and sides, and decorate with cherries and angelica. The first uncooked Christmas cake I saw was made by Mrs. Bridget Amies, then Bridget Mitten, in a lovely demonstration in the Country Life Restaurant at Ludgate Hill about ten years ago. I am grateful to her for this recipe, but as I remember, the coconut cream icing was my own addition

MERINGUES – No. 510

4 egg whites: 6 oz caster sugar: few drops of colouring and flavouring, if required: pinch of salt: pinch of baking powder

Whisk egg whites with salt until really stiff and dry. Lift up with palette knife and tilt bowl to see if there remains any unwhisked white. Whisk till no liquid remaining. With palette knife gently fold in sugar and baking powder, and if needed, flavouring and colouring – both very discreetly.

Have ready a sheet of greaseproof paper on a baking sheet, and with 2 dessert spoons, shape oval heaps and place 2 inches apart on paper. When finished dredge over sieved icing sugar, or caster sugar, to form a crust. Heat oven to 200°F or less than Mark $\frac{1}{4}$. Place meringues in oven, switch off and leave for $1\frac{1}{2}$ hours or till dry and firm. Handling carefully scoop out a little from the flat side with a thin teaspoon and leave to dry with this side up, on a wire rack. Serve with either whipped cream or ice cream between 2 meringues. Very tiny teaspoonsful, shaped and rounded, may be made just as No. 510 for serving with fruit salads, etc. These will, of course, take less time to dry out, and will not need scoop-out. Meringues can be stored in airtight tins.

SHORTBREAD – No. 511

4 oz wholewheat flour: 2 oz butter: 1 oz soft pieces sugar

Mix sugar and flour together in a bowl, then cut butter into pieces and add. Knead and press butter into flour, and sugar, and continue until you can knead the mass easily into a round on a floured board, that is about $\frac{1}{2}$ inch thick. It should be easily moulded, if kneaded well, and I find that it makes a cake that will easily stand in a victoria sandwich tin, which will protect the edges whilst cooking.

It is usual to pinch the edges to crimp them, between thumb and first finger, on the surface. I usually mark portions to indicate cutting lines, and perhaps mark some design with fork prongs. Bake in an oven at 375°F or Mark 4.

APPLE TEA CAKE – No. 512

Apples: sugar: cloves: shortcrust pastry No. 529

This is really a kind of pie, but usually served at teatime, hot. Line an ovenware dish with shortcrust pastry. Fill with thick wedges of cooking apple, well sprinkled with demerara sugar and dotted with cloves, either a few whole cloves, or some ground. Firmly stand a pie funnel in centre. Add a sprinkling of water to start off the juice and after damping edges of paste, cover with a lid of pastry and seal edges by cutting and finishing. Make a tiny hole on top of funnel. Add some damped pastry "leaves" to trim.

Heat oven to 450°F or Mark 8 and place cake in centre of oven and reset oven to 400°F or Mark 6, then bake for up to an hour, or until careful investigation with a sharp knife through pastry close to a trimming, reveals that apple is soft.

Serve with thick cream, hot or cold. We had it cold and cut in squares. Nothing has ever tasted so good made on a smaller scale, for those in my childhood were as large as the oven would take!

BISCUITS

CORN FLAKE BISCUITS – No. 513

3 cups corn flakes: ¾ cup chopped walnuts: 1 cup demerara sugar: 2 egg whites

Beat egg whites to stiff froth, add sugar, walnuts and corn flakes. Pile mixture in paper cake cases and bake in moderate oven – 300°F or Mark 1 until set.

This recipe, along with the one for nut bread, I owe to an Australian friend who gave them to me on her first arrival in this country in 1934. I hope she will be here still when this appears in print and will recall our early cooking efforts.

WHOLEWHEAT BISCUITS – No. 514

3 cups wholewheat flour: 1 cup margarine or butter: 2 tsp baking powder: 1 egg: 1 Tbs demerara sugar: water to mix

Mix dry ingredients, then add fat as for pastry No. 525 until breadcrumb consistency. Mix now with well beaten egg and enough water to make a really moist paste. Turn out onto floured board and roll quite thinly. Shape with cutter and bake in moderate oven for about 15 minutes, 375° or Mark 4.

NUTTY BISCUITS – No. 515

2 cups wholewheat flour: 1 tsp baking powder: 1 cup chopped nuts: 1 Tbs butter or margarine: pinch salt: milk to mix

Make a firm paste with blended dry ingredients, shredded butter and milk. Blend well together on floured board and then roll out thinly. Cut into circles and prick well, then bake in gentle oven on well greased tin.

COCONUT BISCUITS – No. 516

1 cup wholewheat flour: 2 cups desiccated coconut: 1 cup sugar: 2 eggs

Blend all together, adding a little milk, if necessary, to make a slack mixture. Place in tiny heaps on well greased tins and bake in moderate oven for 20 minutes.

OAT AND NUT BISCUITS – No. 517

1 cup rolled oats: 3 oz margarine: 2 oz brown sugar: 1 Tbs black treacle: ½ cup milled nuts: 4 drops almond essence

Melt margarine with treacle in oven, and add other ingredients. Warm and grease a shallow tin about 10 by 5 inches and spread mixture evenly. Bake for 20 minutes in moderately hot oven. Mark into sections. When done leave to cool. Cut again and remove from tin. (I am sorry that I am unable to recall the author of this delicious recipe, given to me some ten years ago. We have much enjoyed it.)

GINGER NUTS – No. 518

2 oz margarine: 2 oz syrup: 1 cup wholewheat flour: 1 tsp ground ginger: ½ tsp cinnamon: ½ tsp mixed spice: ½ tsp bicarbonate of soda

Melt fat and syrup. Blend flour, spices and soda, and stir in just warm fat and syrup. Knead for ½ minute, then break off walnut sized pieces, roll into ball and bake on greased and floured tin for 10–12 minutes at 375°F or Mark 4.

ALMOND BISCUITS – No. 519

8 oz wholewheat flour: 5 oz vegetarian shortening: 3 oz soft brown sugar: 6 oz ground almonds: 1 egg yolk: a few milled or coarsely chopped almonds

Cream together fat, sugar and egg and gradually add flour and almonds in small quantities alternately. Work well till possible to shape, roll out to a rectangle, sprinkle over chopped nuts and roll lightly with rolling pin. Cut into fingers 1 inch by 3 inches. Bake in fairly hot oven, 375°F or Mark 4 for about 20 minutes or a good colour. Cool and store in a tin.

GINGER SNAPS – No. 520

2 oz butter: 2 oz soft brown sugar: 2 oz wholewheat flour: ½ tsp ground ginger: 1 tsp fresh or bottled lemon juice: 1 Tbs golden syrup

The mixture is prepared in a saucepan. Over low heat blend butter, syrup and sugar. Remove from heat and add juice, ginger and flour. Blend thoroughly.

On a well greased and floured baking sheet drop heaped teaspoonsful of mixture 6 inches apart. Bake at 350°F or Mark 3 for 10 minutes or till real golden colour. Leave on sheet for the moment. With a butter paper grease the handle of a wooden spoon. With a palette knife carefully lift each "snap" onto the spoon handle and wrap it around to form the shape. Remove and repeat with the rest of the biscuits. If you are not quick the later ones may be too cool to shape until you return them to the oven for a moment.

Fill with either fresh whipped cream or a mixture and mashed banana and whipped cream, or just mashed banana. Favourite children's party sweet. Filling is simple with a forcing bag and nozzle.

CELEBRATION BISCUITS – No. 521

2 oz butter: 2 oz soft brown sugar: 1 Tbs syrup from preserved ginger, or 1 dspn golden syrup: ½ tsp grated lemon or orange zest: 2 heaped Tbs wholewheat flour: 1 piece preserved ginger – moderate size: 2 glacé cherries: 1 dspn sultanas: 1 Tbs candied peel (if orange zest used, use lemon peel, if lemon – orange peel): 12 almonds with brown skin on, chopped: ¼ lb bar dark chocolate for coating

These are mixed in a saucepan. Over low heat blend butter, syrup and sugar. Remove from heat and add flour, zest and very finely chopped fruit and nuts. Have a baking sheet ready, well greased and floured. Drop heaped teaspoonsful of mixture on to tin allowing room for spreading. Bake at moderate heat – 350°F or Mark 3.

Cool on wire rack. When cold, coat with chocolate melted in double saucepan, or in basin over pan of very hot water. Chocolate will melt more quickly if grated.

OATMEAL BISCUITS – No. 522

2 oz wholewheat flour: 2 oz coarse oatmeal: 1 oz shortening: 1 oz sugar: pinch of soda bicarbonate: pinch of salt: ¼ tsp mixed spice: water to mix

Blend fat with flour, oatmeal, spice, salt and sugar. Dissolve soda in a tablespoon water and then add, adding enough water to make paste that will roll out very thinly. Roll on a floured board and cut into rounds. Prick with fork. Bake at 425°F or Mark 6 for about 10 minutes.

HAZEL WAFERS – No. 523

2 oz butter: 2 oz fine sugar: 1 standard egg: 2 oz wholewheat flour: ¼ tsp baking powder: a few drops of vanilla essence, or use Vanilla Sugar No. 564 instead: 1 Tbs chopped hazels

Cream butter and sugar till light, add egg and beat well, finally flour, baking powder and essence, unless using vanilla sugar. Drop small teaspoonsful onto greased baking sheet well apart as they will spread, and with hazels sprinkled on top.

Cook about 5 minutes at 400°F or Mark 5 till they are getting brown, then remove carefully with palette knife onto handle of wooden spoon and curl. Cool well and store in tins, if necessary.

FLORENTINE BISCUITS – No. 524

Short pastry No. 529, cut into fancy shapes with biscuit cutters, or puff pastry No. 527, cut into fingers, and for either kind, cool after cooking before decorating with a little jam on top and then dipping sticky side into coarsely chopped nuts.

PASTRIES

NOTES ON MAKING PASTRY WITH VEGETABLE FAT AND WHOLEWHEAT FLOUR – No. 525

The method of short pastry making with these materials is quite different from that used with the conventional white flour and greasy lard. There you keep everything very cold and you have a glutenous flour that sticks together easily. With wholewheat flour many have been unsuccessful with pastry, but I have always found it very easy to handle and get an excellent result by using tepid water and quick mixing. For years I have used a square holed sieve grater rather like a square table-tennis bat, to blend my fat quickly with flour. By pushing handfuls of fat and flour through these holes 3 or 4 times I have achieved breadcrumb consistency in a few moments. On one occasion I mixed 5 lb. of perfectly blended pastry in 5 minutes. My methods will seem outrageous to the uninitiated, but with this material, wholewheat flour, a really delightful and beautiful pastry can be achieved by using them.

When covering a large pie or dish with pastry, roll to required size, then roll up and laying on one side of dish unroll like a carpet.

Puff paste does need to be chilled during the making, the vegetable fat soon "warms" again with rolling and hand work. This is much less easy than short paste, but one does not make it often.

TO USE PUFF PASTRY – No. 526

It depends upon what you wish to make of course. For a large puff pastry case leave $\frac{3}{4}$ to inch thick. Cut oblong to fit baking tin about 6 x 9 inches, lay pastry in tin then make a score round $\frac{1}{2}$ inch from edge, and *not* cutting right through pastry, like marking a frame. Within this frame score lightly across making diamond shapes.

Bake in a really hot oven 450°F or Mark 8. The pastry will rise high, and when a real golden brown, place in hot serving dish, and carefully lift up centre "lid" and pour in hot filling, replacing lid and keeping very hot. For small *vol au vents* roll pastry to $\frac{1}{4}$ inch thick before cutting. These also can be cut square to save wasting pastry, and cut another square, to slight depth only, inside edge, to lift up and remove for filling after cooking. If desired round, use a smaller cutter to mark second round for lifting.

Lids must always be lifted off whilst pastry is hot.

PUFF PASTRY – No. 527

1 lb fine wholewheat flour: 1 lb butter or margarine or vegetable shortening: 1 tsp lemon juice: tepid water to mix

Mix flour, lemon juice and water to a soft dough, knead gently till well blended and soft then roll out on a floured board till twice the size of shortening. It should be ¼ inch thick but less thick at edges. Lay shortening in centre of pastry and cover with first one sidepiece of pastry then the other completely wrapping up fat. Well press edges with rolling pin and leave in a cool place for 15 minutes or so preferably in a refrigerator. Flour board or table well, also rolling pin, allowing plenty of length to roll away from you as you stand at table.

Place pastry before you without any joined edges on your right, and do this each time you shift pastry.

Press out pastry rather flat with rolling pin and lightly roll until ¼ inch thick or less, keeping board and pin floured as you work. Fold pastry in three again, pressing outside edges together. Arrange as before and repeat rolling, same size, and again fold in three.

If you have time and patience now rest the pastry again 15 minutes in refrigerator and repeat for three more rollings and foldings. Pastry is at last ready for use. Keep very neat so as not to waste pastry which cannot be rolled into a ball and used up. Roll out lightly keeping well floured so that fat does not come through.

ROUGH PUFF PASTRY – No. 528

As for puff pastry No. 527 but folding only three times before using.

SHORT PASTRY – No. 529

8 oz wholewheat flour: 4 oz vegetable shortening or butter: tepid water to mix: 1 tsp lemon juice

Blend fat finely into flour of breadcrumb consistency. Make a well in centre and with a palette knife add lemon and water in small quantities, working well and not making wet but sufficiently soft to handle easily.

Roll out on floured board with floured rolling pin to required thickness.

If a slightly sweet pastry is required add 1 tablespoon sugar to flour.

FLAN PASTRY – No. 530

6 oz wholewheat flour: 3 oz vegetable shortening or butter: 1 egg yolk: tepid water to mix

Blend fat with flour, making a well in centre, add egg yolk and mix with palette knife, and adding water as necessary, till a soft but firm dough results.

Roll out on floured board and with floured rolling pin to about ½ inch thickness for flans. Using a flan ring, if you have one, or inverting and covering the underside of a round sponge sandwich tin and baking it inverted, after neatly covering.

NUT-SUET CRUST – No. 531

8 oz wholewheat flour: 3 oz Suenut, vegetable nut suet: 2 tsp baking powder: tepid water to mix

Into a mixing bowl put flour and baking powder and grate Suenut into it. Mix to a dough with water, soft and easy to handle, but still dry. Use for all suet puddings, dumplings, baked rolls or fresh, bottled, or dried fruit puddings.

CHEESE PASTRY – No. 532

4 oz wholewheat flour: 3 oz vegetable fat: 3 oz finely grated cheddar: 2 oz Parmesan: 2 egg yolks: a little water: a little cayenne or paprika

Blend fat with flour, add cheese and seasonings and mix to a firm soft dough with egg yolk and water. Roll out and use as required.

POTATO PASTRY – No. 533

1 cup wholewheat flour: 1 cup mashed potatoes: 1 tsp baking powder: salt if liked: 4 oz margarine: a little tepid water

Add baking powder and salt if used, to flour and blend with margarine. Add mashed potato and blend well, and finally a little tepid water as necessary to form a firm, stiff paste that will roll out and handle.

CHOUX PASTE – No. 534

½ pt water: 3 oz butter or margarine: 4 oz wholewheat flour: 4 small or 3 standard eggs

Boil water and butter together and when foaming add, all at once, the flour, having freed it from lumps. Remove pan from heat and beat well till smooth. Return again to gentle heat and stir till paste forms a ball that can be moved around pan. Remove at once from heat, or butter will ooze and panada, or paste, will be wasted. Cool a little, then beat in eggs one by one, making smooth after each egg, before adding the next. If sweet cream buns or éclairs **are** to be made, now is the time to slightly sweeten and flavour paste, with either vanilla sugar or sugar and a few drops of vanilla essence.

Use as directed for cream buns, éclairs, cheese puffs, etc.

CREAM BUNS – No. 535

Choux paste No. 534 either forced into small heaps or spoonsful placed on greased baking tins and cooked at 450°F or Mark 8 for 12–15 minutes. Cool on wire rack for a while before filling with whipped cream. Cream may be squirted into centre with a forcing bag or else open and fill then close again. Dust top with a little icing sugar.

ÉCLAIRS – No. 536

Choux paste No. 534. When coolish, either shape fingers of paste with the hands or with a large plain nozzle in a forcing bag. Bake on a well greased baking sheet, well spaced to allow for rising, at 425°F or Mark 6 for about 25 minutes.

When cold fill with fresh whipped cream No. 670 or a made cream No. 555, with the help of the forcing bag.

Ice top of éclairs with either chocolate No. 549 or coffee No. 550 icings.

BATTERS

ON MAKING AND USING BATTERS – No. 537

When making white flour batters it is usual to sift flour into bowl.

It is not possible to sift wholewheat flour without removing some of the necessary parts of it. Therefore it is necessary to ensure that there are no lumps, and this can be done by whisking the flour in the bowl with either a whisking spoon or by rubbing it through a coarse square-holed sieve.

Next, add either whole egg or yolk only if it is advised in recipe.

Next, with the back of a wooden spoon starting at the centre, commence blending batter with a circular movement. Gradually adding liquid continue stirring, taking in a very little more flour each time, until an evenly blended smooth batter results. For Yorkshire puddings, fruit batters and pancakes, the mixture is thin – for fritters the batter is thicker and if properly made you will find that the batter will coat the wooden spoon. I like to add the egg whites separately for fritters to give a light and fluffy fritter.

Cook as advised in individual recipe. Some fritters need deep frying, others are more suitably cooked in a frying pan in deep fat.

All need draining on crumpled kitchen paper and keeping hot for serving.

Pancakes are made with the thin batter No. 541, and are cooked by pouring the batter into a hot frying pan containing a little hot fat. The batter is spread over the bottom of pan thinly and the pancake is turned over either with a palette knife or by tossing it over, and the other side cooked. The cake is then placed on a hot dish, filled either with a sweet or savoury mixture and rolled up neatly. Repeat process until all are cooked, and keep them hot till ready to serve.

Yorkshire puddings are cooked in a shallow dish in the oven, the dish always contains smoking hot fat, enough to thinly cover the bottom of the tin or dish. The pudding rises high especially at the edges and must be served immediately it is removed from the oven. It is usually cut into squares. Sweet and savoury puddings are made by adding batter to fruit or savoury foods. These methods are indicated in individual recipes.

FRITTER BATTER 1 – No. 538

4 oz wholewheat flour: 1 Tbs olive oil: 1 egg: ¼ pt milk: 2 tsp cider vinegar: a pinch of salt

Make batter with flour, egg yolk and milk, oil and cider vinegar. Stiffly beat egg white with salt and lightly fold into batter. Use for any fritters; especially good for savoury fritters, spinach, lettuce, cauliflower, sage, asparagus, cheese and elderflowers.

FRITTER BATTER 2 – No. 539

4 oz wholewheat flour: 2 eggs: ¼ pt milk: 1 Tbs olive oil: a pinch of salt

Make as fritter batter 1. Use for any kind of fritter.

FRITTER BATTER 3 – No. 540

4 oz wholewheat flour: ¼ pt white wine or apple juice: 2 egg whites: 1 egg yolk: a pinch of salt: 1 Tbs olive oil

Slightly warm juice or wine and make as fritter batter 1. Use for fruit fritters, especially apple, pear, banana and elderflower. For apple, add a saltspoon of cinnamon.

PANCAKE AND YORKSHIRE PUDDING BATTER – No. 541
(Yorkshire Pudding)

4 oz wholewheat flour: 1 or 2 eggs: ½ pt milk: a pinch of salt, if liked: fat for cooking

Make as instructed and have ready a shallow dish not less than about 10 by 6 inches. Heat the oven to what is convenient between 450°F or 500°F or Mark 10. Heat ½ oz or so of fat in tin, and when smoking pour in batter. Reduce heat to 450°F or Mark 8 and cook for about half an hour.

INDIVIDUAL YORKSHIRE PUDDINGS – No. 542
Using batter No. 541, well grease and heat 2 patty tins with room for 12 puddings on each, or if liked used dariole tins. Bake at 450°F or Mark 8 for about 10–15 minutes.

Can be used sweet or with savoury course. Serve with warm jam and clotted cream for a sweet. A little sieved icing sugar dusted over before serving adds attraction. Serve very hot in either case.

ICINGS

ROYAL ICING – No. 543

1 lb sieved icing sugar: 2 egg whites, small to standard size:
1 small tsp of glycerine: 1 dspn lemon juice

Beat egg white and lemon in a mixing bowl till slightly frothy,
then add sugar gradually, beating with the back of a wooden
spoon, and glycerine, and continue to beat till, when peaks are
formed, they stay pointed and do not turn over, which may take
up to 20 minutes. This will ensure your icing staying as you put
it on the cake.

If giving two coats of icing over almond paste one coat can be
given just before icing is perfect for decorating. In this case
spread with a palette knife – it is very, very easy. The cake should
be on a board or a turntable to work easily, then turn it as you
cover with icing. Now the cake should be placed in a dry, safe
place for setting, but the remaining icing must be covered with
muslin or a teacloth wrung out in cold water and firmly covered,
and also with a plate or tray to seal. Next day you can give icing
another beating with the back of the wooden spoon till the peaks
stand. As long as you keep the icing bowl covered as described
you can spend three days over the coating and decoration of the
cake. If liked the whole can be coloured in varying colours with
the aid of vegetable dyes sold for colouring food, from palest pink
to shocking pink, and delicate lilac to deep purple, and all shades
of yellow, orange and green. I have never used the often advised
washing blue for tinting or even for whitening a cake. Mine have
been quite dazzlingly white without it and I could not quite fancy
the blue. Up to some months ago I was unable to buy a blue
vegetable dye – I should advise reading the labels of your dyes,
as anything else, to see what you are buying.

For decoration, use either a calico forcing bag with a slip-in
nozzle to give the right pattern, or use a metal one sold for the
purpose. I think the calico bag is very satisfactory and is easily
washed and stored for use at any time. It is better still to have
several in case you are embarking on a two-colour scheme. I suggest that if inexperienced, you practise icing patterns on a piece
of kitchen parchment. Draw a design and holding the bag in both
hands, thumbs uppermost, straight in front of you, and with the

open end turned over firmly and held down, force the icing over your lines and curves. You should soon get the hang of it, as it really is very simple. If doing lettering it is wise to mark this and any other design on your cake with a large darning needle; if you go wrong you can easily repair damage with a knife made hot in a jug of hot water.

Use a fine nozzle for a name or greeting, or for making basket-like patterns. The star nozzle is fascinating to use and I have taught many a small child to decorate a plain sponge with it. A tiny squeeze downwards onto the cake and off quickly, and you have a star. These look magnificent if topped with a silver ball before they dry. A row of stars round top and bottom of the cake look attractive for a beginning, and a simple red satin ribbon tied round into a small bow (tying left bow first to get it straight). This for a Christmas cake with some washed holly leaves and berries in a garland – a leaf, three berries, then another leaf – circling the top of the cake, would be easy for a beginner to carry out. You will not want ever again to pin a paper frill on your cake to hide the sides!

ON USING GLACÉ ICING – No. 544

Glacé icing is poured over the cake or pastry or biscuits. It is to cover and is not smoothed with a palette knife as are Royal and butter icings.

Stand the cake on a cooling rack that is over clean kitchen parchment in case you spill icing. Pour on the centre of cake and it will spread. Use a spoon for icing biscuits and éclairs. This icing should dry with a shine.

GLACÉ ICING – No. 545

½ lb sieved icing sugar: 3 Tbs of either just warm water or orange juice, lemon and water, consisting of 1 of lemon to 2 of water, black currant juice or any juice fancied

Stir in a pan over minimum heat until warm only. Colour if necessary, and delicately, then test for coating with the back of the wooden spoon.

CHOCOLATE GLACÉ ICING – No. 546

To No. 545, add 2 oz of cocoa and a few drops of vanilla essence after mixing with 2 tablespoons of sieved icing sugar, and blend-

ing with the minimum of boiling water to make a smooth paste.
Do this before stirring over hot water, and it would be wiser to
add only 2 tablespoons water unless more needed.

I lightly butter my basin for chocolate glacé icing.

COFFEE GLACÉ ICING – No. 547

As for No. 546, but substituting 2 level tablespoons Nescafé for
cocoa and vanilla. This can be added to sugar without pouring on
boiling water and 3 tablespoons may be just right; only add more
if necessary, and then, literally, a few drops at a time.

BUTTER ICING – No. 548

*8 oz sieved icing sugar: 1 oz butter or good margarine: top milk,
water or fruit juice for mixing*

Have a roomy mixing bowl and – my favourite tool – a rubber
bladed squeegee on a strong handle. Cut the margarine or butter
into slices then start to beat with the squeegee, or a wooden spoon
if you have not a squeegee. When butter is getting fluffy gradually
add sugar and until all blended, then add a little liquid at a time,
beating well with the back if using a spoon, until you have a nice
soft icing that will be smooth to spread and easy to decorate by
forcing bag. This soon dries crisp in a cool place.

CHOCOLATE BUTTER ICING – No. 549

To No. 548 add a few drops of vanilla essence and 2 or more
tablespoons of cocoa according to the depth of colour required,
i.e. milk chocolate or dark chocolate. Mix with milk or water.

COFFEE BUTTER ICING – No. 550

To No. 548 add from 2 tablespoons Nescafé, according to how
strong you need it. I always add 1 tablespoon of cocoa to this for
a perfect flavour, and it is a general favourite.

ORANGE BUTTER ICING – No. 551

As for No. 548, but using grated zest and juice of orange for
mixing.

LEMON BUTTER ICING – No. 552

As No. 548 but using grated lemon zest and juice for mixing.

ALMOND PASTE – No. 553

½ lb ground almonds: ½ lb fine sugar: juice of half a lemon: little shredded margarine: 1 raw egg to bind

Blend all very well until easily manageable paste results, that can be rolled on a floured board. Use as required. Paste can be coloured and if other flavouring required, leave out orange and lemon unless they blend with chosen flavouring. Add any flavouring and colouring in mixing process.

MARZIPAN – No. 554

¾ breakfast cup ground almonds: 1 breakfast cup lump sugar or vanilla sugar: 1 gill hot water: 1 egg: lemon juice, orange flower water

Dissolve sugar in water over gentle heat, cover pan and boil to 240°F or "soft ball". Have a clean pastry brush and occasionally dip into cold water and brush sides of pan inside, to prevent sugar browning and colouring, and to prevent sugar granulating. When right heat is reached remove pan from heat and add almonds, stirring meanwhile. Allow to cool, then add beaten egg, then returning to heat cook till mixture will leave sides of pan. Turn onto cold slab and knead till really smooth and almost cold, add flavouring to required taste and when cold it is ready for use.

Colouring, if required, can be added with flavourings. Marzipan can be divided and flavoured and coloured differently. If a white marzipan is required use only egg white instead of yolk and white, using 2 if necessary.

Several layers, very thin indeed, of differing colours can be placed together, brushing each with water before adding another, then the top covered with melted chocolate and from this tiny fancy shapes cut to serve for dessert for gala occasions.

CONFECTIONER'S CREAM – No. 555

2 oz sieved icing sugar: 2 oz unsalted margarine or butter: 1 Tbs top milk

Beat butter and sugar until fluffy and light, gradually add milk, getting the desired consistency. Flavour if liked, or colour. If coffee cream needed add a little powdered, prepared coffee, such as is sold for using in the cup with hot water. If chocolate, use a little cocoa powder and a few drops of vanilla essence or add praline No. 589.

MERINGUE – No. 556

To the stiffly whisked whites of 2 eggs add 2 tablespoons of sugar and a pinch of baking powder. For appearance sake, either caster or granulated sugar serves best, but demerara can be used if principles are against white. (Personally I feel the *very* occasional use of white for a dish not often served, gives a spice of adventure!)

CASHEW CREAM – No. 557
(or other nut cream)

Cashew nut cream can be bought at a Health Food Store, and must be diluted according to need. It can be used as another accompaniment to fruit dishes, when it is used as consistency of fresh cream, or thinner to accompany Muesli, or thin as dairy milk for coffee, etc. If you have an electric mixer with a liquidizer you can make nut creams in a minute or two by blending half a cup of kernels with same quantity of cold water. Make thinner if you require a thinner cream.

COCONUT CREAM – No. 558

Finely grate some of a bar of coconut *crème* available at a Health Food Store and either blend in a liquidizer or by whisking cream and half the quantity of tepid, not hot, water, in a warm basin, until desired cream results.

RUM BUTTER – No. 559

1 lb soft "pieces" sugar: ½ lb butter: 1 saltsp of nutmeg: 1 saltsp of cinnamon: 2 small wine glasses of rum

Cream butter and sugar with spices and when absolutely blended very gradually add rum and blend till all smooth. Pot and tie down, and keep cold.

BRANDY BUTTER – No. 560
OR HARD SAUCE FOR CHRISTMAS PUDDING

4 oz butter: 8 oz soft "pieces" sugar: 1 small wine glass brandy: squeeze of lemon or a few drops of vanilla flavouring

Blend as for Rum Butter No. 559, and serve cold and firm.

SHERRY BUTTER – No. 561

As for Brandy Butter No. 560 but substituting sherry for brandy.

ORANGE BUTTER – No. 562

As for Brandy Butter No. 560, but substituting either concentrated orange juice or the zest and juice of an orange, or more than one if necessary.

GERANIUM SUGAR – No. 563

Bruise several geranium leaves and place in screw top jar with fine sugar for a couple of days before using, say for a special celebration meal or party buffet. Shake the jar occasionally when it catches your eye, and use sugar to flavour and sweeten thickly whipped cream in one of the fruit cream sweets without too much flavour. Do not try to keep the sugar and leaves indefinitely, but make fresh for each occasion.

VANILLA SUGAR – No. 564

Vanilla bean: sugar, caster, pieces or demerara

Score down each side of vanilla bean with a sharp knife, then place in screw top jar with sugar; I use a 1 lb size preserving jar but you could use a smaller jar if you wished. Pour sugar all round it, give it a shaking occasionally, and use for flavouring instead of plain sugar and vanilla flavourings. Refill jar as sugar is used.

CONFECTIONERY

ALMOND NOUGAT – No. 565

1 lb coffee sugar (large dry brown crystals) or 1 lb loaf sugar: juice and zest of 1 lemon: ½ lb sweet almonds: rice paper to line plate and cover

Blanch almonds and slowly and gently dry in oven till crisp but not browned. Chop coarsely.

Gently boil sugar and lemon, stirring till dissolved, and then keeping heat gentle, boil till bubbling all over. Add almonds and stir in. Pour onto plate covered with rice paper and press paper also on top evenly. When cold cut into fingers. Store in wax paper lined tins.

ALMOND ROCK – No. 566

2 cups demerara sugar: 1 breakfast cup blanched almonds: 1 gill water: 4 tsp butter: pinch of cream of tartar

Roast almonds on baking sheet in oven till light golden colour. Into a pan put butter, sugar and water and gently dissolve over heat. Add cream of tartar and boil to almost 240°F then stir in almonds and boil till 312°F. Into a prepared oiled tin pour mixture and when cold, break up and store in tins or jars.

CHOCOLATE ALMONDS – No. 567

Shelled and blanched almonds (see No. 659 for preparing almonds) lightly browned on a baking sheet in oven. Bitter chocolate grated and melted in a basin on a pan of boiling water, is used to coat almonds when they are quite cold. Dip each into chocolate with the help of a long darning needle to spear each one. When dipped place on an oiled sheet on waxed paper to harden. Store in jar or tin with fitting lid.

SUGARED ALMONDS – No. 568

1 lb "coffee sugar" or loaf sugar: 1 cup sweet almonds: ¼ p water

Blanch almonds and dry them with a clean napkin. Heat sugar and water gently till sugar is dissolved, then bring to boil. Stir in almonds and then boil for 5 minutes. Stand pan aside from heat till cooling and thickening, and then remove almonds one by one keeping some sugar on each one, and placing on waxed paper to dry. Store in tins or jars.

To make coloured sugared almonds of course delicately tint the sugar before adding almonds.

STUFFED CHERRIES 1 – No. 569

Glacé cherries: almond paste No. 553: caster sugar

Slit cherries on one side, open and insert tiny balls of paste rolled in hands. Make round with hands, roll in sugar and place in tiny sweetmeat paper case.

STUFFED CHERRIES 2 – No. 570

Alternatively stuff with a piece of brazil or a cashew nut kernel.

HAZEL AND DATE BALLS – No. 571

Stoned dates: hazel nut kernels

Mince together, shape into tiny balls and roll in milled hazels.

ALMOND AND GINGER BALLS – No. 572

2 oz preserved ginger No. 584: 4 oz blanched almonds

Put ginger through mincer set for fine mincing, and follow with most of almonds. Mill remaining almonds finely for rolling balls in to coat, after blending minced mixture. Place in tiny sweet papers and store in airtight tin till needed.

STUFFED DATES – No. 573

As for Carlsbad plums No. 574 and stuffed cherries Nos. 570 and 569 or with pieces of Oranzini No. 583, and then roll dates in either milled nuts or desiccated coconut. Place dates in tiny paper cases and pack neatly into wax paper lined boxes. Very acceptable as presents on festive occasions.

STUFFED CARLSBAD PLUMS 1 – No. 574

As for cherries No. 569, but first removing stones with sharp knife.

STUFFED CARLSBAD PLUMS 2 – No. 575

Remove stones and replace with a whole shelled almond or Brazil kernel.

CHERRY NOUGAT – No. 576

*1 lb icing sugar: a dozen sweet almonds: ¼ lb glacé cherries:
whites of 3 standard eggs: rice paper to line and cover plates*

Blanch, then dry almonds in oven till crisp, then chop coarsely.
Have cherries chopped or minced finely.

Beat egg whites with sugar in saucepan, and when well blended
place over very gentle heat and continue stirring until mixture
thickens, but do not boil.

Take from heat and stir in cherries and almonds. Pour onto
plate covered with rice paper and cover with more, making as
flat as possible. Cool and when cold cut in fingers.

CHOCOLATE FUDGE – No. 577

*¼ lb demerara sugar: 1 oz butter: 2 oz bar chocolate grated:
saltsp of cream of tartar: 1 cup top milk*

With a wooden spoon, stir sugar in milk over gentle heat till it
has dissolved, then add chocolate, butter and cream of tartar.
Still stirring, bring to boil and continue for about three minutes.
Remove pan from heat and beat mixture until it suddenly is
creamy. This is the time to pour it into a buttered or oiled tin.
Smooth it over and mark into squares and when quite cold remove and store in airtight tins or jars. Mine has never reached
this stage! I like to vary this with chopped preserved ginger No.
584 or Oranzini No. 583, in the first case adding a level teaspoon
ground ginger and in the second, zest of an orange.

CHOCOLATE ORANGE SWEETMEAT – No. 578

Strips of Oranzini No. 583 dipped into melted chocolate as for
chocolate almonds No. 567.

CHOCOLATE GINGER – No. 579

As No. 578 using pieces of crystallized ginger.

CHOCOLATE PINEAPPLE – No. 580

As No. 578 using pieces of crystallized pineapple.

DEVON TOFFEE – No. 581

*½ lb demerara sugar flavoured with vanilla bean: 3 oz butter or
margarine: 1 Tbs golden syrup: 4 Tbs water*

Stir sugar, water and butter over gentle heat till sugar has dissolved, then bring to boil and continue till about 250°F or hard ball is reached (see No. 587), then remove from heat and in a few minutes pour into oiled tin to set. When beginning to set mark in suitable squares with back of knife, so that it will break easily when cold.

MARRONS GLACÉS – No. 582

1 cup sugar: 1 cup water: chestnuts

Select perfect nuts from a pound of eating chestnuts after peeling and skinning. Some will get broken or not be perfect. Boil sugar and water for three minutes lowering heat so that it does not burn. Drop in chestnuts and boil for three minutes. Remove chestnuts with draining spoon and cool on wire tray whilst boiling sugar again till it begins to thicken. Again drop in chestnuts, one by one, using the spoon again, bring to boil again for 3 minutes then remove as before. Do this all again twice more and finally dry out on wire tray, before storing in an airtight tin or jar.

ORANZINI – No. 583

Peeled orange peel, preferably jaffas: sugar

Soak peel for three days in cold water changing water daily, cut into strips, strain. Add weight of peel in sugar, add fresh water just to cover when boiling – boil for 10 minutes and stand aside. Repeat this 10 minute boiling on two days following, then cool, strain and roll pieces in coarse sugar on a plate, dry and store in airtight tins, lined with waxed paper. Use syrup for fruit salad, or cake making. A delightful sweet; this recipe given many years ago by a Viennese friend. Use for dessert as it is, or chocolate coated No. 578, or add to trifles or on top of cream, to garnish sweet dishes. The more pith inside the peel the more luscious the result!

CRYSTALLIZED GINGER – No. 584

As above, using root ginger soaked for 3 days before first boiling and weighing. It may take a few days longer before it is tender right through. Test with steel needle after third boiling. Store in airtight tins lined with waxed paper. Store in preserving jars in syrup, or slice, drain and roll in sugar as for Oranzini.

CANDIED GOOSEBERRIES – No. 585

These are delicious for winter desserts. Trim sound, fine green gooseberries. Boil 1 lb sugar in half a pint of water till thick. Remove pan from heat and leave aside to get cold. Boil up again, then carefully lift up onto a wire cooling rack to drain. When sugar has ceased to drip, roll gooseberries in caster sugar till well coated and put on dry rack in a very cool oven with the door not fastened though closed. When dry pack in tiny waxed paper cases and into airtight tins, with waxed paper between the layers.

CANDIED PLUMS – No. 586

Make use of a plum glut and store away for Christmas!

Ripe dessert plums: for each 1 lb of plums 1 lb sugar and ½ pt water

Stone plums carefully, and boil sugar and water till thick, taking care not to burn. Carefully drop in plums and bringing to boil again reduce heat to the minimum to allow plums to simmer gently. Continue simmering till plums are transparent. Remove plums to lay separately on a large dish till next day. Next day boil up in syrup again and again remove plums. Repeat this once more then drain for several hours before drying on a rack in a cool oven very slowly till dry, with oven door ajar. When really cold, next day, pack in waxed papers in tins with waxed paper between layers.

MARZIPAN FRUITS – No. 587

½ lb ground almonds: ½ lb fine sugar: ¼ lb icing sugar: 1 egg: a little orange flower water: cherries and angelica, and blanched almonds for decorating: colourings

Blend ground almonds and sugar and bind with egg and orange flower water till a firm soft paste that will easily handle results. Divide into three gradually adding drops of colouring and kneading to blend. Colour ⅓ green, ⅓ yellow and leave ⅓ natural. Shape green apples, colouring rosy side with red vegetable dye and a brush, pears, pods of green peas, etc.; with yellow mould oranges, lemons, and bananas, adding with brush, more colour where needed, and using plain for potatoes, rolled in cocoa, cherries, painted red, strawberries, etc. Ready for use when firm.

SUGAR BOILING FOR TOFFEE – No. 588

For small ball or soft ball boil to 235°F–240°F when a little of the syrup dropped into cold water will form a little lump that can be rolled into a soft ball.

For hard or large ball, boil to 247°F–252°F.

For small crack, boil to 290°F when the sugar should be brittle or till a little sticky to handle.

PRALINE 1 – No. 589

8 oz demerara sugar: 4 Tbs water: 2 oz nut kernels, preferably almonds

Boil without stirring till it reaches "cracking" point, when a little is dropped into cold water. Pour onto a plate to set. When set and brittle, break up and either roll out with a rolling pin, crushing and rolling till a pleasant chippy powdered state is reached, or pound with a pestle and mortar. Store in screw-top jars and use for topping creamy sweets or cakes.

PRALINE 2 – No. 590

For topping and decorating and flavouring sweets, cakes, trifles, etc. Almond rock No. 566, either pounded in a pestle and mortar or broken into small pieces and crushed to coarse powder with a rolling pin.

PRESERVES

ON MAKING JAM – No. 591

Fruit should be sound, very fresh, not under or over ripe, with the exception of gooseberries which I cannot resist making into preserves, green as well as ripe.

Most jams can be made with real demerara sugar – some like raspberry need fine white sugar to preserve the colour. If one sacrifices colour one could use demerara sugar.

An enamelled iron or stainless steel preserving pan is ideal. Use large wooden spoon for stirring. As a rule 1 lb sugar to each pound of fruit.

The amount of water must vary with kind and juiciness of fruit. Boil carefully but quickly unless otherwise advised in recipe. A little knob of butter used will mostly prevent scum forming in pan after sugar is added.

Cook till a teaspoonful on a cold plate that is tilted, will show a skin forming over it, and then sets to a jelly.

Pot up as soon as jam is done, into scrupulously clean pots, warmed and standing ready to use. I use a large oven tin to stand mine on to warm in a cool oven, or warm them in a heated drawer under oven. Fill with a kitchen cup. Wipe jars when filled, with a very clean cloth, tie down or fasten down with rubber bands, the prepared cellophane jam covers, with waxed disc on top of jam, first label carefully and neatly with date and name of jam and, if you have several recipes, the identification of recipe in case you wish to repeat or discontinue a recipe.

Finally, keep jam on shelf in cool airy pantry that is as dry as possible.

I do advise making any necessary notes at the foot of your recipe for future guidance. Often one makes a particular kind of jam or preserve once only in a year, and memory may be faulty.

ON MAKING JELLY – No. 592

Most fruit makes good jelly, but I have failed to produce it from pears, strawberries or cherries. That was many years ago it is true, but I don't think it is possible at all.

All fruits should be cleaned, large fruits cut into small pieces, but none of them need be topped and tailed. I do not peel or core apples, but of course, do remove all damaged parts of any fruits, and have all fruits as fresh as possible.

Lemon juice or prepared and bottled pectin from the chemists will help to set fruits with little pectin. On the whole, you cannot fail with the berries such as blackberries, loganberries, red, black and white currants, apples, crab-apples, cranberries, rowans, etc.

The method is simply to just cover fruit with water, to boil until tender, then to let drip until juice is collected in a bowl, and to boil this juice with a pound of sugar per pint. Lemons are added either for flavour or to help setting. Liquid is then boiled till it sets when tested by putting about a teaspoonful onto a cold plate. Almost immediately, on tilting the plate you will see a skin has formed over the juice if it is done, and it will soon set to a real jelly, and is ready for potting. Apple jelly turns a delicious pink colour, as does crab-apple. Indeed, the colour of jellies thrills the housewife as she arranges her jars, clean and carefully labelled, on her shelf. To strain my jelly I upturn a kitchen chair on the kitchen table, the seat on the table. Dust off carefully first, especially under seat and the rungs. Now knot a piece of old clean linen or a couple of thicknesses of butter muslin, kept for the purpose, at each corner. It will need to be about a yard square. Arrange the knots over the chair legs now sticking up in the air, so that they are firmly held, the leg sticking into the linen beside the knot and being held on by it. Stand a large bowl under the linen bag now hanging down – the bowl stands on the upturned seat of the chair. Tip the fruit into the bag, the juice will drip, and whilst you are permitted to turn it about once or twice, you should never squeeze it or the jelly will be cloudy.

Next day measure juice and boil up with sugar. Carefully label jars and give date, name of preserve and recipe guidance and even source of fruit as well as recipe. For instance, "Blackberry, August '58. Garden. Own recipe."

APPLE GINGER – No. 593

3 lb cooking apples, after preparation: 3 lb sugar: 2 oz root ginger: ½ lb preserved ginger

Cover root ginger overnight with ½ pt boiling water. Next day peel, core and cut up apples into fairly evenly sized pieces and place in pan. Strain on liquor from ginger, stir in sugar then tie root ginger in a piece of muslin and add this to fruit and sugar, and boil together till apple is soft and mixture is quite clear, and jellies when tested. Just before completion, add preserved ginger cut into tiny pieces. Pot when ready. Delicious for tarts, etc.

APRICOT JAM – No. 594

5 lb ripe apricots: 4 lb sugar: juice of 1 lemon: ½ cup kernels from apricot stones

Make as for peach jam No. 603.

BLACK CHERRY JAM – No. 595

4 lb preserving sugar: ½ pt water or fruit juice (preferably goose-berry): 4 lb stoned black cherries: ½ cup kernels from cracked stones: 1 tsp salt: nut of butter

Boil sugar, salt, butter and water or juice together, add stoned cherries and kernels and boil till cherries are tender and jam will set if a little is cooled on a plate.

BLACKCURRANT JAM – No. 596

1½ lb blackcurrants: 3 lb demerara sugar: 1 pt water: nut of butter: ½ tsp salt

Boil water, currants and butter until currants are really tender, 15–20 minutes. Add sugar and boil for about 15–20 minutes or until jam sets when tested.

DAMSON CHEESE – No. 597

Fill a casserole with damsons and cover with lid. Cook in gentle oven 300°F or Mark 1 until damsons are tender and stones slip out easily. Cool them by tipping onto a large dish and leaving till they can be handled.

When cool, remove stones and weigh pulp (weigh pan empty and then again, after filling) and allowing 1 lb demerara sugar for each 1 lb of pulp, stir over gentle heat till it thickens, when it is ready for potting.

GOOSEBERRY JAM – No. 598

3 lb gooseberries: 4 lb sugar: 1 pt water

Top and tail gooseberries and mince them, taking care not to lose any juice. This will enable you to cook the jam quickly and so preserve the lovely green colour. Boil gooseberries in water till pieces of skin are tender (keeping lid on pan), this should be about five minutes. Remove lid, add sugar and boil till setting on testing. 10–15 minutes.

LEMON CURD – No. 599

4 oz butter: 2 eggs: 2 lemons: 6 oz fine sugar

Into the top pan of a double cooker place butter, sugar, grated zest and juice of lemons. Bring water in bottom of pan to boiling and stir pan contents until sugar has dissolved. Beat and strain eggs and add, stirring, to mixture, continuing to stir until it obviously thickens. Pot and use as preserve for spread, tarts, etc.

MARROW PINEAPPLE JAM – No. 600

2 lb marrow when prepared: 2 lb cooking apples: 1 lb tin pine-apple chunks: 3 lb preserving sugar: ½ lb crystallized ginger

Cube everything, cut up pineapple and ginger in very small pieces. Leave in bowl for 12 hours. Simmer slowly for 1 hour or until it sets.

ORANGE CURD – No. 601

As for lemon curd No. 599, but substituting orange for lemon.

ORANGE OR LEMON AND GRAPEFRUIT MARMALADE – No. 602

Follow instructions for tangerine marmalade No. 609. I have made mine this way for very many years and have found no reason for changing. It takes only a quarter of the time taken by the conventional method, and is less messy and wasteful.

PEACH JAM – No. 603

5 lb ripe peaches: 4 lb sugar: juice of 1 lemon: kernels from some peaches – ½ cup

Gently wipe peaches with cloth, split and stone them and lay on large dishes with sugar sprinkled all over cut sides for 24 hours. Next day place fruit and juice in pan with lemon juice and slowly bring to boil, then gently simmer till jam will set, about 60 minutes in all. Add kernels for last 10 minutes. Pot daintily in jars, small and best jars, for this is a choice jam

PEAR MARMALADE – No. 604

*Ripe pears: sugar: rind of a lemon to each 4 lb pears: juice of a
lemon to each 4 lb pears*

Peel, core and halve pears, just cover with water and simmer till
tender. Strain off liquid, and tip pears onto large dish and return
liquid to pan. Adding lemon rind, cores and peelings, boil till
liquid is reduced to half quantity and strain.

Weigh fruit and for each pound put 1 lb sugar and 1 lb water
and lemon juice into large pan with strained liquid from pears.
Boil till jelling on test, then add thickly diced pears and bring to
boil again for two or three minutes.

PLUM JAM – No. 605

4 lb ripe plums: 3 lb sugar: 1 pt water

Wipe and halve and stone plums; removing stone kernels to add to
jam. Gently simmer plums, kernels and water till plums are nearly
tender, then add sugar and stir till it is dissolved. Boil rather fast
till some jam sets on testing.

RASPBERRY JAM – No. 606
This is a quick method that I have found excellent over many
years, and leaves the jam tasting like fresh raspberries.

2 lb raspberries: 2½ lb sugar, fine

Warm sugar in a bowl over hot water till warmed through, stirring it about occasionally hastens this.

Press raspberries with wooden spoon in preserving pan to
release juice, then gently bring to boil whilst stirring, and continue for about 15 minutes. Add warmed sugar and bring again
to boil, still stirring, and boil exactly two minutes longer. Jam
is now ready to pot up.

SUMMER JELLY – No. 607
When summer soft fruits are available use equal quantities of
raspberries, red currants, loganberries and gooseberries. To 4 pt
measures of fruit, add one pint water and cook to extract juices.
Leave to drip overnight and next day measure and boil with 1 lb
sugar for each pint of juice, 20–30 minutes. When setting is
assured by testing, pot and cover.

STRAWBERRY JAM – No. 608

*Strawberries: ¾ lb sugar, per lb of strawberries: 1 tsp glycerine:
juice of 1 lemon per 2 lb strawberries*

Prepare strawberries, then place in layers with sugar, juice and
glycerine in preserving pan. Leave in warm place till some juice
shows, 1 hour approximately. Gently bring to boil, stirring till
all sugar dissolved, but taking care not to break berries. Fast boil
till jam sets on testing.

TANGERINE MARMALADE – No. 609

12 tangerines: sugar: lemon

After wiping tangerines place them in a pan and barely covering
with water, cook till skins are tender when tested, keeping lid on
pan. Strain and tip oranges into large dish, returning liquid to
pan, after weighing.

Finely slice oranges and remove pips. Weigh pulp when ready,
and allowing 1 lb of sugar for each pound of fruit and juice, boil
sugar and liquid together with juice of lemon till it is thick, then
adding pulp boil again till mixture jellies on testing.

RIPE TOMATO JAM – No. 610

Tomatoes: lemon: sugar: nut of butter

When tomatoes are plentiful select ripe, sound ones and remove
skins by covering in bowl with boiling· water. Place each peeled
tomato in another bowl, after weighing it. Allowing 1 lb sugar to
each pound peeled tomatoes, cover them with sugar and leave till
next day. Next day, strain off syrup and boil in preserving pan
with a nut of butter. When boiling, add tomatoes and juice of
1 lemon to each 2 lb tomatoes. Boil till setting results. Pot whilst
hot.

APPLE CHUTNEY – No. 611

*1 lb cooking apples, after preparing: ½ lb onions, after preparing:
½ lb dates, stoned: ¼ lb figs: ½ lb tomatoes: 1 lb barbados sugar:
2 pts vinegar: 1 oz pickling spices: 1 Tbs salt*

Cut up apples, tomatoes and onions and mince figs and dates·
Tie spices in a piece of muslin, leaving string to tie to pan handle·

Boil everything together and simmer till tender. Remove and
squeeze spice bag. Pack into jars and cover when cold. Label
clearly.

GREEN TOMATO CHUTNEY – No. 612

*4 lb green tomatoes: 1¼ lb brown sugar: 1 lb stoned raisins:
2 lb apples: 1 lb onions: 1 quart vinegar: 1 oz mustard seed:
1 tsp ginger: 1 tsp allspice*

This recipe, given by my friend Dorothy Miller, had very brief
instructions. "Mince tomatoes, raisins, onions and apples. Add
to vinegar, spices and sugar and boil for ¾ hour."

I followed this and boiled pickling spices in a muslin bag at-
tached to pan handle with string for easy removal. Mincing gives
nice evenly sized pieces, but I would have preferred 1½ pts of
vinegar, I think, although I thought Miss Miller's results from
this recipe were perfect. Mine more than filled three 2 lb preserving jars; screwed down immediately and the following day they
were found to be sealed.

If liked the chutney could be passed through a sieve when a
thick purée would result.

ELDERFLOWER AND GREEN GOOSEBERRY
JELLY – No. 613

As for mint and gooseberry jelly No. 614, but substituting elderflowers for mint. The only difference in procedure is to boil the
elderflowers with the gooseberries before dripping. Remove
flowers from stalks by rubbing between palms.

FRESH MINT AND GREEN GOOSEBERRY
JELLY – No. 614

4 lb green gooseberries: 1 pt water

Wash and mince berries without topping and tailing. Boil in
water for 5 minutes with lid on, and only a minute or two longer
if skin pieces are not tender then. When tender, with cooking
shortest possible time to preserve colour, put to drip and leave
overnight. Next day measure juice and to each pint allow:

*1 lb preserving sugar: ½ cup very finely chopped mint: 1 Tbs
cider vinegar*

Boil juice with mint and vinegar for about two minutes – again
timing so as not to lose colour – then add sugar and boil till
setting is reached on testing.

Pot and use with hot nutty savouries, peas, potatoes, or as you
fancy.

GREEN TOMATO CHEESE – No. 615

To each 1 lb green tomatoes, add 2 lb green cooking or windfall apples. To each pound of cooked pulp, after sieving, add ¾ lb sugar. Make as damson cheese No. 597. Do not peel apples. ,sieve fruit when tender. A small bunch of spinach leaves in the casserole will keep the green colour. Scald them first.

MINT CHUTNEY – No. 616

1 cup finely chopped fresh mint: 1 lb minced dates: ⅓ cup cider vinegar: paprika and salt to taste

Blend well then pack into tiny jars and seal down. Keep cool, or cold, and once opened a jar must be used.

PARSLEY JELLY – No. 617

1 lb parsley: 2 lemons: cider vinegar: sugar

Boil parsley for about 15 minutes with enough water to cover easily, and juice of the lemons.

Strain and boil again adding 1 lb sugar to each pint of juice and to each pint, 1 tablespoon cider vinegar. Boil till jellying is achieved, then pot in tiny pots, for serving with hot or cold savouries, or hot vegetables or vegetable salads.

MINCEMEAT – No. 618

½ lb shredded "Suenut" nut suet: ½ lb peeled and cored apples: ¼ lb currants: ¼ lb sultanas: ¼ lb dates: ½ lb soaked prunes: ¼ lb mixed lemon and orange peel: ¼ lb barbados sugar: ¼ lb chopped nuts: grated zest and juice of 1½ lemons: ½ grated nutmeg: ¼ oz ground ginger: ¼ oz mixed spice: ¼ pt apple juice (bottled or No. 746).

Wash and dry fruit. Stone dates and prunes and pass all fruits and nuts through mincer. Blend in spices, juice, zest, sugar and salt. Stir really well, pot, and tie down.

ELDER VINEGAR – No. 619

As tarragon vinegar No. 622 using 1 oz of dried flowers to ½ pt vinegar and soaking for 2 weeks. Filter and bottle, using as a gargle or to promote perspiration in warding off a chill. 1 tablespoon to a glass of hot water.

GARLIC OR SHALLOT VINEGAR – No. 620

Crush 2 cloves of garlic or one shallot to one quart of vinegar, and shake daily for about 10 days, then strain and bottle.

MINT VINEGAR – No. 621
As tarragon vinegar No. 622.

TARRAGON VINEGAR – No. 622
Either fresh or dried tarragon left in a jar of vinegar, with lid in place, for about six weeks. Strain then, and bottle.

No. 623
Using either croutons of bread No. 695 stamped into attractive shapes with biscuit cutter, or shaped cheese on plain short pastry No. 529, small plain biscuits, or toast shapes. Spread with butter, butter and yeast extract blended, peanut butter, Tartex or savoury butter No. 694.

Arrange, with every care, on any of the above. Either a whole slice of hard-boiled egg No. 127 or two half slices. Pipe cream cheese round the edges and across centre, or on centre sprinkle finely chopped parsley or chives, or capers.

Spread with parsley, mint, or watercress butters Nos. 339, 333, 343.

Pounded hard-boiled egg spread on and topped with half a stuffed olive, or chopped stoned olive.

Spread thickly with cream cheese on which is a round of cucumber cut into 2 halves and put on butterfly-wise with capers down centre.

A slice of cucumber without rind removed but with rind scored down length of cucumber, and top the slice with a shape of Dutch cheese cut with a tiny biscuit cutter. Make a tiny nick in centre and press in a caper.

Spread thickly with cream cheese and place on a stamped cut shape of cucumber dipped in lemon juice.

Thickly spread cream cheese and top with stuffed olive.

Thickly spread cream cheese and finely chopped celery mixed.

Peanut butter spread and top with salted peanut.

Spread with cold Fondue No. 679 and top with slice of gherkin.

Spread with cream cheese and chopped ginger mixed.

Spread with peanut butter and top with gherkin.

No. 624
Halve hard-boiled eggs No. 127 lengthwise, remove yolk and pound with butter and a little paprika and celery salt, then pipe back into egg whites.

No. 625
With a pastry brush, oil plain small biscuits, sprinkle with parmesan and paprika then bake in moderate oven 350°F or Mark 4 for a few minutes.

No. 626
On biscuits as No. 625, place a piece of stoned date dipped in lemon juice and drained, and on this a salted peanut, cashew or almond.

No. 627
A slice of tomato dipped into cool vegetable jelly before arranging on base, piped with cream cheese and the centre filled with slice of pickle.

No. 628
For a buffet, have either a grapefruit, a scrubbed swede – till it is really beautiful – a compact red cabbage or a colourful marrow, arranged as a centrepiece and with the help of cocktail sticks, impale attractive morsels of food and push the stick into the chosen vegetable.

Suggestions for this are as follows:
Cut ½ inch pieces of celery and impale with a ¾ inch cube of cheese
or a stuffed olive and cheese
a piece of ginger and cheese
a tiny pickled onion and cheese
a tiny gherkin and cheese
a tiny gherkin alone
a cube of cucumber and cheese
a radish and cheese
a radish cut like a flower, black or green grapes
a pineapple cube dipped in oil and lemon, balls of double cream cheese rolled in milled nuts
a pickled walnut
Party chestnuts No. 662
and many other items will doubtless present themselves.

No. 629
Using cheese pastry No. 532 roll out very long and very thinly, and spreading paste used for savoury eggs No. 136 make the thinnest possible rolls, sealing edge with water to fasten. Make this roll only finger thick. Brush whole length with raw egg and sprinkle with finely grated cheese, or parmesan, then cut into inch long lengths and bake.

No. 630
With thin pastry No. 530 cover the outside of boat shaped moulds and cook upside down on a baking sheet. Fill with fondue No. 679 or mushroom filling No. 92 or tartex, or mint and pea paste No. 687. Or fill with an asparagus tip and some *béchamel* sauce No. 345.

No. 631
Or serve tiny cheese and potato cakes No. 118 well drained on paper and served cold.

No. 632
Or thinly rolled pastry No. 530 spread with yeast extract and butter mixture and made into tiny rolls as already described. Asparagus tips on fingers of buttered toast, halves of bridge rolls or fingers of fried bread, hot or cold.

ROLLED ASPARAGUS SANDWICHES – No. 633
Spread a damp clean cloth on the table. Cut very thin slices of bread, cut to right size for asparagus tips and butter after removing crusts, place pieces of bread on cloth, and asparagus on each piece. Then roll up and stack on foil or greaseproof paper with open side down. Stack neatly till all complete then wrap carefully till required.

No. 634
As No. 633 using cream cheese and capers, chutney, a pinch of curry powder, or ginger.
Or potted cheese No. 677.
Or peanut butter and celery seeds.
Or Tartex and fennel.

RYE BREAD DICE – No. 635

Butter slices of darkest rye bread, sprinkle with chopped celery, finely crumbled Cheshire or blue cheese, etc., or celery seed and finely grated gouda, and pile slice upon slice, pressing down well. Wrap up in slightly damp cloth for an hour or so, then remove block. Cut crusts off all round, cut into inch wide slices across with sharp knife, keeping together. Cut across other way to get portions of convenient size. Arrange on dish garnished with watercress or mustard and cress.

ROLLED SANDWICHES – No. 636

Cut top, side and end crusts from a sandwich loaf, cut long thin slices along length, butter and lay on damp cloth. Spread with chosen filling and roll each slice into a neat roll. Stack as advised in rolled asparagus sandwiches and when set, slice into ½ inch slices.

THREE OR MORE DECKER SANDWICHES – No. 637

Cut and spread as No. 636 only placing layer upon layer. Wrap tightly after ending with a piece of bread and butter, butter side down, and when set cut into inch wide slices.

ROLLED CINNAMON TOAST – No. 638

Very thin, toasted one side only and brush with melted butter, sprinkle a little powdered cinnamon and a little moist sugar. Roll up immediately and spear with cocktail stick. Keep hot in napkin till served.

TOASTED CHEESE ROLLS – No. 639

As for cinnamon toast, substituting potted cheese or cream cheese.

As rolled stack in grill pan tightly and when all finished, grill till golden, watching carefully, tops only. Garnish with mustard and cress. Serve immediately.

CHEESE WHEELS – No. 640

Cheese pastry No. 532 adding 1 teaspoon made or tube french mustard to mixing liquid. 2 oz extra grated cheese.

Make pastry and roll out to ¼ inch thickness on floured board. Sprinkle cheese over paste, roll up and cut into ¼ inch thick slices. Bake on greased baking sheet till golden, in hot oven 425°F or Mark 6. If liked a little celery salt may be sprinkled at same time as cheese.

CHEESE AIGRETTES – No. 641

Choux paste No. 534 adding to flour before mixing:

1 tsp paprika or ½ tsp cayenne: 1 tsp dry mustard

When panada is made as directed, beat in ½ cup finely grated cheese, after eggs.

Deep fry teaspoonsful, very hot, and trying one teasoonful first for heat.

Fry till golden. Drain on kitchen paper. Serve hot or cold but preferably hot.

If required for buffet they can be heated at last minute in oven.

TOAST FONDUE – No. 642

Serve fingers of toast or croutons, or whole slices, if desired, with fondue No. 679.

Serve with just warmed tomato slices and garnish with parsley finely chopped.

TINY VOL-AU-VENTS – No. 643

Fill tiny *vol-au-vents* made from puff pastry No. 527, with any savoury mixture and serve hot or cold. Use the very tiniest of cutters. Larger *vol-au-vents* as desired.

KEBABS – No. 644

On skewers stick oiled button mushrooms, pieces of tinned vegetarian sausages, pieces of pineapple, pickled onions, cubes of cheese and halves of small tomatoes, and grill in pan, turning over when necessary.

HORSERADISH BALLS – No. 645

Horseradish sauce No. 358 made thicker as instructed. Roll in fine fried crumbs or milled nuts.

CELERY STICKS – No. 646

Dry crisp celery sticks with a cloth and selecting the larger ones cut into 2–3-inch lengths.

Into the hollows press fillings made from cream cheese, cream cheese with chopped preserved ginger, or with chopped hard-boiled eggs, or chopped chives, or grated orange zest. Chill and serve with salad or as buffet snacks.

CHEESE FRITTERS – No. 647
Using Fritter Batter No. 1 or 2, with the addition of:

> 1 *small grated onion: 1–2 oz grated cheddar or 1 Tbs parmesan: a good pinch of marjoram*

Have hot fat in a pan over heat and drop in tablespoonsful well spaced. Carefully cook till golden and turn to cook other side. Drain on kitchen paper and serve. These may be served with vegetables and tomato sauce No. 371 as main course.

WHOLEWHEAT ROLLS WITH CREAMED MUSHROOMS – No. 648
Bake wholewheat rolls No. 476 rather small to medium size. When cold cut through centre and pull out soft centres. (These can be dried out in slow oven and used for pulled bread.)

Make *béchamel* sauce No. 345 and heat roll shells in oven. Fill shells with sauce when both are ready. These can be assembled in a short while for a hot addition to a cold buffet. A chopped hard-boiled egg may be added to the sauce, if liked.

MUSHROOM ON TOAST – No. 649
Grill mushrooms as for No. 67 and serve on rounds of buttered wholewheat toast, or use any fat in pan for oiling toast with a pastry brush. Serve very hot. Omit shallots and garlic if preferred.

LEEKS ON TOAST – No. 650
Gently cook white ends of leeks split down centre, drain and coat with béchamel sauce No. 345 and using some of the liquor from leeks, then serve on rounds, two deep, of wholewheat toast. If liked a sprinkling of grated cheese, a delicately flavoured one, may be browned under the grill before serving.

TOASTED CHEESE SANDWICHES – No. 651
Butter 4 slices medium thick wholewheat bread, cover with generous slices of Cheese – Cheddar – Cheshire – Guda or Caerphilly are all excellent – and place under grill for a little while to start melting the cheese. When cheese starts to melt, spread a little chutney, or mint, or chopped olive, on the cheese and cover with four more slices of buttered bread. Toast sandwiches till rich golden, turn, and toast other side. Cut sandwiches in halves, garnish with parsley and serve on hot plates immediately. If you

wish to serve these sandwiches for a party, a buffet, everything can be prepared beforehand. Cover with napkin when toasted.

SAVOURY PASTIES – No. 652
Tiny pasties made with short pastry No. 529 and filled with any savoury filling.

Roll out to ⅛ inch thickness and cut 3 inch rounds, damp edges, fill and fold, pressing edges to seal. These may be baked or deep fried.

GREEN RAREBIT – No. 653
Using gorgonzola or blue cheese, mash and then beat gently in a pan with a generous lump of butter, stirring till smooth and soft.

Have some watercress ready chopped and add sufficient to make mixture green.

Serve on rounds of wholewheat toast, very hot, and garnished with more cress or criss-cross of red or yellow pimento. If liked a slice of hard-boiled egg could be placed on rarebit before garnish.

SCRAMBLED EGGS ON TOAST – No. 654
As No. 129.

POACHED EGGS ON TOAST – No. 655
As No. 128.

CHEESE FLUFFS – No. 656
1 cup grated cheese: ½ cup wholewheat flour: 2 egg whites: a little made mustard: a pinch of marjoram: a pinch of onion salt

To stiffly beaten egg whites, add flour, seasoning and cheese, blending well. Roll into tiny balls and then in breadcrumbs. In deep fat fry till golden and drain onto paper d'oyly and serve hot or cold.

No. 657
Always have some plain brown bread and butter available at parties. It's very refreshing to come upon.

Also bowls of crisp celery in conveniently sized pieces.

Crisp lettuce and radishes, as well as the conventional olives,

potato crisps, etc. A bowl of soaked prunes with a nut kernel
instead of a stone will be refreshing.

And a bowl of crisp apples!

POPCORN – No. 658

A special basket with sliding lid, the "Weasel" corn popper can
be obtained for making popcorn. It is well made and will last a
lifetime. Full instructions are given with the basket and it takes
only a minute to pop the corn over heat. It is a great favourite
with the young and the not so young – either sweet or savoury.

To make popcorn without a special pan heat 1 oz of butter in
the bottom of a heavy and large saucepan that has fitting lid, tip
in 1 tablespoon of special popping corn that can be bought in any
large grocers. With the lid on the pan and fairly good heat, if the
pan is thick, you will soon hear the corn popping. Lower heat –
or with a very thick pan – switch off heat as soon as you hear the
first "pops".

With a thinner pan, keep moving the pan over heat, sliding
back and forth to keep corn moving and prevent burning.

If you remove lid whilst popping is in process you will not only
slow down cooking but will probably have to collect the corn
from all over the kitchen floor.

For savoury popcorn add a little celery salt and grated parmesan with the corn.

For sweet popcorn, after cooking tip into a bowl, boil a nut of
butter and 1 tablespoon, rounded, brown sugar for a minute, or
the same amount of golden syrup, then remove from heat, add
any favoured flavouring and tip in corn and stir about with
spoon. The simple butter flavour is good. Turn out and cool,
when ready.

SALTED ALMONDS – No. 659

Blanch almonds by pouring over boiling water, leaving a short
while, then squeezing skin will release nut easily. Dry. To each
¼ lb kernels add 2 tablespoons olive oil in large frying pan, turn
about till all are coated with oil then over moderate heat fry till
golden. Remove onto clean blotting paper, sprinkle with salt and
paprika and turn about. Store in jars when quite cold.

SALTED CASHEWS – No. 660

As salted almonds No. 659.

SALTED PEANUTS – No. 661
Shell peanuts, bake nuts on oven sheet at 350°F or Mark 3 until skins rub off easily.

Follow recipe for salted almonds No. 659.

PARTY CHESTNUTS – No. 662
1 lb chestnuts: ¼ lb cream cheese: finely chopped parsley: paprika for garnish: cocktail sticks: either a small red cabbage, marrow, or a well scrubbed swede turnip

Wash chestnuts then boil them for 30 minutes. Remove a few at a time from pan and shell very carefully, keeping nuts whole, then set aside to cool. When cold coat nuts with cream cheese after impaling each on a stick. Do this carefully and daintily, then half dip in parsley and sprinkle remainder with paprika. As each nut is completed push stick in cabbage, marrow or swede for buffet.

CELERY APÉRITIF – No. 663
Finely chop and use with cream sauce as for No. 672 and tinted green, and use as for No. 664 on a little shredded lettuce. A black olive would decorate this well.

CELERIAC – No. 664
As hors-d'œuvres serve very thin slices of carefully cleaned, peeled and trimmed celeriac, with either lemon to squeeze, or oil and lemon blended, to pour over.

Young and smallish plants are preferable for this method of serving. Garnish with mustard and cress.

May be shredded for cocktail on lettuce with lemon as No. 663.

FENNEL APÉRITIF – No. 665
Scrubbed root, scraped and shredded finely and served as apéritif or cocktail as No. 663.

SALISFY APÉRITIF – No. 666
Wash and scrape salsify, then very finely shred immediately before use. Dress with lemon juice and serve on shredded lettuce in a tiny cup or glass, about a tablespoonful. A cream sauce such as No. 670, 671 or 672 with or without lemon may be served instead.

SPROUTED CORN OR BEAN COCKTAIL
AS HORS-D'OEUVRES – No. 667

Sprout as for corn No. 199. Arrange on tiny lettuce heart leaves in a small glass, using about a dessertspoonful of either corn or beans, or a mixture of both, after blending with oil and lemon No. 335.

Garnish with a radish split nearly to the stalk several times and left in chilled water for half an hour, when it will open like a flower.

FILLINGS

APPLE VELVET FILLING – No. 668
Equal parts of shredded apple and cashew nut cream.

APPLE AND RAISIN – No. 669
Chopped or sliced ripe apple with a few drops of lemon juice and seeded or seedless raisins.

FRESH WHIPPED CREAM – No. 670
Cream and basin should be as cold as possible. Using either a rotary whisk or your favourite whisk, and a basin only large enough to work with – not larger than a 1 pt basin for $\frac{1}{4}$ or $\frac{1}{2}$ pt cream for instance – whisk until cream suddenly becomes bulky, but no longer as it will go to butter.
  If liked some sieved icing sugar and vanilla may be added.

ASPARAGUS CREAM – No. 671
  1 cup asparagus tips cooked and cold: 1 cup whipped cream:
  $\frac{1}{2}$ cup water boiled with $\frac{1}{2}$ tsp agar-agar or Gelozone

Blend gelatin and water in double saucepan and stirring occasionally, simmer for 15 minutes then leave to cool. Sieve asparagus and blend with jelly, then fold in cream gently. Use for sandwiches, tiny *vol-au-vents*, pastry shells, etc. or to garnish canapés.

LEEK CREAM – No. 672
As for asparagus cream No. 671 but substituting the soft white part of cooked leeks.

BANANA AND NUT FILLING – No. 673
Mash ripe bananas and add a few chopped nuts.

CARROT AND CELERY FILLING – No. 674
Finely chopped with or without cheese.

CREAM CHEESE FILLING – No. 675
  2 oz finely grated cheese: 4 oz cream or cottage cheese: 2 Tbs
  top milk or thin cream

Blend together. If needed hot, blend over hot water. Equally good hot or cold.

Chopped chives, parsley, finely chopped tiny spring onions, a little finely shredded horseradish, chopped ginger or nut kernels may be added if liked.

Do not add chives or parsley before heating, if using hot.

CHEESE, RADISH AND OLIVE FILLING – No. 676

Thin cheese, chopped olives and radishes, then cheese again, and bread and butter or roll and butter both sides.

POTTED CHEESE – No. 677

8 oz crumbly Cheshire: 2 oz butter: 1 tsp French mustard: 1 Tbs cider vinegar: butter for sealing

Mash cheese very finely and blend with butter, mustard and vinegar till a paste results. Press into tiny jars, leaving an eighth of an inch space at the top. Pour over melted butter, tie down and keep cold. Chopped walnuts may be added to some pots, if desired.

SOUR MILK CHEESE – No. 678

Warm milk that is "on the turn" gently to lukewarm in double saucepan. Place a piece of muslin across a large strainer and pour milk into this and allow it to drain. Tie up muslin and let curd drain for several hours.

Turn out curd, blend in a little cream or top milk, add salt, if liked, and keep cool till ready to use. Carraway seeds may be added, or chopped chives.

FONDUE 1 – No. 679

2 eggs: 2 oz Gruyère: 1 oz butter: 1 tsp mustard: seasoning: pinch garlic salt and paprika: 2 tsp cornflour

Grate cheese, beat eggs. Melt butter over gentle heat, add eggs, cheese and seasoning and keep beating till creamy. Serve hot over a tea light and serve crusty bread to dip in. A $\frac{1}{2}$ cup of cider or apple juice may be added, if liked, and stirred till all heated.

This may be used cold or made beforehand and heated over hot water.

May be used to fill peppers, aubergines, *vol-au-vents*, etc.

FONDUE 2 – No. 680

1$\frac{1}{2}$ lb grated Gruyère, or other favoured cheese: $\frac{1}{2}$ pt cider or apple juice: 1 oz butter: 1 Tbs cornflour: 1 Tbs paprika or a pinch of cayenne: a clove of garlic

Have a thick ovenware dish and a hot plate where fondue will be served. Rub garlic around dish.

Blend cornflour with some of the cider and boil the rest, adding cornflour and butter and stirring. Then add seasoning and cheese, stirring all the while. Keep heat low, all will melt, and is served over gentle heat and with bread to dip in – in large crusty chunks.

DATE PASTE – No. 681

1 lb dates stoned and chopped or minced: 3 Tbs water: juice of half a lemon

Boil together, stirring till a thick paste results. Use for filling cakes, sandwiches, etc., hot or cold.

DATE AND BANANA FILLING – No. 682

As No. 683 but mincing dates alone and blending with sliced or mashed banana.

DATE AND HAZEL FILLING – No. 683

A cup of dates: 1½ cup hazel kernels: a squeeze of lemon, or a scraping of lemon zest

Stone dates and mince together with nuts. Add lemon. If no mincer, chop dates and nuts and blend.

DATE AND WALNUT FILLING – No. 684

As date and hazel No. 683.

SCRAMBLED EGG FILLING – No. 685

Use scrambled egg No. 129 and sandwich with either bread and butter or toast and serve hot or cold. Butter with parsley or watercress butter.

EGG AND TOMATO FILLING – No. 686

Skin two large tomatoes, mash and blend with chopped hard-boiled egg No. 127. Season as desired.

GREEN PEA AND MINT SPREAD – No. 687

Cook garden peas for shortest time to achieve *just* tenderness and no more. This time cannot be laid down but will depend upon age and freshness of peas – some needing no more than 2–3 minutes and others up to 7 or even 10.

To each cup of peas chop 1 tablespoon mint finely, with a little sugar. Mash peas, blend with mint and add just a squeeze of lemon and a small nut of butter.

Use in wholewheat sandwiches, whilst fresh, or keep potted and covered in a fridge for a few days and use as needed. Best fresh made and used, but if you keep it, do not regard it as a preserve. It is very little trouble to make, taking only a matter of minutes.

HARD-BOILED EGG FILLING – No. 688

Hard-boiled egg as No. 127, shelled and chopped finely, then either butter or mayonnaise added to moisten, add a little paprika. May be used between pieces of hot toast.

HONEY AND ALMOND – No. 689

Mill or chop almonds and sprinkle on sandwich spread with butter and honey.

PEANUT BUTTER AND CHUTNEY FILLING – No. 690

Spread peanut butter and add a little chutney, cover with plain buttered slice. Salad may of course be added first.

PEANUT BUTTER AND YEAST EXTRACT FILLING – No. 691

Spread with yeast extract first, then with peanut butter, and butter the second slice of the sandwich.

PEANUT AND SPRING ONION FILLING – No. 692

This explains itself, but needs a good digestion.

RUM BUTTER FILLING – No. 693

¾ lb (1¾ cups) barbados or soft brown sugar (pieces): ½ lb melted butter: 1 level tsp nutmeg: ½ level tsp cinnamon: an egg-cupful of rum

Beat all together till clear then pot in small pots, and seal down when set.

SAVOURY BUTTER FILLING – No. 694

Blend 1 tablespoon E.M. Soup with 2 oz butter and spread. These soups are dehydrated vegetables, herbs and milk, so a nourishing as well as savoury paste results, and a number of flavours are obtainable.

CROUTONS – No. 695

As fried bread No. 696, but with bread either cut into tiny cubes or stamped out into fancy shapes with a cutter.

Quickly wet and drain croutons, a sieve is useful here; drop bread in, quickly wet and then shake off surplus moisture. Place croutons on paper to drain, and they are ready to fry. For temperatures of fat try one cube first.

A frying basket is really a necessity if doing any quantity. It is easily possible to cook a smaller quantity in a frying pan. Have plenty of fat for speedy cooking.

Drain croutons on kitchen paper and keep hot for serving with soups, curries, etc.

FRIED BREAD – No. 696

Slices of wholewheat bread preferably several days old, cut and trimmed to desired shape and size. Dip quickly into water or milk and water, and fry both sides in hot vegetable fat or butter till golden and crisp. Drain on paper and serve hot or cold as needed.

FRIED CRUMBS – No. 697

1 *oz butter: 2 rounded Tbs wholewheat crumbs*

Melt butter in frying pan and when hot shake in crumbs and turn them about gently until a bright golden colour. Drain on kitchen paper in warm place till crisp. Use for garnishing sauce-coated or other dishes.

PULLED BREAD – No. 698

With a fork roughly pull to neat and evenly sized pieces a day old wholewheat loaf. Place on baking sheet in moderate oven, 350°F or Mark 3, until crisp right through, but not tough. Serve with cheese or soups or curries. Excellent for young teething children.

BREADCRUMBS FOR KEEPING – No. 699

Pulled bread No. 698 rolled out with rolling pin or put through a nut mill and stored in screw-top jars.

ROLLED BREAD AND BUTTER – No. 700

Cut crusts from top, bottom and sides of sandwich loaf. With a sharp knife or slicer, slice loaf lengthways and butter generously. Either roll up whole long slices and fasten in roll of parchment, later, slice as for swiss roll, having kept roll very cool, or if wished small individual rolls.

TOAST – No. 701

About three slices to the inch for buttering and serving with some savoury on, and very much thinner to eat dry or with butter added at table before soup, or with soup.

Make the thicker kind quickly, at the top of the grill pan and with top heat.

Make the thinner kind slowly at the bottom of the pan to dry out the bread. When finished, stand on edge to allow steam to escape.

CINNAMON SUGAR – No. 702

As for vanilla sugar No. 564 but substituting cinnamon sticks. For cinnamon sugar to serve with melon, etc., powdered cinnamon may be blended with fine caster sugar.

TANGERINE SUGAR – No. 703

Take lump sugar and rub over tangerine or mandarin oranges to allow sugar to absorb beautifully perfumed oil. Several oranges will be good for several dozen sugar lumps which can be stored in sealed preserving bottles and used to give their delightful flavour to custards, etc.

Alternatively, grated zest may be blended with fine sugar and kept in screw-topped jars, and used as necessary.

TO DRY HERBS – No. 704

Gather on dry day immediately before flowering. Strip leaves and, if possible, dry on parchment in hot sun first, then in very cool oven with door open till you can crumble them. Bottle and seal to keep airtight, labelling each variety. To make certain of right label, write name of herb on parchment when first picked, and keep separate during drying and packing process.

HOW TO SEPARATE EGG YOLK AND WHITE – No. 705

If you have not a gadget for separating the yolks from white of eggs, break egg carefully onto a saucer. Invert an egg cup over yolk, and tip off white into another vessel, carefully lifting egg cup only just enough to let white slide off yolk, and taking pains not to pinch yolk and break surrounding membrane.

CHESTNUTS – TO SHELL – No. 706

Melt a little margarine on a shallow baking tin in moderate oven. After a few minutes shake about well to coat each nut then leave for about 10 minutes.

Remove from oven and it will be found that skins come away easily.

BAKING POWDER – No. 707

4 oz rice or cornflour: 1 oz bicarbonate of soda: ½ oz cream of tartar: ½ oz tartaric acid

Blend by passing through a fine sieve into a bowl, passing it through several times. Store in screw-top jars.

CATERING QUANTITIES – No. 708

A party of 20 folk will require:

3 of my wholewheat loaves (if made 2 large and 1 small per 3 lb bag of flour use that quantity): 2 dozen small rolls: 1½ lb butter: ¼ lb tea: 1 sliced lemon for tea: 1 pt milk per 20 cups of tea: 1 lb sugar for tea or 1 lb coffee or a small tin of dandelion coffee and rather more milk – twice as much as for tea: 3 quarts of fruit cup or 3 pts cider or wine cup, and 2 pts fruit cup: 12 bottles of ginger ale

DRIED FRUITS – No. 709

A cheap and very valuable source of nourishment. Should not be cooked unless for cakes, puddings, etc. Remember only water has been removed so only water should be added. Wash well in hot water then soak in cold for 36 hours when fruit will be ready to eat.

When counting cost remember that it takes:

6–9 lb apples to make 1 lb dried: 5½ lb apricots to make 1 lb dried: 3 lb prunes to make 1 lb dried: 4 lb bananas to make 1 lb dried: 3 lb figs to make 1 lb dried

So you see what good value for money you have, quite apart from food value.

ORANGE AND LEMON ZEST – No. 710

The zest is the finely grated orange or lemon covering to the skin of these fruits, is rich in vitamins and the full flavour of the fruit. If you have no immediate use for the zest it can be stored with fine sugar in a screw-top jar, allowing plenty of sugar to coat the zest.

This is delicious in cakes, puddings, fruit drinks, fruit salads, etc.

TOMATO PULP – No. 711

For relieving tired and burning feet, squash a ripe tomato onto clean linen and bind to feet with a *crêpe* bandage. Relief will be immediate as the alkaline juices reach the acid pores, and further relief will be obtained if a short rest with feet so poulticed is taken with feet a little above waist height.

BEVERAGES

COFFEE – No. 712

Warm coffee pot. When it is really warm place in it one tablespoon of ground coffee for each person, with 4 to each pint of boiling water. When water is poured on, place lid on pot and keep hot. After about 4 minutes lift lid, and touch coffee, which will be on top, with a spoon, when it will sink to the bottom of pot. Give it a moment to settle and then pour. Serve hot milk with coffee for English guests, and cold, a very little, for continentals.

Some of the ways I have served coffee may be of interest. Hot coffee with peppermint fingers, chocolate outside, cream inside. Stir the black coffee with it instead of a spoon. With dark sweet chocolate grated finely, mixed with brown sugar. With Oranzini No. 583 to nibble; the hot coffee brings out the orange flavour. With grated lemon zest and brown sugar mixed. Pass as sugar. A few drops of angostura bitters gives a party flavour. There are of course many ways of making coffee and many kinds to be made. I am not an authority of coffees but have found that the best was good and the cheapest very bad. I have used caffeine-free coffee happily. Whilst being interested in this subject, I am not, as I say, competent to do more than offer instructions for making a good pot of coffee.

ICED COFFEE 1 – No. 713

Make coffee double strength, which applies also to dandelion coffee. When drawn, pour over ice cubes in a jug, and when cold serve in glasses with more cubes. If coffee is not made very strong it will not be drinkable when diluted with melted ice.

Freeze cream into cubes to serve with coffee, or pour freshly made coffee over milk cubes and add ice cubes when serving. Or serve with whipped cream.

ICED COFFEE 2 – No. 714

Hot strong coffee poured over ice cubes and given a spoonful of whipped cream.

DANDELION COFFEE – No. 715

This can be bought ready packaged at any Health Store and is a delicious drink. Made as coffee but using only one teaspoon instead of four tablespoons to the pint. It will soothe an unhappy liver and make the well feel even better. Serve as for ordinary coffee. A delicious flavour.

If you have access to dandelion roots, simply wash well and trim away leaves, then roast on a shallow tray in the oven till well brown and dried right through and really dark. Then grind as ordinary coffee. Store in tins.

TEA – No. 716

The golden rule for tea-making is to have the water boiling madly and to take the teapot to the kettle – *never* the kettle to the pot.

Most folk like it made strong, with one spoonful per person and one for the pot.

As a family we like it not just weak, but *helpless* and use one spoon per large pot. Weak with water is the rule if tea is liked weak – not chilled and thickened with milk.

I personally feel that the homely teapot is seldom kept clean enough. I like to use detergent and a brush inside pot and spout, down to the bottom of the spout, then run water down the spout till it runs clean into the pot. Most people will be shocked at what comes out of that spout!

Indian and Ceylon teas are made stronger than China tea which needs to be weak, and is better served with lemon than with milk, I think. Hand thin slices of lemon with rind on. Tea and hot water need to be kept hot on the table. Tea cosies are used and they too need to be washable. Often the outside cover is washable and the inside quite unmentionable!

I can recommend a dish with a grid on top for a lid, and two little night lights inside, that keep tea and hot water really hot, also the coffee and hot milk.

ICED TEA – No. 717

Make tea twice as strong as you require it to be for drinking and then pour it over ice cubes in a jug as soon as drawn. Add slices of lemon or orange or tangerine to cubes in jug, and when cold serve with another cube to chill further. Lemon or orange juice or slices may be frozen to use instead of ice in glasses. Tiny pieces of mint *frozen* into ice cubes are attractive for serving with lemon tea iced.

APPLE TEA – No. 718

Apple parings, preferably sun-ripened, and dried either in the sun or in a very cool oven may be used for making tea. Half a handful of dried parings with boiling water and used as tea, with or without milk. I like it best without, and with a thin slice of lemon. Fresh parings may be used, of course, as available. Apple tea may be strained off and used cold when it will be found refreshing. Either way it is good for bladder trouble if skins are from really ripe apples. Has vitamins B and C, and is sub-acid.

BALM TEA – No. 719

One ounce balm leaves to 1 pt of cold water and leave to infuse for half a day.

Can be made hot instead, with boiling water, to ward off a cold. Otherwise it is invaluable for the nervous and hysterical, as its name suggests.

CARROT AND CELERY TEA – No. 720

For acidosis make a tea with 1 tablespoon grated carrot and one of celery and 2 teaspoons medium oatmeal. Make as for tea with one pint of boiling water and leave under cosy for 15 minutes. Contains vitamin C.

Beet, shredded and cucumber serve the same purpose.

DANDELION FLOWER TEA – No. 721

*1 cup dandelion petals: zest and juice of ½ lemon: 1 Tbs honey:
¾ pt boiling water*

Pour boiling water onto other ingredients in a warmed jug. Cover and leave till cold. A good tonic and a refreshing drink – hot or cold.

JASMINE TEA – No. 722

Jasmine tea may be enjoyed in this country. I have never made it from fresh jasmine, but have purchased it from the Bombay Emporium in London.

A delicious, refreshing and fragrant drink. Make as other herb teas, and use either hot, cold or as a basis of fruit cup.

LAVENDER FLOWER TEA – No. 723

Make as tea, use as a tea for nervous headaches, or use the tea as a base for fruit drinks.

LIME TEA – No. 724

Lime flowers may be dried, or bought ready dried, and used as tea. Very refreshing either hot or iced, and used extensively in France, Italy and Greece. Excellent for nerves.

LINSEED TEA – No. 725

For colds:

½ oz linseed: ½ oz barbados sugar: ¼ oz liquorice: 1 pt water

Well rinse linseed in sieve under cold tap, then put into double saucepan with water, broken liquorice and sugar. Slowly simmer for 2 hours until liquid thickens. Strain through muslin when it is ready for use.

MINT TEA – No. 726

For a one person teapot use 2 teaspoons chopped mint. Make as tea, serve honey and a thin slice of lemon.

Excellent for the digestion, and for nervous headache. If feeling really too much under the weather to make the tea – rest with a handful of mint leaves, bruising them and inhaling the rising aroma. The spirit will readily respond and brighten considerably.

OAT STRAW TEA – No. 727

For silicon, to help eyes, skin, teeth, nails, hair, the finest source is the straw of oats.

Well cleanse, cut into very short lengths, or powder in electric liquidizer. Use 1 teaspoon powder or 1 tablespoon short pieces to one pint of boiling water.

Make as for tea and leave covered with cosy to "brew" for about 20–30 minutes. Serve with fresh mint leaves and a slice of lemon and honey if liked.

PARSLEY TEA – No. 728

As a healthy drink between meals and especially for kidney and rheumatic sufferers. Root and green leaves can be used. Chop and infuse with boiling water. Better still, if you have an electric liquidizer simply blend parsley and water in liquidizer and drink.

A handful, before chopping, to 1 pt water is a good guide. Contains vitamins C and E and is an alkaline drink and specially good for diabetics and kidney sufferers.

PEPPERMINT TEA – No. 729

If you grow peppermint in the garden you might like to benefit by making tea from it.

A small bunch in the teapot, or jug, boiling water and leave to draw for 10 minutes.

Good for flatulence of course, and a cheering drink.

RASPBERRY LEAF TEA – No. 730

Use fresh or dried – which are easily obtainable from a Health Store or herbalist. Really quite invaluable in pregnancy and after childbirth, and a healthsome drink for all.

Make as for ordinary tea by infusing 1 oz of the dried or a few of the fresh, to a pint of boiling water. Do not spoil with milk or sugar, but enjoy the natural flavour.

ROSE HIP TEA – No. 731

1 handful rose hips: 1 quart water

Boil together for an hour, strain and use hot or cold as liked. Hot it can be used with milk and sugar or a lemon or orange slice and honey or sugar. Cold, sweeten with honey, if liked. Rich in vitamin C.

ROSEMARY TEA – No. 732

As mint tea No. 726 and for the nervous or unhappy. Effective if used in the hand, for headaches, again as in mint No. 726.

BARLEY WATER 1 – No. 733

Wash a tablespoon of pearl barley well, then put in a jug with either thin peel or grated zest and juice of 2 medium sized or 1 large lemon. Pour on 2 pts boiling water, cover and leave till next day. Strain and sweeten to taste.

BARLEY WATER 2 – No. 734

Into a jug put 1 tablespoon flaked barley, after rinsing in a strainer under cold tap. Add juice and rind, thinly peeled, of a lemon. Pour on 2 pts boiling water, use after an hour. Sweeten with a little honey as desired, or use without. Barley water can also be quickly made in emergency with tinned Patent Barley in powder form.

PIP AND PEEL WATER – No. 735

Skins of oranges and lemons: boiling water to cover

Place skins and pips in large bowl and cover with boiling water. When cold, strain and drink as required, either as it is or as the basis of fruit drinks.

Do not keep more than two days, and keep under muslin.

COCKTAILS FOR HEALTH

TOMATO SPECIAL – No. 736
Tomato juice with 1 teaspoon cider vinegar.

TOMATO COOLER – No. 737
Equal parts tomato and cucumber juice.

TOMATO TONE-UP – No. 738
Tomato juice with 1 tablespoon lemon juice.

TOMATO WARMER – No. 739
Tomato with a pinch of curry powder.

EGG NOG – No. 740

1 egg: 1 tsp honey: four-fifths glass hot milk

Beat egg thoroughly and pour on it, still stirring, hot milk with honey dissolved in it. Strain into glass and serve. A tablespoon sherry may be added or it may be flavoured with one of the many delicious herbs, coriander or elderflowers or lavender for instance, or a few drops of angostura bitters.

TREACLE POSSETT – No. 741
Stir one teaspoon of black treacle into a tumbler of hot milk and drink if shivery, keeping warm, or better still, going to bed.

HONEY POSSETT – No. 742

1 glass hot milk: 2 tsp honey

Stir in and serve immediately.

WHEAT GERM POSSETT – No. 743

1 glass hot milk: 1 tsp honey: 1 Tbs wheat germ

Blend in glass and serve hot. A fine nerve restorer.

MALT POSSETT – No. 744

1 glass hot milk: 2 or more tsp malt extract

Stir in and serve immediately.

ROSE HIP SYRUP – No. 745

4 lb rose hips: 2 lb sugar: 6 pts water

Mince cleaned hips and boil for two minutes only with half of the water. Allow to drip as for jelly No. 592 without squeezing. Return pulp to pan with remainder of water and again boil for two minutes. Leave standing for half an hour before placing in jelly cloth to drip as before.

Later place both lots of liquor in enamelled pan to boil, then simmer until reduced by half. To the liquor now add sugar and boil for about 5 minutes.

Have bottles, small ones, heating in oven from cold to 200°F. Remove with oven cloth to a dry surface and pour in syrup. Fill as near to the top as possible allowing for insertion of cork, previously boiled, and cooled in the water, drained and covered with a lid till used.

During the war I made eight pints of this one autumn and we had a wonderful winter, each taking the syrup on cereal and porridge, and making delicious fruit salads with what came to hand, and our rose hip syrup.

A valuable source of vitamin C, and good for young and old alike.

At least 1 dessertspoonful a day each.

APPLE JUICE – No. 746

Use any apples after washing, wiping and looking over. Windfalls are excellent if a grub search is made before grating.

Halve apples. Over a bowl spread two thicknesses of muslin or old linen, scrupulously clean. Stand grater on muslin in bowl and grate down apples. When all finished remove grater and squeeze. If you do the job properly you will find nothing of value, except to the compost heap, remaining in the cloth. I have obtained a whole tumbler of juice from one large Charles Ross apple in a T.V. demonstration.

Drink as it is or chilled. It is a great vitamin and mineral source and a dissolver of toxins.

BEET JUICE – No. 747
As apple juice No. 746. If too sweet add a little lemon. For vitamin C and a quick supply of energy.

CARROT JUICE – No. 748
As apple juice No. 746. A little lemon may be added if too sweet. Use as pre-meal cocktail. Contains vitamins A and C, and a valuable alkaline drink, therefore very good for an acid condition.

CARROT TOP JUICE – No. 749
This can best be made with an electric liquidizer, when stalks and leaves should, after washing, be broken into short lengths and dropped into the liquidizer with a cup of water and liquidized. If no liquidizer is available, break or chop into half inch lengths then scald with only enough boiling water to cover barely, press well under and then either through a Mouli Légume sieve or an ordinary sieve, after steeping 15 minutes or so. For health and vitality.

CELERY JUICE – No. 750
As for apple juice No. 746. A fine vital drink for health or sickness, especially for rheumatic sufferers who cannot have too much. Vitamins A, B and C.

CUCUMBER JUICE – No. 751
Wash and wipe and prepare as for apple juice No. 746. A little lemon may be added, or parsley, or celery juice. Good for the complexion. Also with endive, for rheumatism, neuritis, etc.

ORANGE, LEMON AND GRAPEFRUIT JUICES – No. 752
Squeeze and strain, using a lemon squeezer. Roll under the hand on the table with plenty of pressure before squeezing for maximum amount of juice.

All valuable sources of vitamins C and D and invaluable in health and sickness. Do not waste the skins.

PINEAPPLE JUICE – No. 753
Make as for apple juice No. 746. Use with radish for liver disorders, or with carrot for the heart, adding a little honey.

Excellent for the healthy and a delicious addition to fruit cups. Vitamins B and C.

SWEDE JUICE – No. 754
Especially good as a winter drink. Make as apple juice No. 746. Contains vitamin C.

TOMATO JUICE – No. 755
If no liquidizer, make with an ordinary sieve, cutting tomatoes in half and rubbing through.

A valuable alkaline drink for any acid condition. Containing vitamin C.

LEMONADE – No. 756
Juice and zest of 4 lemons: 3 oz demerara sugar or ½ cup honey: 2 pts water

Blend sugar or honey with lemon juice and zest and ½ pt boiling water. Cool and chill then add 1½ pts cold water. Garnish with lemon slices and mint sprigs.

Soda water or seltzer may be used instead of plain water.

ORANGE CUP – No. 757
Juice of 6 oranges: juice of 2 lemons: zest grated from skins: ½ cup honey: 1 pt lime flower tea: 1 pt of soda water

Blend juices with honey, zest and tea. Add soda water just before serving. Chill with ice cubes.

QUICK FRUIT PUNCH – No. 758
1 large can orange juice: juice of 1 lemon or 2 Tbs pure lemon juice: 2 Tbs sugar or honey: 2 pts bottled ginger ale or soda water: garnish with mint sprigs

HERBS

My study of this subject is not adequate to giving anything like a comprehensive section. I give some of the knowledge I have acquired however, in order to stimulate other housewives towards making their own studies. This subject really is of great value and merits adequate time and care being spent.

ANGELICA – No. 759
Use fresh leaves chopped for salads. Eat stems as one eats celery.

Candy the stems as for other fruits and use for decorating sweets, cakes, etc.

A tea may be made from leaves and this is especially good for aiding digestion.

BALM – No. 760
A few young leaves make an interesting and healthful addition to salads.

Use for flavouring soups, hot pots, etc., and for making savoury stuffings.

Make balm vinegar as for garlic or tarragon vinegar.

For balm tea prepare as for other herb teas. About an ounce of fresh or 1 teaspoon dried leaves to a pint of boiling water, and infuse a few minutes, or fresh cold water and infuse for a day or night. Good for nerves and is said to cheer the spirit.

Drink hot balm tea to ward off a cold, adding a little honey.

BAY LEAVES – No. 761
No bouquet garni is complete without a bay leaf, and indeed it may be used for flavouring slow cooked milk puddings, or any stew.

Remove the leaf before serving the dish it has flavoured.

BOUQUET GARNI – No. 762
A bunch of herbs, thyme, parsley, marjoram, bay leaf, chives, etc., used for giving a fine flavour to soups, casseroles, etc.

Tie round with thread for easy removal after cooking.

CARAWAY – No. 763
Use fresh leaves as an addition to salads. Use seeds for flavouring

cakes, biscuits and sweets, also for vegetables. (See Bircher potatoes).

Make a tea of 2 teaspoons ground or crushed seed to 1 pt of boiling water. Cover and leave to infuse till next day when strain and bottle.

A very little in a little warm water will relieve flatulence.

CELERY SEED – No. 764
Of utmost health value. Use for flavouring soups and stews, for teas and crushed, for the table. Invaluable for those with tendency to rheumatism.

CHERVIL – No. 765
Use this delicate herb for flavouring salads, soups, gravies, consommés, etc. Do not use it with very strongly flavoured vegetables as it will be "lost" in the dish. Gives a delicate piquancy to cooked vegetable salad, or combines well with lettuce, tomato and cucumber.

CHIVES – No. 766
Chives are green almost all the year round and are very useful for quickly adding a slight onion flavour to food. Used chopped with cottage cheese, in salads or as a dressing for soups.

CORIANDER – No. 767
A few leaves of coriander are an attractive addition to a summer salad.

The seeds, ground, may be used to flavour sweets, sweetmeats, and biscuits.

FENNEL – No. 768
For flavouring – see vegetables.

Use for salads – aids digestion. Use for colic as caraway seed tea recipe. For other fennel recipes – see sauces.

GARLIC – No. 769
This wonderful plant needs a book to itself. Use it as much and as often as possible for health. It seems impossible to spoil it, and one should certainly regard it as a gem in the kitchen.

Apart from all culinary uses it has amazing healing powers. A clove held in the cheek will clean up the most wretched throat or mouth condition. A tiny heart of a boiled garlic clove will heal a bad ear condition, but care must be taken as to temperatures before inserting and I would slip it into a tiny piece of sterile muslin for easy removal.

Keep garlic powder and garlic salt in the store cupboard for improving savoury dishes.

ELDER – No. 770
See elder vinegar No. 619 and other recipes in savouries and pre-serves.

I would like to know much more of this wonderful shrub. We have used elderflower and peppermint (known as "elp" in the family) over a long period. We have purchased this from a Health Food Stores. I look forward to making a study of herbs that would, I know, be really rewarding.

MINT – No. 771
Culpepper says, "All mints have wholesome properties beyond most plants. By their scent they stimulate and reduce reflex ner-vous irritability. This is because their leaves and flowers contain camphor which refreshes the spirits and stirs up the appetite. Good for wind colic of the stomach."

Use as directed for teas, sauces, adding chopped to potatoes, etc., when cooked.

When jaded or depressed it will be found really refreshing to cup fresh mint leaves in the hand, the warmth helping the mint aroma to rise, it can be inhaled with great benefit.

PARSLEY – No. 772
I suppose that parsley will be at one and the same time the most, yet least, used of herbs.

Most, because it is the most used for garnishing savoury foods, sandwiches, fish dishes, etc., etc., and least because it is usually pushed to the side of the plate and thrown away by the washer-up. This is utter folly, for parsley is one of our most important foods. It should be eaten on every possible occasion for as well as acting as garnisher and appetizer it contains valuable mineral salts, iron and vitamins and also acts as a cleaner in removing odours of food, etc., from the mouth of the eater.

Serve chopped with soups and stews, over fresh boiled vege-tables, in stuffings, etc., etc.

If you have a liquidizer make wonderful parsley cocktails for health and beauty alone or blended with carrot or carrot tops, celery or celery tops.

These are wonderful for fevers, rheumatic and arthritic conditions, anæmic and kidney conditions.

In fact, it is a gem of a herb and should be in daily use, and not as a garnish only. See parsley butter No. 339.

ROSEMARY – No. 773

Use leaves for flavouring stews, hot pots and sauces.

Use powdered for nut roasts and rissoles, add a little powdered to salad dressing.

Gather the newly flowered tips of sprays for teas for nervous conditions.

A rosemary wash is good for hair, for preserving colour if fading. Steep in boiling water and leave several hours, then strain and use as a rinse.

SAGE – No. 774

Culpepper says, "Used for many complaints, night sweats, T.B., shivering fever" (I should give tea from the sage for this) "and externally for bruises and sprains" (I suggest poultice of fresh or dried leaves) "gargles and washes. A brain tonic."

A gargle of lemon juice made hot on red sage leaves is very effective. ¼ pt lemon juice, 1 oz red sage leaves, steep an hour or two, then strain and bottle. Use 1 tablespoon to ¼ tumbler of water.

Use sage for seasoning and stuffings also.

SAGE AND ONION STUFFING

2 large onions: 1 round tsp dried sage or 6 sage leaves: 1 oz Suenut nut suet or butter: ⅓ cup wholewheat crumbs: seasoning if required: 1 beaten egg for binding or ⅓ cup milk or water if needed

Mince scalded sage leaves and onions and blend with crumbs and shredded suet. Mix together and bind with egg or milk if desired to make balls. Or use between two layers of nut roast mixture.

THYME – No. 775

Lemon thyme is the most commonly used in the kitchen and may be used as all herbs, fresh or dried.

Use for seasoning soups and stews and for stuffings. An easily prepared recipe being:

> 2 oz nut suet: 2 oz wholewheat crumbs: 1 beaten egg: zest from
> ½ lemon: juice of ½ lemon: 4 tsp chopped parsley: 1 tsp dried or
> 2 tsp fresh thyme: ¼ tsp marjoram: a pinch of celery salt

Blend all together and use either to fold in nut meat roast or to make balls to roast around it, or amongst potatoes roasting in a tin. Do not cook as long as nutmeat roast of course, add to dish about 15 minutes from end of cooking time.

HOW TO CHOP HERBS – No. 776

Herbs are very quickly chopped in a cup with a pair of scissors.

Or mint, on a board can be more quickly chopped if sprinkled with a little sugar. Hold knife firmly above point with finger and thumb, and whilst chopping swing handle in a semicircle, and slowly make this movement backwards and forwards.

VINE LEAVES – No. 777

Apart from the use of vine leaves for savouries, they will impart a delicious flavour to delicately flavoured fruits as gooseberries or apples when these are being stewed. Add a few leaves to the pan or casserole and allow to steep for a while before cooking and later remove when fruit reaches simmering point.

INDEX

Numbers are recipe numbers not page numbers

VEGETABLES

WINTER SALADS

SUMMER SALADS

DRESSINGS

SAUCES – SAVOURY

SAUCES – SWEET

SWEETS AND DESSERTS

BREAD, SCONES, CAKES, BISCUITS, PASTRIES,
BATTERS, ICINGS, CONFECTIONERY

PRESERVES

BUFFET, SNACKS, ETC.

FILLINGS

MISCELLANEOUS

BEVERAGES

HERBS